Living Dragons

Living Dragons

A Natural History of the World's Monitor Lizards

RODNEY STEEL

Ralph Curtis-Books
P.O. Box 349
Sanibel Island, FL 33957-0349

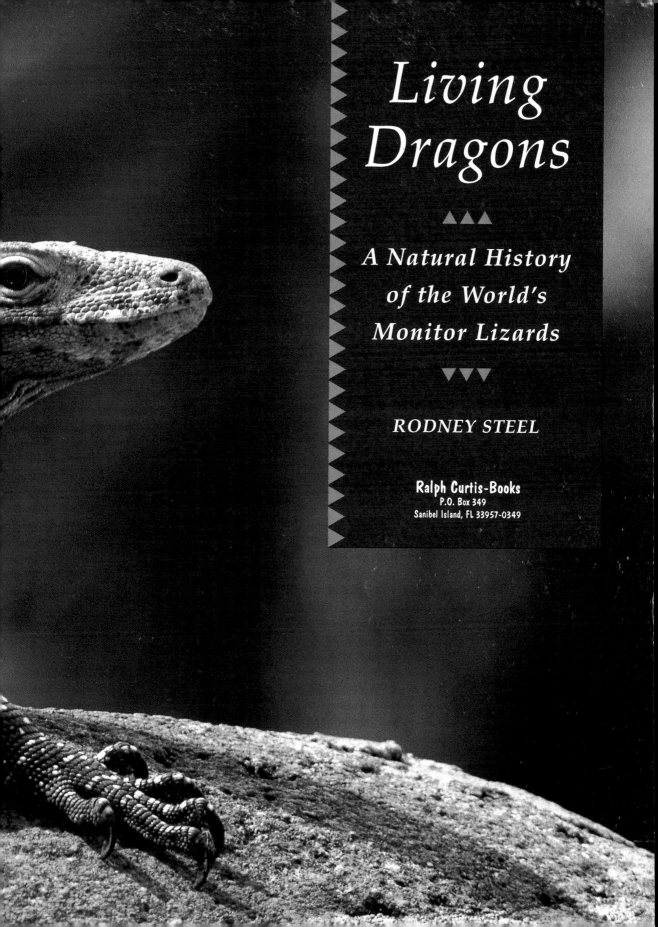

RALPH CURTIS BOOKS

First published in the UK 1996
by Blandford, an imprint of the Cassell Group
CASSELL PLC
Wellington House
125 Strand
London WC2R 0BB

Distributed in U.S. and Canada by: Ralph Curtis Publishing, Inc.
P.O. Box 349, Sanibel Island, Florida 33957-0349

Library of Congress Catalog Number: 96-84557

ISBN 0-88359-040-9

Typeset by York House Typographic Ltd
Printed and bound in Spain by Bookprint, S.L.

Previous page: Komodo dragon *(Varanus komodoensis)*.

Contents

CHAPTER 1

Varanids – the Real Dragons

Belief in the existence of winged, fire-breathing dragons was a common feature of medieval folklore and eastern mythology. The sort of dragon so nobly slain by St George, or to be found writhing across Chinese tapestries, never existed, save in the over-vivid imaginations of superstitious artists and story-tellers. But there are dragons living – dragons of sufficient size and ferocity to have taken a toll of human life.

To find them, you would have to travel to Indonesia. There, half way along the chain of islands which stretches from the eastern tip of Java into the Banda Sea, between the islands of Sumbawa and Flores, lies tiny Komodo, a mere 29km (18 miles) long and just 19km (12 miles) across at its widest part. On the rocky hills of this tropical islet are to be found real-life dragons – Komodo dragons, more properly Komodo monitors, more properly still *Varanus komodoensis,* giant members of the extensive family of monitor lizards which today extends across the Old World from Africa to Australia, but which once was also represented in North America and Europe. Some of their distant relatives still persist in the USA and Mexico – the Gila monster and the Mexican beaded lizard. These are apparently primitive survivors of an ancient stage of monitor evolution and hold the distinction of being the only living poisonous lizards – poisonous enough to have killed people on occasion.

Fossils from rocks dating back to the Age of Reptiles, over 65 million years ago, disclose a race of extinct sea dragons that were also relatives of the monitor lizards and reached lengths of 15m (50ft) or more. Denizens of Cretaceous seas, in the days when *Tyrannosaurus* stalked the land preying on its fellow dinosaurs, the sea dragons were mosasaurs, totally adapted to life in shallow tropical waters and apparently living mostly on fish and the now defunct cephalopods which are known as ammonites.

◀ A komodo dragon *(Varanus komodoensis)* on the lookout for prey or larger rival lizards of its own species.

THE KOMODO DRAGON

Komodo dragons do not fly and do not breathe fire but, in every other respect, they fully merit their emotive name. It is a measure of Komodo's remoteness that this massive reptile, up to 3.5m (11ft) long, was unknown to science until just before the First World War. One of the Lesser Sunda islands, Komodo is only about 520km^2 (200 sq. miles) in area. It is very hilly, rising to 825m (2,700ft) in the interior, and covered largely by savannah, although the hilltops are clothed in forest. For an Indonesian island it is surprisingly dry, most of the January monsoon rains falling on Java and Bali before they reach Komodo on their southeasterly track. Human habitation, even towards the end of the twentieth century, was limited essentially to a small village of native huts. In the nineteenth century, this obscure corner of the Dutch colonial empire was truly an outpost of Western civilization.

In December 1910, P.A. Ouwens, who was connected with the botanical gardens at Buitenzorg (now Bogor, 19km/30 miles south of Jakarta in Java), was introduced to J.K.H. van Steyn van Hensbroek, an infantry lieutenant at that time serving as a civil administrator on the island of Flores. Komodo is located in the narrow strait between Flores and Sumbawa and, as part of his duties, Hensbroek was required to visit it on a periodical basis. He heard stories of the huge dragons living on Komodo, which allegedly reached 7m (23ft) in length, and, on his next call, was persuaded by Ouwens to try and secure one of these *boeaja darat*, or 'land crocodiles', as the natives called them. A skipper from the pearling fleet based at Komodo claimed to have shot several of these 7m (23ft) monsters and furnished Hensbroek with information on their habits, warning him that human settlement along the coast had forced the reptiles to retreat into the hills. The lieutenant was successful in his quest and sent the skin of a 2.2m (7¼ft) specimen to Ouwens, together with a photograph of the carcass.

An excited Ouwens immediately arranged for a native collector from the zoological museum at Buitenzorg to go with Hensbroek to Komodo in search of more specimens. Unfortunately, Hensbroek was transferred to Timor at this time, but the collector enlisted the aid of a native chief and his dogs. Four dragons were caught: two adults, measuring 2.9m (9½ft) and 2.35m (7¾ft) long, and two juveniles less than 1m (3¼ft) long. The two young animals survived in captivity long enough for tests to be carried out that satisfied the observers that Komodo dragons were, as alleged, deaf – this was despite the fact that they noticed the unusually large ear drums which these creatures possess. A further specimen, reputedly 4m (13ft) in length, was shot shortly afterwards by a Sergeant Beker and, on the basis of all this evidence, Ouwens published, in 1912, the first scientific description of the Komodo monitor, *Varanus komodoensis*, for so he correctly defined its affinities.

Later investigations demonstrated that Komodo monitors occur on Flores, as well as on several islets (Padar, Rintja, Gili Mota, Oewada Sami), and also restored a semblance of rationality to exaggerated claims of 7m (23ft) monsters. In fact, the Komodo dragon reaches about 3.5m (11ft) in length but, with a weight of 50kg (112lb) or more, it is still a formidable predatory reptile. A fully grown male represents a very real threat to a human being and a number of attacks on people have been recorded, several resulting in fatalities. Normally, adult Komodo dragons take deer, wild boar and occasional domestic animals (goats, buffalo, horses, cows), as well as gorging indiscriminately on carrion – special precautions have to be taken by the natives when burying their dead or the lizards will dig up the corpses.

Komodo monitors are largely solitary and live in burrows, naturally occurring cavities or beneath overhanging vegetation. They emerge by day to hunt for food across the savannah country and through the monsoon forest which grows along streamsides, sometimes emerging onto the beaches or prowling the mangrove swamps, and even extending their activities to offshore reefs or sand-bars.

Is this fearsome creature, the largest living lizard, a prehistoric left-over? Its origins probably date back to Miocene times, some 15 million years ago, which, although a venerable ancestry in human terms, is not so very ancient in an evolutionary context. The great reptiles to which the Komodo dragon has sometimes been compared vanished 65 million years ago, although fossils dating back to this remote time suggest that monitor lizards of some sort – although not Komodo dragons – had already emerged and they shared the closing days of the Mesozoic world with the dinosaurs.

DRAGONS AROUND THE WORLD

Almost as large as the Komodo monitor, but very different in appearance and habits, is the water monitor *(Varanus salvator)*, which ranges from eastern Bengal through Burma, Thailand and southern China to the Philippines and the Indo-Australian islands. A denizen of humid forests and river shores, the water monitor will cross quite wide stretches of sea-way (which explains its extensive range), grows to about 3m (10ft) in length, and lives principally on frogs, rats, crabs, and birds and their eggs. However, it is large enough to kill small deer and has a predilection for carrion, as a result of which it is, like the Komodo monitor, notorious for digging up human corpses in burial grounds.

Australia is the home of the 2.5m (8¼ft) gigantic lace lizard *(Varanus giganteus)*, which lives in arid areas of the continent's interior, taking refuge from mid-day heat in burrows and living on lizards, snakes, small mammals (including rabbits), birds and birds' eggs, as well as carrion. Until some 20 000 years ago, Australia included in its bizarre and now largely extinct fauna the largest of all known terrestrial lizards, the giant *Megalania*, which really did grow to 7m (23ft) long. This formidable predator probably weighed about 600kg (1320lb) and, in all likelihood, lived on diprotodonts (enormous marsupial herbivores that have now died out), the huge Pleistocene kangaroos, giant wombats, and possibly large flightless birds. Whether *Megalania* evolved from a monitor line that had been present in Australia for millions of years or was a descendant of relatively recent immigrant stock is not known; the island continent had been cut off for the best part of 50 million years and accommodated a wide range of marsupials but hardly any indigenous placental mammals at all (only a few bats and rats managed to secure a foothold). It is noteworthy, for example, that there was no cat-like creature to fill the ecological niche that lions, tigers or jaguars occupy on other continents. *Megalania* seems to have been the animal most likely to have assumed this role.

In contrast to the mighty *Megalania*, some of the other monitors in Australia are dwarfs. They belong to a uniquely Australasian subgenus *(Odatria)* and, in some cases, e.g. the short-tailed monitor, *Varanus (Odatria) brevicauda*, do not exceed 20cm (8in) in length, although most reach 60–90cm (24–36in). They live on insects, mice, skinks and other appropriately diminutive prey, and probably evolved within Australia, subsequently spreading to Timor and New Guinea – perhaps when water levels fell during the Pleistocene glaciations and land connections were established.

Other Australian monitors, intermediate in size between the large *Varanus giganteus* and the little *Odatria* group, include: the sand goanna *(Varanus gouldi)*, which occurs in sandy areas throughout the continent, except southeastern Victoria and Tasmania; the water-dependent mangrove monitor *(Varanus indicus)*, with a foothold along the northern tropical coasts; Mertens' monitor *(Varanus mertensi)* and Mitchell's water monitor *(Varanus mitchelli)*, also from the humid areas of the north and similarly water-adapted; *Varanus panoptes* from eastern Australia, with its strikingly spotted skin; and the plains goanna *(Varanus spenceri)*, which prefers arid areas of northern Australia. The name 'goanna', popularly applied in Australia to so many of these species, seems to be a corruption of the word 'iguana'; early European visitors to the continent, who were familiar with the iguanas of the western hemisphere, probably confused Australian varanids with the superficially similar, but only very distantly related, New World lizards of the iguana group.

New Guinea has two monitors that are exclusively its own: Salvador's monitor *(Varanus salvadori)* is an arboreal form, widely distributed in the island, which attains a length of about 2m (6½ft), while Schmidt's monitor *(Varanus karlschmidti)* is an obscure species represented in scientific collections principally by a handful of specimens collected in 1929 on the Sepik River by Karl Schmidt of the Chicago Natural History Museum.

The monitor lizards of Africa and Asia have apparently been largely prevented from reaching Australasia by sea barriers to the east of Java, Borneo and Luzon. Several species range widely across this vast region, notably the 1.5m (5ft) long desert monitor *(Varanus griseus)*, which is found from Morocco right across north Africa to Asia Minor, Trans-Caspia and central India, living in holes or below rocks to escape the arid mid-day heat of this desert belt and feeding on insects, other reptiles and small mammals. In the cold season, it hibernates for as long as 6 months, an ambient temperature of at least 30°C (86°F) being necessary for it to become active and emerge from its hiding place.

Overlapping the range of the desert monitor across Iran and Afghanistan, but extending further eastwards through Assam and Burma to Malaysia and Java, the Bengal or common monitor *(Varanus bengalensis)* grows to 2m (6½ft) and is an agile, fast-moving hunter of small mammals, amphibians, lizards, snakes and birds. Although living most of the time in a burrow or a hole in the ground, the Bengal monitor will readily climb trees; however, although largely independent of water, it avoids the sandy deserts that are home

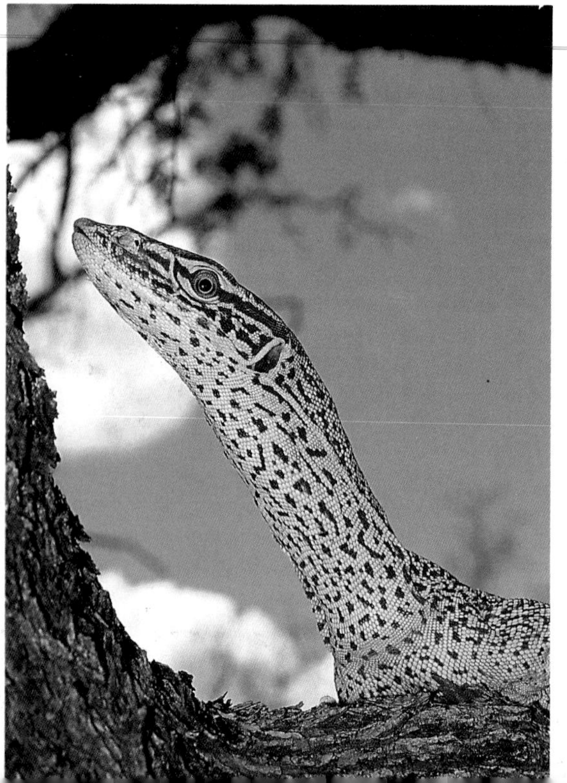

▲ The largest living Australian monitor, the gigantic lace lizard *(Varanus giganteus).*

◀ An alert young sand goanna *(Varanus gouldi)* in the Northern Territory of Australia.

▶ *Varanus bengalensis* is found from southeast Iran and Afghanistan eastwards to Malaysia and Java, occurring in almost every environment except sandy deserts and dense rain forests.

to *Varanus griseus*. The eggs of other reptiles (especially crocodiles) and birds are regularly eaten by this species and it is a notorious raider of domestic poultry in native settlements.

The typical varanid of Africa is the Nile monitor *(Varanus niloticus)*, which is found throughout the continent except in the northwestern region and the western rainforests. Attaining nearly 2m (6½ft) in length, Nile monitors are catholic feeders, taking birds, mice, slugs, snails, crabs, rats and crocodile eggs, as well as feeding on carrion. Good swimmers and capable of climbing quite tall trees, Nile monitors nonetheless usually live in burrows near water or in crevices among rocks. Their sharp teeth administer a painful, crushing bite and their claws are powerful lacerating weapons: if threatened, they become exceedingly aggressive, hissing and lashing their tails. The Arabs know the Nile monitor as the *waral*, *ouran* or *varan*, hence the Latin name *Varanus*, which is applied to all living members of the group. Rendering the Arab name *varan* as 'waran' led to confusion with the German *Warnen* (to warn), hence *Warn-eidechsen* (warning lizard), which translated loosely into the English 'monitor lizard'.

In South Africa, this species is known as the iguana, *lagavaan* or *leguann* by settlers of Dutch origin, presumably because (as in the case of Australia) early settlers confused it with the true iguanas of the New World.

Also widespread in Africa is the stockily proportioned savannah monitor *(Varanus exanthematicus)*, up to about 1.5m (5ft) in length, which lives, as its common name suggests, in dry areas south of the Sahara (the western African rainforests excepted). It has an unusually short tail for a monitor and lives mostly on insects, molluscs, birds and small mammals. Despite a preference for relatively arid surroundings, the savannah monitor is, in fact, a competent swimmer and, in some parts of its range (e.g. Guinea and the northern Congo), frequently enters water.

At the eastern end of the Afro-Asian monitor population's range, South-East Asia is home to several species. One of the most widespread is the yellow monitor *(Varanus flavescens)*, which is possibly a close relative of *Varanus exanthematicus* and occurs from Pakistan through northern India to Burma, Thailand, Indo-China and Peninsular Malaysia. A moderate-sized monitor of terrestrial habits that prefers to live in the vicinity of water, it is now becoming increasingly rare due to paddy-field encroachment on its marshland habitat. The rough-necked monitor *(Varanus rudicollis)* is an arboreal lizard, found from Burma to Sumatra, Borneo, Sarawak and the Riouw archipelago, that attains less than 1m (3¼ft) in length and is distinguished by prominent, keeled scutes protecting the neck, while Dumeril's monitor *(Varanus dumerili)* is a sizeable reptile, up to 1.5m (5ft) long, favouring mangrove swamps and coastal evergreen forest and found from Thailand, through Sumatra and Java, to Borneo. The mangrove monitor *(Varanus indicus)* has its principal domain through Celebes, Timor, the Indo-Australian islands, New Guinea and the Marshall Islands, as well as maintaining a presence in northernmost Australia.

Isolated in the northern Philippine island of Luzon is a uniquely curious monitor that lives to a large extent on a diet of fruit. Gray's monitor *(Varanus olivaceus)*, also known as the *butaan*, grows to a total body length of 1.5m (5ft) and was for many years regarded as a very rare species. It was first described by John Edward Gray of London's Natural History Museum as long ago as 1845, on the basis of a single immature specimen, and, for nearly a century, that was all anybody knew about what became known as Gray's monitor.

In 1942, the German authority, Robert Mertens, published details of a skull that he thought probably belonged to this species, but it was left to Walter Auffenberg, the dedicated American student of monitor lizards, to discover that, in fact, *Varanus olivaceus* is relatively common in southeastern Luzon. It lives in the rapidly disappearing lowland forests of this Philippine island, spending much of its time basking or sleeping in the tree canopy, where tangled vegetation provides a refuge, sheltering from inclement weather in rocky crevices and foraging by day on the forest floor for land snails, insects, hermit crabs and the fallen fruit upon which it subsists.

SEA DRAGONS

Varanids are therefore still numerous and varied today and, as long ago as the Mesozoic Age of Reptiles, there were varanids among the ruling reptile cohorts, although they played only a very minor role in the land faunas of that remote lost world. Towards the end of the Mesozoic, the group of varanoids that had returned to the vertebrates' ancestral watery home became spectacular predators of warm, semi-tropical, Late Cretaceous seas: the ferocious mosasaurs included in their number the largest lizards of all time.

Mosasaurs had typically varanoid skulls, constructed from five basic assemblies between which a degree of movement (cranial kinesis) was originally possible, as is the case in the skulls of modern varanoids. Shortly before they became extinct, mosasaurs acquired skulls in which this capacity for movement was lost, presumably because aquatic predation was more effectively accomplished by a rigid skull. The mosasaurs' long, slender bodies lacked the sophisticated adaptations for swimming seen, for example, in the ichthyosaurs and porpoises, but their paddle-like limbs would have made locomotion on land difficult or impossible. Swimming was probably accomplished by sculling movements of the rather short, but flat and deep tail, enabling them to generate considerable speed for the pursuit of fish in the open water, and an adequate degree of manoeuvrability for hunting along the sea floor in quest of the ammonites that were so abundant in Mesozoic seas, as well as belemnites (relatives of the present-day cuttlefish).

The first known mosasaurs appeared nearly 100 million years ago and they quickly proliferated to become major predatory elements in the marine faunas of the Late Cretaceous period (Fig. 1.1). They were particularly common in the warm-temperate chalk seas of North America and Europe, but their remains also occur in such far-flung places as the former USSR, Nigeria, Argentina, Israel, New Zealand, Sweden, Poland, Bulgaria, Brazil, Jordan, Timor, Egypt and even Antarctica. At the time when the mosasaurs lived there, these places were, of course, either under the sea or, at any rate, represented a coastal environment, for it seems unlikely that mosasaurs could ever have emerged from the water. This raises the unsolved problem of how they reproduced. The ichthyosaurs were another group of wholly aquatic reptiles, almost totally fish-like in outward appearance, and there is evidence that, instead of laying eggs, they gave birth to live young. Whether the mosasaurs had also evolved this more sophisticated means of reproduction is unknown, but it is scarcely conceivable that they could have laid eggs unless they still retained some capacity for emergence on land.

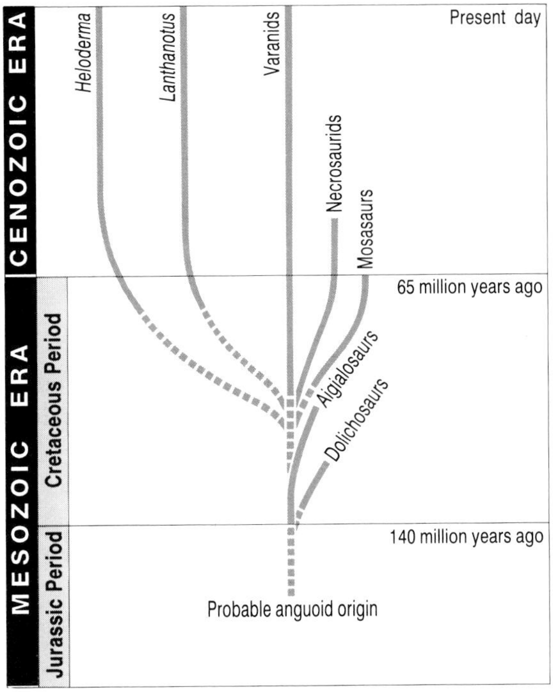

▲ **Fig. 1.1 Family tree of the Varanoidea, the living dragons and their relatives.**

At the end of the Age of Reptiles, the mosasaurs, in common with the dinosaurs, became extinct with a still largely unexplained abruptness. As major predators at the summit of food chains in Mesozoic seas, any environmental changes, however caused, that affected prey species lower down the food chain would have threatened the mosasaurs' existence. At the end of the Cretaceous, there were profound geographic and climatic disturbances, and many of the fish stocks that had typified life in the Mesozoic oceans were replaced by modern species, while major invertebrate groups, such as

▲ The desert monitor *(Varanus griseus)* has adapted to the harshest and most arid of desert environments, occurring from North Africa to India.

the ammonites, died out altogether. Too specialized to adapt, the great sea dragons became extinct and their fossil remains subsequently gave rise to much speculation, and even became involved in the dramatic events of the French Revolution.

The first real inkling that scientists had of this race of extinct sea dragons was a celebrated

specimen recovered in 1770 from one of the extensive quarries in the vicinity of Maastricht, in the Netherlands. Near this city, the River Meuse is bordered by the almost vertical cliff of an eminence called St Peter's Mount, formed from Cretaceous rocks that had been tunnelled and excavated for centuries as a source of sandstone. Fossils often came to light in the course of these activities. Mostly they were shells, corals, crustaceans and fish bones – relics of former denizens of the ancient sea that covered this area of northwestern Europe in the Late Cretaceous. An assiduous collector of these relics in around 1770 was a Dutch army surgeon called Hoffman, who became well known to the quarry workmen. So when the dust from a blasting operation deep underground cleared, to reveal the fossilized toothed jaws of a large animal exposed in the gallery roof, the enthusiastic Hoffman was immediately summoned. Realizing the importance of the find, Hoffman spent weeks carefully removing the specimen from its ancient resting place. It was, in fact, the remains of a mosasaur, but no one knew anything about mosasaurs at that time and the jaws were widely believed to be those of a huge crocodile.

Word of the find spread rapidly and the fossil speedily became a celebrated and covetable specimen. Accordingly, the canon of the cathedral that stood on St Peter's Mount sued through the courts for possession of the relic, on the grounds that he was lord of the manor in which the find was made, and, after long drawn-out legal wrangling, successfully annexed it from the unfortunate Hoffman. Following the outbreak of the French Revolution, Maastricht came under attack from the Republican armies, but members of the committee of savans, who accompanied the French troops to supervise the selection of plunder, were aware of the famous fossil reposing in the residence of the canon of St Peter's and suggested that the artillery should avoid bombarding that area of the town in which the house was situated. The canon had in fact concealed the specimen in a vault but, once Maastricht fell to the Republican troops in 1794, he was obliged inevitably to surrender it. Despatched to the Jardin des Plantes in Paris, it was examined by the celebrated French zoologist, Georges Cuvier, and pronounced to be the remains of a reptile intermediate between iguanas and monitors. Cuvier's deduction is remarkable, considering that the science of zoology was still in its infancy early in the nineteenth century, and that an understanding of the mechanism of evolution was not unravelled by Charles Darwin until

50 years later. In 1822, the English geologist, William Conybeare, named the St Peter's Mount fossil *Mosasaurus*, or 'lizard of the Meuse'. Thus the mosasaurs first became known to modern science.

DRAGONS IN LEGEND AND SUPERSTITION

The larger, living monitor lizards are such imposing creatures that it is not surprising they were held in superstitious awe by primitive native societies, many tribes even believing that some people had the power to turn themselves into 'weremonitors'. The natives of the Garo hills in Assam distinguished three different types of water monitor: Aringga, with a very clearly defined pattern of yellow spots, friendly to humans, and Matphu and Phusil, with less prominent yellow spotting, believed to be dangerous animals, dragging people under water and sucking their blood.

The Garos both feared and revered water monitors, regarding them as not far removed from water spirits. Carved figures of Aringgas occur on the Bachelors' Houses of the Atong and Ganching Garos, who live in riverside villages, and the Dawas claimed descent from a man called Dawa, who was a friend of the Aringga. (The Lushais, who did not live beside rivers, had no water monitor legends.)

The legend of Dawa recounted how Dawa caught a small Aringga and caged it. The creature's parents came from the river every day to visit the captive and Dawa became afraid to venture into the river or to go out in a boat for fear they might take revenge upon him. Eventually he released the small Aringga, placing rings in its ears and dressing it in a yellow coat, promising never to catch any monitors again and persuading his former prisoner to agree not to try and kill anyone swimming in the river who called out 'I am a son of Dawa'. Subsequently the small Aringga became Dawa's friend and would carry him across the water on its back. The Garos would always call out 'I am a son of Dawa' before crossing a river, never killed an Aringga, and released any that they caught. Aringgas were carved on the beams of Bachelors' Houses because of the story of Aning Krang Ratcha and Chanang Gitting Pante, two young men who built a Bachelors' House (Nokpante) in the Lower Regions, from which the sounds of singing and general merriment reached a man on Earth called Katchipa.

This worthy pulled aside the screen between Earth and the Lower Regions, saw the Bachelors' House, and persuaded his people to build one on Earth – the first village Bachelors' House. Figures of Aringgas were carved on the beams of the Bachelors' House in the Lower Regions, so the Garos subsequently always carved Aringgas on the beams of their own Bachelors' Houses.

In connection with these beliefs in the Aringga, Matphu and Phusil, it is noteworthy that the young of both the common monitor and the water monitor are marked with ocelli, arranged in bands which disappear with age, although in water monitors the markings on the belly and lower flanks still remain visible in adults (common monitors generally become a rather drab grey colour).

Australian folklore attributes goanna oil or fat with incredible powers of penetration (even through glass) and it is claimed that goannas eat a legendary plant to neutralize the venom of the snakes they feed on (immortalized in Banjo Paterson's poem 'Johnson's Antidote'). Goanna bites are said to be liable to break out annually or every 7 years and, in many cases, never completely heal (secondary infections may account for this myth).

In South-East Asia, tribes place water-monitor effigies made of wood among crops to protect against rodents, insects and disease. It is believed that, if a monitor crosses the path of a war party, it is an ill omen and the raid should be abandoned, while the sight of a monitor is also held to indicate the near presence of an enemy. Shields decorated with water-monitor images are supposed to bring bad luck to adversaries.

It is considered unlucky in parts of Thailand if a water monitor enters a house and a Buddhist monk is needed to exorcize it, while the Kalabits of Borneo consider it to be bad luck if a monitor is seen during a marriage ceremony. In India, young common monitors were once regarded as deadly poisonous and were associated with the mythical 'Bis Cobra', which was said to poison people from a distance of several metres.

DRAGONS AS FOOD

Monitors are eaten quite extensively by human beings. The Nile monitor is esteemed by Africans in the Victoria–Nyanza region, where fishermen also flay the creatures alive (the skin is more easily removed). In Ghana, both this species and *Varanus exanthematicus* are eaten; the flesh provides thick white steaks, rather like fish, or can be dried and added to palm soup. *Varanus niloticus* and *Varanus exanthematicus* are also eaten in Nigeria and by South African Bushmen. Australian Aborigines eat the tail and legs of *Varanus gouldi* (roasted, stewed, grilled or baked in clay), as well as the white and allegedly tasty flesh of *Varanus giganteus,* whose abdomen also provides long fillets of fat.

Low-caste Hindus will eat *Varanus bengalensis,* and both the eggs and the flesh of monitors are regularly eaten in Asia. The eggs fetch high market prices in Burma, commanding a higher figure than hens' eggs and the flesh allegedly has the flavour of chicken or fish.

VENOMOUS DRAGONS

Apparently related to the monitors, but ascribed to a separate family of their own, are the poisonous helodermatids of the southwestern USA, western Mexico and Guatemala. Sluggish, heavily built lizards, up to about 90cm (36in) in length, the Gila monster and its southerly cousin, the Mexican beaded lizard, are usually brightly coloured, with yellow, red and black markings. Up to 95 per cent of their time is spent hiding in burrows or other similar underground refuges, either hibernating during cold, dry winter months or seeking shelter from the strong midday heat in the summer. Helodermas feed mostly on the eggs of reptiles and of ground-nesting birds, as well as seeking out the young of small mammals, such as ground squirrels or jack rabbits. They can even go without food for months on end during inclement weather, frequently emerging from hibernation in an emaciated condition when the spring arrives.

Unaggressive if left alone, they will not attack people unless teased or threatened, but modified salivary glands in the lower jaw secrete a powerful venom; helodermas will bite savagely if provoked and the poison is injected deep into the wound by grooves running up the long, pointed teeth. The venom is as toxic as that of a cobra, although differently constituted, and will cause severe pain, accompanied by profuse sweating, faintness or vomiting. An elderly person, or someone in a reduced state of health, might well be in danger of succumbing to the poison and, indeed, a number of deaths have been recorded over the years.

LANTHANOTUS

Also probably a member of the varanoid assemblage is an obscure, poorly known little reptile from the island of Borneo, known to science as *Lanthanotus.* Only some 45cm (18in) long, and an elongate, subterranean denizen of waterlogged ditches, perhaps sometimes hiding under rocks and logs, it seems to live principally on earthworms. Its short legs suggest that it does not move efficiently on land, although it is a very good swimmer, and an apparent lack of response to sound led to it becoming known as the 'earless monitor', although it does have quite well-developed ears beneath the skin. Some scientists have suggested that *Lanthanotus,* in some respects, may be structurally intermediate between the helodermatids on one hand and *Varanus* on the other, despite its evident specializations and snake-like means of progression on land.

* * *

Highly adaptable, capable of exploiting a wide variety of ecological niches within the tropical and subtropical zones, the varanoids are an immensely successful group of reptiles with a long evolutionary history during the course of which they have included among their number the largest lizards ever known to have existed – mosasaurs in the seas and *Megalania* on land. Their story is a fascinating and intriguing study of reptile life and they fully deserve to be known as 'the living dragons'.

CHAPTER 2

Anatomy of a Dragon

It may seem surprising that such diverse reptiles as the Komodo dragon, the Gila monster, the tiny obscure *Lanthanotus* and the huge extinct sea-dwelling mosasaurs all belong together in a single animal assemblage, customarily referred to as the superfamily Varanoidea (from the generic name *Varanus,* which embraces all the living monitor lizards). Varanoids are all lizards in the broadest sense and therefore share with iguanas, geckos, skinks, and other similar forms, a skull structure which basically incorporates two pairs of temporal openings for the accommodation of jaw musculature.

THE VARANOID SKULL

During their long evolutionary history, all the various lizard groups have undergone substantial skull modification, notably the loss of the bony bar which connects the cheek to the quadrate bone and forms the lower edge of the lateral temporal opening. This modification is also a feature of varanoid skulls, which, in addition, typically exhibit cranial kinesis – joints between the bones that permit a degree of movement (Fig. 2.1).

In the living monitor lizards, there are five basic skull assemblies. A central unit, to which it may (for convenience of explanation) be assumed that the rest of the skull articulates, is formed by the braincase (the occipital unit). The skull roof (parietal unit) articulates with the upper part of the occipital unit, and the palate (basal unit) hinges to its lower part. Both the parietal unit and the basal unit have joints which connect them to the muzzle unit. The paired quadrate bones, which form the upper part of the jaw articulation and support the tympanum (ear drum), constitute the fifth skull unit. At the top, they are braced against the braincase, while their lower ends are effectively free to move backwards and forwards, restrained only by ligaments and able to generate a backward and forward sawing movement of the lower jaw. A further joint occurs half way along each side of the lower jaw, where the dentary and splenial bones at the front hinge against the rest of the lower jaw bones at the back of the jaw.

The purpose of this kinetic skull structure is difficult to determine but it seems likely that it serves to increase the gape when the animal is striking at prey. The muzzle unit is raised relative to the parietal unit by the action of muscles and ligaments, while the front of the lower jaw is depressed. As the mouth snaps shut, a reverse movement lowers the muzzle unit on the parietal unit and pulls up the front of the lower jaw, thus increasing the power of the bite. To some extent, the structure may also act as a shock-absorber, cushioning the impact of the strike and the savage jaw closure.

All living monitors have this type of kinetic skull and some members of the Gila monster group (*Heloderma)* exhibit a lower jaw joint which is strongly indicative of varanoid relationship. Little *Lanthanotus* also possesses a joint in its lower jaw, perhaps more elaborate than that of *Heloderma* but less sophisticated than the *Varanus* structure, which suggests that this obscure species is a varanoid. The huge extinct mosasaurs all had fully kinetic varanoid-like skulls initially, although, towards the end of their spectacular career, these massive sea dragons tended to lose the skull jointing, and were left with only the lower jaw hinge.

▶ **Fig. 2.1 The skull of: (a) a mosasaur (*Clidastes velox*) and (b) a monitor lizard (*Varanus salvator*), showing kinetic elements of the structure.**

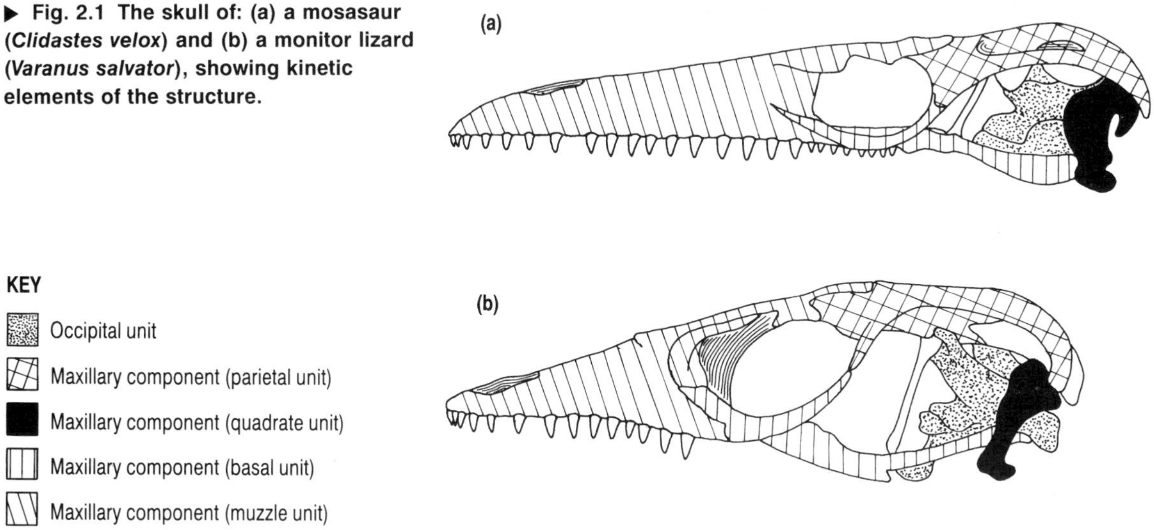

TONGUE

A further characteristic common to varanoids is the presence of a long, forked tongue, the anterior portion of which can be retracted into a basal sheath while the hind region is broad and elastic. A similar structure is also present in lizards of the anguoid group (the glass snakes, slow worm, alligator lizards, galliwasps). This group is probably antecedent to the varanoids and the fact that snakes also have this type of tongue suggests that they may be of varanoid derivation. The oldest known snakes are Late Cretaceous in age, so their evolutionary divergence obviously took place at least 80 million or 90 million years ago. The origins of monitor lizards, however, extend even further back, so a line of snake descent tracing to early varanoids is entirely feasible.

POST-CRANIAL SKELETON

The post-cranial skeleton of monitors (Fig. 2.2) is that of a typical terrestrial lizard with five-toed feet, a relatively long tail and sprawling limbs that are, nonetheless, capable of supporting the animal sufficiently well to permit rapid locomotion, with the belly held clear of the ground, as well as enabling many species to climb effectively. During the propulsive phase of a monitor's stride, the humerus (the upper bone of the forelimb) moves 40–55 degrees antero-posteriorly and rotates a total of 30–40 degrees. Simultaneously, the coracoid element of the scapulo-coracoid (shoulder girdle) translates posteriorly along the tongue-and-groove coraco-sternal joint by a distance equivalent to about 40 per cent of the coracoid's length. Because the humerus and

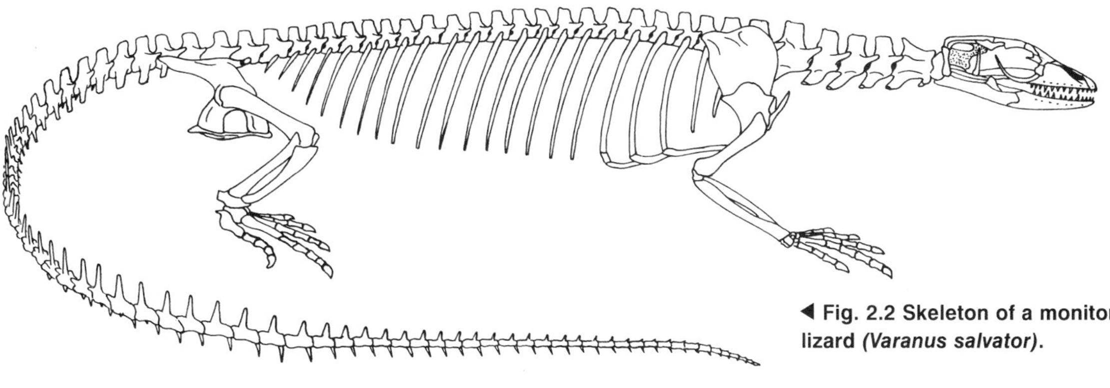

◀ **Fig. 2.2 Skeleton of a monitor lizard (*Varanus salvator*).**

scapulo-coracoid move forward in a fixed relationship, the undulatory movement of the trunk that helps to advance the limb is accommodated only at the coraco-sternal joint, whereas, if the scapulo-coracoid was fixed to the trunk, the trunk would tend to pivot about the gleno-humeral (shoulder girdle/upper arm) joint of the supporting limb.

The tendon of the forelimb's triceps muscle has a bony ulnar patella but the radial/carpal joint lacks an inter-osseous ligament in the interior of the cavity. Instead, the radius carries a hemispherical projection which engages with the socket on the radiale. Pronation/supination encompasses about 60 degrees, with some of the carpal rotation being taken up at the freely movable radial/carpal joint and at the elbow, the articular surfaces of which are not particularly complex and so move freely.

A distinctive feature of the vertebrae is an oblique articulation between the centra, and the bones of the neck are somewhat elongate – a specialization regarded as an advanced feature. Varanoids also have nine neck vertebrae instead of the eight present in lizards generally: the shoulder girdle has in effect moved back one segment along the spinal column, presumably to endow the neck with greater flexibility for seizing prey. In large monitors, there is a tendency for the tail to be laterally flattened, but no member of the varanoid group is able to shed its tail as a means of escape from predators, unlike many other lizards.

TAIL

The tail of a monitor is adapted for use as a weapon. It can be lashed from side to side and has a tough skin incorporating a strongly developed dermis immediately overlying the musculature. This corresponds with the structure found in other lizards that possess an 'active tail'; less mobile tails of lacertilians have a more delicate caudal epithelium only loosely connected with the underlying musculature. It is noteworthy that, in the regenerated tails of species that can shed their tails as a means of escape, the epithelium is of a tough texture, with scalation suggesting reversion to the presumed ancestral type, as found in monitors.

The caudal scales of varanids are arranged in longitudinal rows crossed by transverse rows. The slightly imbricate ventral scales have their long sides parallel to the longitudinal axis of the tail and pass upwards into juxtaposed laterals. Where a dorsal ridge is present, it is usually formed by a double row of slightly recurved tubercles, which become more distinct posteriorly and have a fine furrow between them. The ventral scales retain their length posteriorly but the laterals become shorter. Thus the two transverse rows of ventrals come to correspond to three rows of laterals, all of which are separated by grooves bearing microscopic scales to facilitate extension of the skin during flexion. The backbone runs down the middle of the tail, with strong, compactly constructed vertebrae that have tall neural and haemal spines, diminishing in length posteriorly and dividing the tail into right and left sides. There are strong ball and socket articulations between the caudal centra but the vertebrae are short dorso-ventrally, broadened from side to side and have relatively small zygapophyses. Up and down movement is somewhat limited. Towards the end of the tail, the vertebrae become elongate, hollow cylinders, higher than broad.

Anteriorly, there are five pairs of muscle trunks (three dorsal pairs, two ventral pairs) with flexors located immediately beneath the skin. The right and left sides are separated by a vertical partition composed of tough connective tissue that embraces the neural spines and the haemal arches. Of the three epi-axonic (upper) pairs of muscles, only the transverso-spinalis and the ilio-costalis (which perform creeping movements of the trunk in other lizards) continue to the end; the other pair (the longissimus) extends only a third of the way along the tail. The hypaxonic (ventral) muscles are the ilio-caudalis and the infero-caudalis. Lashing movements of the tail are apparently initiated in the trunk, a series of sinuous contractions passing alternately down each side from the base of the tail backwards towards its tip.

LOCOMOTION

Locomotion in monitor lizards is normally quadrupedal, the legs being advanced in a diagonal pattern when walking, e.g. the left foreleg and the right hind leg are advanced while the opposite pair of legs propels the body forward, the head, trunk and tail undulating from side to side in rhythm with the limb movements and the tail swinging in the opposite direction to the head. The soles of the feet are placed flat on the ground and the legs are thrust out to the side as they swing forward, then come back under the body. When running, monitors tend to hold the body and tail relatively rigid. Some species can allegedly run on their hind legs with the forelegs folded against their sides, the body assuming an almost vertical position at maximum speed, although it is doubtful whether large specimens of, e.g., the Komodo dragon (*Varanus komodoensis*) would be capable of such agility (or even need to move so quickly, either to escape predators or catch prey, since a Komodo dragon of substantial size has no real enemies and secures its prey by ambush).

All monitors are accomplished swimmers, although only the more specialized aquatic species regularly enter the water. The tail is the principal organ of propulsion; the legs are normally held against the sides but are sometimes used to assist ascent to the surface after a dive. Monitors can remain submerged for long periods (up to 1 hour) and regularly aquatic species, at least, close and seal their external nostrils to prevent the ingress of water.

ACTION OF JAWS AND TONGUE WHEN FEEDING

All varanoids are basically predators and monitor lizards will eat almost anything which they are big enough to overpower – one species (*Varanus olivaceus*) has acquired a taste for fruit, but this is an exception. Members of the *Heloderma* group all have stoutly constructed jaws for crushing tough or hard-shelled prey and little *Lanthanotus* probably lives largely on subterranean invertebrates, notably earthworms. The extinct mosasaurs, of course, were marine killers of exceptional magnitude and indicate the frightening potential of the varanoid assemblage to evolve into truly formidable predators given a conducive environment. The Komodo dragon and the extinct *Megalania* are other indications of the size and power these reptiles can achieve in the absence of competition from large mammalian carnivores.

▼ Fig. 2.3 Skull of *Varanus salvator*: (a) side elevation; (b) dorsal view; (c) palatal aspect.

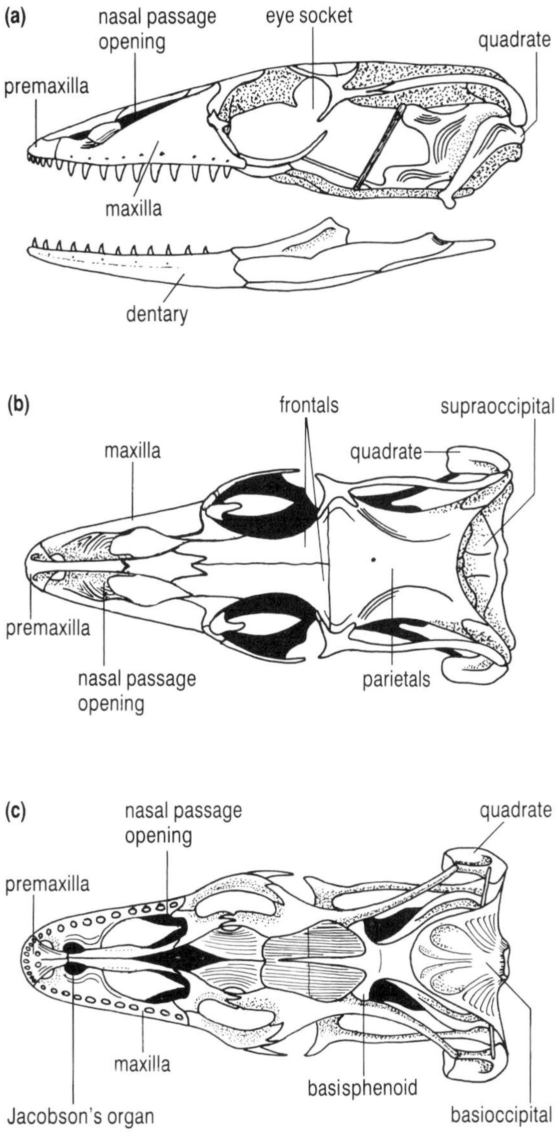

The kinetic skull of monitors (Fig. 2.3) is a key feature of their predatory adaptations, the various joints being held together by elastic fibrous tissue, although they lack the cartilaginous gliding surfaces possessed by limb bones. The mouth is opened principally by raising the head (the

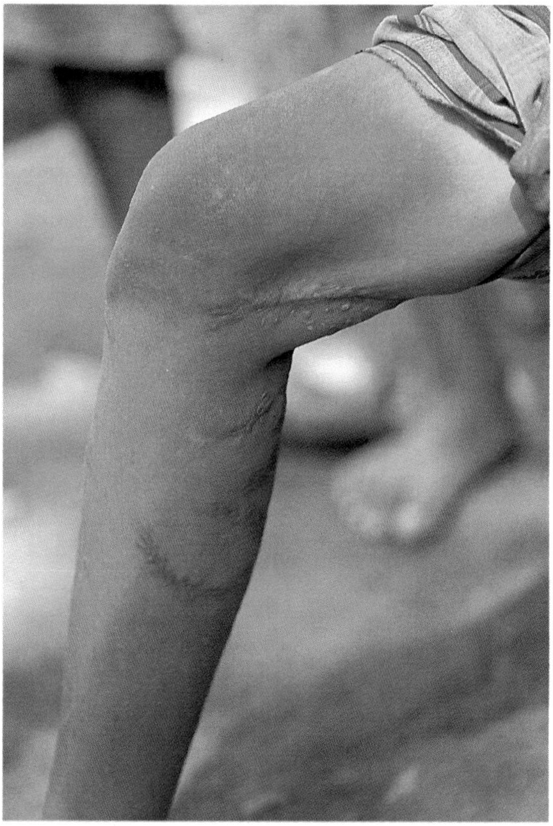

▲ **The badly scarred leg of this man, who was attacked by a Komodo dragon *(Varanus komodoensis)*, bears testimony to the efficiency of a monitor's teeth.**

upper jaw) rather than by lowering the lower jaw (whose function is primarily to support any prey that has been seized). Initially, the muzzle unit of the kinetic skull is elevated about 9 degrees relative to the rest of the skull as the jaw opens, with the quadrate swinging anteriorly through some 21 degrees. During jaw closure, the muzzle is depressed about 15 degrees relative to the rest of the skull (i.e. 6 degrees beyond the resting position), while the quadrate swings back about 27 degrees and imparts a shearing action to the bite.

Cinematic analysis of monitors in the process of seizing their prey indicates that the flexion of the upper jaw is largely independent of the lower jaw's action. It appears that, at the moment the lizard strikes at its prey, the upper and lower jaws are simultaneously adducted so that they both grasp the victim at the same moment. Subsequently, the maintenance of downward flexion in the upper jaw helps to maintain a pincer-like grip, with the maximum number of teeth impaling the victim, while at the same time serving to expand the throat in the gular region to facilitate swallowing. Dorsal flexion of the upper jaw, as the mouth re-opens to throw the prey inertially back into the throat, is probably to clear the teeth from the victim's body.

Embryonic varanoid teeth are almost symmetrical but become progressively more recurved towards the tip as they grow. Fully mature teeth show some slight reduction in recurvature during the final stages of development and the maxillary dentition is more recurved than the teeth of the lower jaw. The crowns are laterally compressed, with anterior and posterior serrations in living species, and exhibit a degree of lingual curvature. Implantation is pleurodont, i.e. individual teeth are ankylosed to an obliquely sloping dental shelf on the tooth-bearing bone. The bases are widely flared, sometimes overgrown by bone, and exhibit striations (plicidentine). This structure provides a strong attachment, and compressive and tensile stresses are taken up along the long axes of the striations during axial or vertical loading of the teeth. (The slope at which the teeth are attached to the jaws is so arranged that these shear stresses are minimized.)

To be properly effective, recurved teeth must strike the prey point first. This requires either a very wide gape or a kinetic skull. The advantage of recurved teeth is that they can hold prey as well or better than a straight tooth of greater length. Monitors employ kinetic inertial feeding, thrusting the head forwards and down once prey has been seized to secure a better purchase with the teeth and initiate swallowing. (Alternatively, monitors have been seen to push apprehended prey against the substrate to force it back into the mouth.) The stronger posterior recurvature of the maxillary teeth enhances their capacity to hold prey without requiring excessive increase in overall length, thus enabling monitors to take relatively large prey.

Tooth replacement occurs in alternating waves so that no substantial gaps are left as worn teeth are shed. Nonetheless, some individuals display gaps where several successive teeth have been lost or have a number of newly developed teeth all in position contiguously, while aged individuals apparently have a tendency to lose the more posterior teeth permanently.

The mandibular joint hinging the lower jaw to the skull is complex so that the lower jaw rotates laterally around its long axis during depression and mesially during elevation. When fully adducted, the dentary and maxillary teeth point slightly inward; as the jaw is depressed, the jaw rotates around the deeper medial side of the glenoid fossa and the teeth rotate outward. When the teeth actually strike the intended prey, they are therefore fully erect.

The tongue plays little part in food transport. The intrinsic muscles are reduced to little more than longitudinal and circular masses and the hyobranchial apparatus is exceptionally strong and mobile, with a well-defined joint between the cerato-hyal and the anterior process, and a series of distinct muscles inserting at the anterior hyobranchial region. *Varanus* relies on hyobranchial movements for drinking and for the pharyngeal packing and compression of food. The long narrow shape of the tongue is probably related to the mechanics of tongue protrusion, while the increased extent, strength and complexity of hyobranchial movement occurs because the hyobranchium replaces the tongue in many functions.

Ingestion is by inertial feeding (effected by rapidly opening the jaws as the head is pulled back, imparting a backward motion to the prey, then thrusting the head forwards, with the jaws at maximum gape), after first grabbing and orienting the prey in the mouth. There is no mastication (big monitors scavenging at a carcass may, of course, bite out lumps of flesh for ingestion) and up to a dozen thrusts may be needed to engulf large victims or substantial mouthfuls of flesh. Once the prey is in the gular or pharyngeal region, the hyoid apparatus squeezes it into the oesophagus and thence it passes to the stomach.

SENSES

Because of their predatory nature, all monitors are to a greater or lesser extent active hunters. Their sensory perception is probably greater than that of lizards in general and they have a capacity for sustained activity which transcends the capabilities of most reptiles and approaches the warm-blooded mammalian level.

Chemoreception

Uniquely among lizards, the varanid tongue has an exclusively sensory function and is devoid of taste buds, although the reason for its deeply forked structure is not really known. It is highly protrusible, lacks a roughened dorsal surface and retracts into a sheath for most of its resting length. It only protrudes and bends – there is no flattening or differential expansion or contraction – moving upwards and downwards during protrusion and wrapping around the outside edges of the mouth during withdrawal.

The sensory function of the monitor's tongue is correlated with the conspicuous development of Jacobson's organ (vomero-nasal organ) – a pair of sensory sacs opening into the roof of the mouth in front of the internal nasal apertures (Fig. 2.4). In monitors, Jacobson's organ is well developed, each side possessing a large dorsal dome, lined by sensory epithelium, and a mushroom body invaginated into the lumen from in front and below. This structure is covered by a non-sensory, ciliated or stratified epithelium, beneath which is a layer of dense connective tissue. It is supported by the cartilage of Jacobson's organ, which projects upwards and backwards from the vomerine concha and is borne on a stalk arising from the dorsal surface of the vomer. The organ's spiral duct, also lined by a non-sensory, ciliated epithelium, has a crescent-shaped opening into the lumen beneath the posterior part of the mushroom body, and passes downwards and forwards into the mouth. The lacrimal duct opens into its medial aspect as it traverses the tissues of the superficial palate.

It was at one time believed that particles were inserted into the lumen of Jacobson's organ by the forked tip of the tongue and then carried by ciliated epithelia up the lateral aspect of the duct, over the mushroom body, and back into the mouth via the medial aspect of the duct, which thus functioned as a one-way circuit. However, while other lizards have long choanal grooves

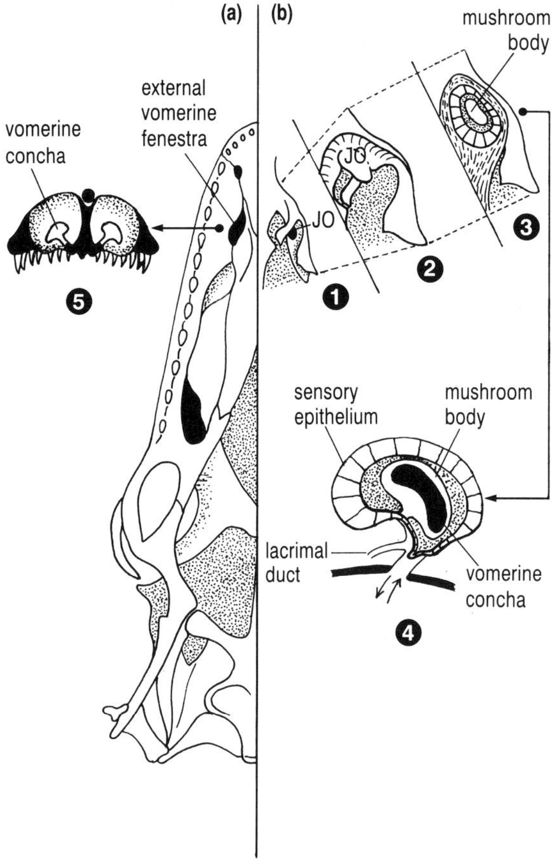

▲ Fig. 2.4 Jacobson's organ (JO) above the palate of *Varanus*. (a) Ventral view of the palate, showing one of the paired exterior vomerine fenestrae into which particles are directed for assessment. (b) 1. The location of Jacobson's organ revealed by removal of the palatal bones. 2. The cartilaginous capsule of Jacobson's organ from the right side, seen from above, after removal of the roof of the nasal capsule. 3. Jacobson' s organ from the right side, seen from above in horizontal section. 4. A transverse section of Jacobson's organ (through 3), viewed from behind. 5. A cross-section through the snout to show the paired cavities for Jacobson' s organ and the vomerine concha each side which supports the mushroom body.

that carry particles by ciliary action to Jacobson's organ, *Varanus* has only short grooves, suggesting that it would be necessary for the tongue to place particles in the lumen of the organ in order for the cilia of the mushroom body to work on them.

In an experiment, radio-dense material, mixed with raw beaten egg and strawberry-flavoured barium sulphate, was fed to a specimen of *Varanus exanthematicus albigularis* whose flicking tongue was then viewed on a video screen while X-rays were taken of its action. It was discovered that the tongue did not in fact enter Jacobson's organ but moved past the openings. No muscle fibres apparently extend into the twin tips of the tongue, which cannot therefore orient itself to enter the ducts leading to Jacobson's organ. Instead, the X-rays showed radio-dense material being spread by the forked tongue in two lines along the floor of the buccal cavity (not along the palate at all), with particles apparently being transported to the ducts of Jacobson's organ by ciliary action. In monitors, the inner cartilaginous capsule of Jacobson's organ is richly supplied with blood vessels while the nerve supply is more comprehensive than that associated with the olfactory centres, emphasizing the importance of the vomero-nasal organ to the varanid group.

The flicking tongue evidently samples particles from ambient air currents, using Jacobson's organ as a major source of sensory input, so that the monitor can assess whether potential prey or enemies are nearby. Olfaction is a very important sense in monitor lizards, all of which are hunters and may, when the opportunity presents itself, carrion eaters. A Komodo dragon can detect a decomposing carcass from a distance of 11km (7 miles) but it seems likely that the nose is of only secondary importance as an olfactory receptor, the primary source of smell detection being Jacobson's organ. Smell and taste are probably not such distinctly separate senses in monitors as they are in mammals or, indeed, in other reptiles that lack a highly developed Jacobson's organ, e.g. crocodiles. A monitor probably 'tastes' the air currents in its vicinity, rather than sniffing them as a mammal does, and its flicking tongue will sample a volume of air at least as great (if not greater) than the similar tongue of structurally advanced snakes.

Hearing

Just how much monitor lizards can hear is unknown. Among reptiles, whose ears are less sensitive than mammals, monitors seem to have quite good hearing, although varanids are apparently incapable of vocalizing and therefore use their ears only to aid defence or foraging. At one time, it was claimed that monitors were deaf, or became deaf with age, because of the apparent lack of response evinced by these lizards to shouting, firecrackers, rattling plates and nearby shotgun discharges. Furthermore, any reaction to auditory stimulus that is displayed seems to be short-lived and captive animals apparently tend to lose interest in sounds that initially elicit at least a flicker of interest. Boredom or familiarity probably account for at least some of this apathy and observations in the field demonstrate that monitors certainly can hear. Komodo dragons, for example, have been seen to raise their heads at the sound of a distant motorcycle engine, the chattering of natives passing from an island village, or sharp noises deliberately produced from a zoologist's observation hide – hand claps, whistling, shouts, a loud radio, etc. These responses seem to be of brief duration, however, and the reptiles tend to ignore these sounds if they are repeated.

The cochlear duct of the varanid ear is a relatively advanced structure, large and elongate (approximately twice as long as wide) to accommodate the substantially proportioned, heavily constructed limbus – the supporting structure of the basilar papilla (a sensory area of the sacculus). The sensory lagenar macula is moderately developed and the groove for the peri-lymphatic duct is quite deep. The limbic recess has a long superior and a short inferior recess, while the basilar papilla is elongate and sometimes divided, with a longer superior portion. In the Bengal monitor *(Varanus bengalensis)*, for instance, there is a constriction about one-third of the way from the ventral end that effectively divides the papilla into two areas of unequal size: a dorsal portion, sensitive to low frequency (2.8–1.1kHz) sounds, and a ventral section responding to higher frequencies (above 1.3kHz). Alligators, which vocalize, have a better developed, longer, partially twisted cochlear duct and a basilar papilla that is two to five times as long and ten to thirty times the area of this feature in lizards.

Sight

There is little hard evidence by which to measure the acuity of a monitor's vision. They are diurnal creatures and there are no nocturnal specializations of the eyes. Slight movement, either close to or at a distance, seems to be instantly detected and large species are believed to have a visual perception of at least 50m (55yd), captive Komodo dragons being able to recognize their keepers from 5–6m (5½–6½yd) in a good light. Prey is apparently located in an arc of about 90 degrees each side (mostly between 30 and 80 degrees), the visual fields possessing an overlap of some 30 degrees, compared with only 10–20 degrees in most other lizards.

RESPIRATORY SYSTEM

Lizards have a compliant body wall and highly compliant lungs that lie not in a pleural cavity, but in the upper region of the general pleuro-peritoneal cavity. The saccular lungs of *Varanus* (Fig. 2.5) are proportionately twice the size of

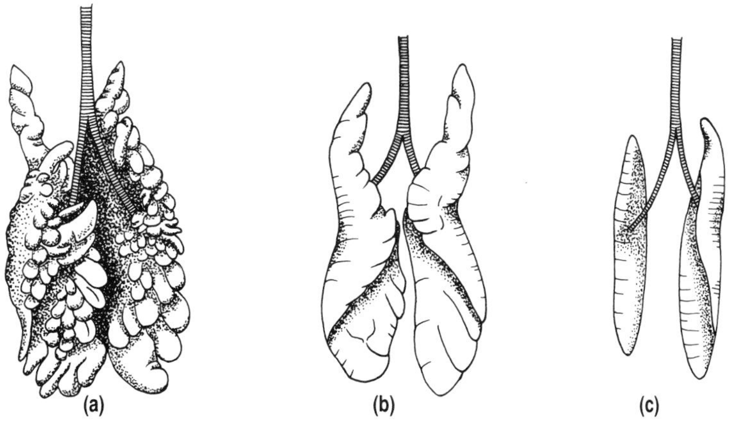

▶ Fig. 2.5 Varanid lung structure, viewed from the ventral aspect. (a) The richly convoluted lungs of *Varanus salvator*, a very large, extremely active monitor with high metabolic requirements. (b) The moderately complex lungs of *Varanus mertensi*, an aquatic species nearly 1.25m (4¹/4ft) long. (c) The extremely simple lungs of *Varanus mitchelli*, a small species less than lm (3¹/4ft) in length.

those normally found in lizards and permit a high level of gas exchange (oxygen acquisition and carbon dioxide release) in a manner that foreshadows the complex ultra-efficient lungs of birds and mammals. The lungs are of the multicameral type, i.e. they have multiple chambers, markedly heterogeneous gas-exchange compartments (of small diameter anteriorly, larger diameter posteriorly), incorporate an unbranched intra-pulmonary bronchus and attach to the body wall where it underlies the rib cage. Anteriorly, the lungs of varanids extend well in advance of the heart and continue forwards, as semi-sacculated structures, into the forelimbs and either side of the neck. The ventral chambers, particularly towards the caudal end of the lungs, have only thin membranous walls, contrasting with the densely partitioned tissue of the upper portions.

Thus the most extensively partitioned region of the lungs, within the rib cage, cannot suffer collapse during normal breathing since lung movement is restricted to that of the overlying ribs. At the same time, the ventral and caudal regions of the lungs are separated from the viscera only by a very thin post-pulmonary septum, so that these membranous areas are sensitive to any small change in intra-peritoneal pressure. With these extensive membranous dilatations, lung compliance is high so that a large tidal volume is possible without the need for energy-consuming respiratory effort.

Although reptiles in general do have large lung volumes for their size compared to mammals, their lungs are normally in the form of simple sacs, with the respiratory area confined to the anterior portion, which is not extensively developed. The ability of monitors to sustain a high level of aerobic activity and to recover rapidly from a substantial activity-induced oxygen debt is evidently due largely to their complex saccular lung structure and the high compliance of the lung membranes, which can be readily dilated by non-respiratory functions to achieve efficient ventilation. In a cold environment, the respiratory rate slows and the period of expiration is more prolonged, while at higher temperatures there is a faster respiratory rate with increased breathing amplitude.

HEART AND CIRCULATORY SYSTEM

The efficiency of gaseous exchange achieved by varanid lung structure is complementary to a heart and circulatory system that also represents an advance on the normal, typically rather conservative, reptilian arrangement. The varanid heart (Fig. 2.6) and the proximal regions of the great arteries and veins are enclosed in a comparatively firm and non-compliant pericardium. The heart is located far behind the axillary region, partly overlapped by the anterior borders of the right and left lobes of the liver and surrounded on its left and right sides by the lungs; it has shifted markedly posteriorly compared to other lizards, possibly because of the long, retractile neck. The cardiac output, heart rate and systemic arterial pressures of *Varanus* are all high by the standards for other lacertilians.

The ventricle of the reptilian heart has two main compartments: the cavum arteriosum, with the imperfectly separated cavum venosum, supplying oxygenated blood from the lungs to the body; and the cavum pulmonale, which pumps deoxygenated blood from the body to the lungs and, in varanids, constitutes a distinct chamber surrounded by a cone of dense trabeculae.

The cavum venosum is reduced in monitors, while the cavum arteriosum has become enlarged and is functionally separated from the cavum venosum by an incomplete vertical septum. During the inflow of blood from the left atrium into the cavum arteriosum, the large left septal atrio-ventricular valve opens against this septum and prevents arterial blood from filling the cavum venosum. Outflow from the cavum pulmonale into the pulmonary artery (to the lungs) is separated from the openings of the right and left aortic arches (emanating from the cavum venosum, communicating with each other, and supplying the body) by a muscular ridge.

Despite this structural sophistication, there nevertheless seems to be some shunting of blood from the lungs directly back to the lungs, and a measure of systemic venous blood by-passing the lungs and being shunted back to the systemic tissues. Tests were undertaken on an anaesthetized specimen of *Varanus exanthematicus*, using microspheres, 25µm in diameter (slightly

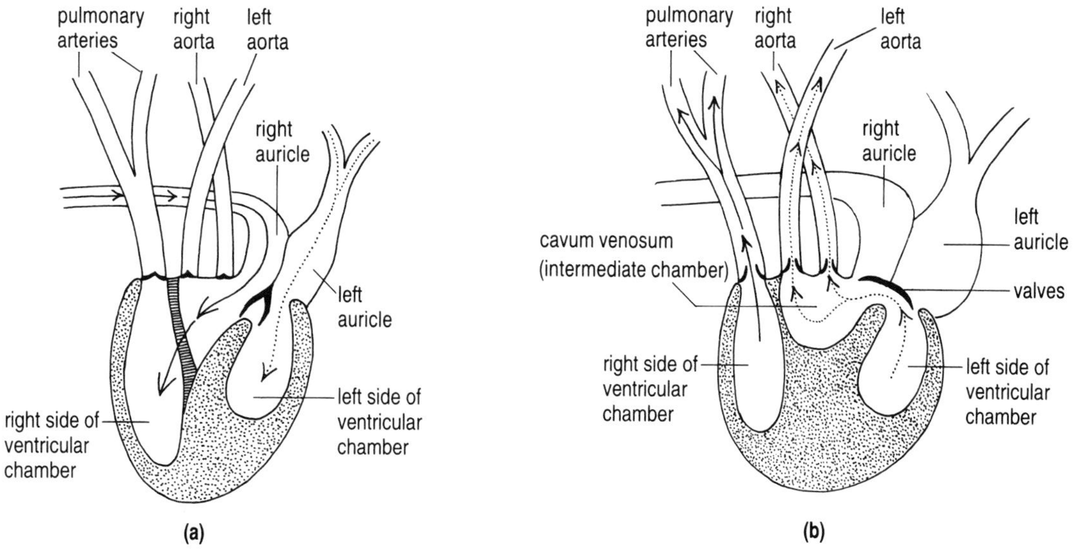

▲ **Fig. 2.6 Semi-schematic visualization of the varanid heart. (a) During diastole (expansion), deoxygenated blood (solid arrows) reaches the right auricle from the body and passes into the right side of the partially divided ventricular chamber prior to being pumped out to the lungs via the pulmonary arteries for reoxygenation; while valves seal off the right and left aortas, oxygenated blood (dotted arrows) from the lungs enters the left auricle and passes into the left side of the ventricular chamber. (b) During systole (contraction), the valves into the right and left aortas, and those that have hitherto sealed the interventricular canal, open. Oxygenated blood from the left side of the ventricle is pumped through the aortas to the body, limbs and head via the cavum venosum (intermediate chamber), which may still contain a residue of deoxygenated blood from the preceding diastole; consequently this may be shunted back up the aortas (mostly the left aorta).**

larger than the erythrocytes, which are about 20μm) and labelled with different gamma-emitting radio-opaque isotopes, to measure left to right and right to left shunting. The microspheres were injected into the left pulmonary vein or the left atrium and disclosed left to right shunting ranging from 28 per cent to 4 per cent (mean 13 per cent), indicating blood returning from the lungs and being shunted back to the lungs; 51 per cent to 3 per cent (mean 16 per cent) right to left shunting occurred as systemic venous blood by-passed the lungs and was shunted back to the systemic tissues.

It seems that the ventricle of the varanid heart is functionally divided during systole into a high-pressure pump (primarily from contraction of the cavum arteriosum) perfusing the systemic artery and a low pressure pump (cavum pulmonale) perfusing the pulmonary arteries, the complex of ventricular compartments being in anatomical continuity during diastole. The blood in the left aortic arch is less highly oxygenated than that in the right aortic arch, apparently because it receives any partially deoxygenated blood left in the cavum venosum after diastole when this is flushed through by the next systole. The exit into the right aorta is so positioned that it receives almost exclusively freshly oxygenated blood from the lungs. Hence, the varanoid circulatory system cannot be regarded as comparable in its efficiency to the mammalian heart, although the degree of intra-ventricular mixing is evidently limited and represents an enhanced level of efficiency compared to typical reptiles.

The resting heart rate of Nile monitors at 20°C (68°F) is 30 beats/minute, the mean pulmonary arterial pressure is 20mb (200mm H_2O/8in H_2O), and the right aortic pressure is 118mb (1200mm H_2O/48in H_2O); as temperature rises, so the heart rate increases, reaching 55 beats/minute at 35°C (95°F). At a heart rate of 25 beats/minute, the pressure rise on ventricular contraction in the pulmonary artery precedes the right aortic pressure rise by 120msec; flow acceleration is equal in the two vessels but outflow through the pulmonary artery decelerates much more slowly. While peak flow values in the right aortic arch, common carotid artery and left pulmonary artery are easily measured, with peak flow values of 80–90cm^3/minute in the right aorta and 40–50cm^3/minute in the left pulmonary artery, the amount of blood passing through the left aortic arch is barely detectable. Flow in the left aortic arch and carotid artery combined (amounting to 120cm^3/minute) balance the flow in the two pulmonary arteries, so that the systemic vascular resistance is about six times the pulmonary resistance during normal breathing, with balanced flow in the two circuits.

Very high blood pressure in the systemic arteries and low pulmonary pressure is unusual in a reptile, the 6 : 1 systemic: pulmonary resistance ratio approaching the value found in homeotherms (e.g. 7–10 : 1 in mammals, 10–12 : 1 in birds). It would appear that the varanid heart is haemodynamically advanced towards the homeotherm condition. During diving, the heart rate of monitor lizards declines in proportion to the duration of the dive (up to 1 hour in the case of *Varanus niloticus*), while pulmonary pressure rises and right aortic pressure simultaneously falls markedly. In the course of a typical dive there is 90 per cent depletion of arterial oxygen and an 85 per cent reduction in heart rate. Arterial pH decreases from 7.5 to 7.1, due to combined respiratory and metabolic acidosis, but high plasma bicarbonate and a buffering capacity increase tolerance to acidosis and they also prolong diving time.

The high oxygen-transporting capability of varanid blood is due not to any increased oxygen affinity on the part of the haemoglobin (which in fact has a low affinity for oxygen, facilitating efficient unloading), but to avoidance of metabolic acidosis during activity. In *Varanus*, high levels of myoglobin, equal to those of mammals, facilitate rapid transfer of oxygen from blood to muscle fibres. A monitor's oxygen consumption rises 5- to 20-fold above resting rate during activity but ventilation frequency does not change. Tidal volume increases greatly, however, and represents the principal ventilatory adjustment to increased oxygen demands. *Varanus* removes oxygen from air more efficiently than most other lizards and it also consumes more oxygen during activity – a function of the complex lung structure with greater surface area found in many species.

Monitors remain largely aerobic during sustained activity and thus avoid the exhaustion inherent in anaerobic work, which causes a release of lactic acid into the blood, lowering blood pH and decreasing the affinity of haemoglobin for oxygen. Some species, however, seem to be less aerobically efficient than others. The water monitor *(Varanus salvator)* starts to employ anaerobic metabolism within 10 minutes if required to run on a treadmill at its maximum sustainable walking speed of 0.5km/h (⅓mph), and blood lactate concentrations rise to in excess of 20mb (200mm H_2O/8in H_2O) after only 4½ minutes at a speed of 1 km/h (⅔mph) because of the use of anaerobic metabolism. Some other lizards approach varanids in aerobic efficiency, e.g. the small desert iguana, *Dipsosaurus*. Very high levels of arterial blood oxygen saturation (up to 94 per cent) have been recorded for varanids, although their cousins in the *Heloderma* group are far less efficient in this respect, with a maximum oxygen blood saturation of only about 40 per cent.

In common with other lizards, *Varanus* suffers a decline in the oxygen capacity and oxygen affinity of its blood when subjected to excessively high temperatures. Unlike other lizards, however, monitors breathe regularly, with none of the periods of breath-holding that commonly occur in lacertilians and during which blood is shunted away from the lungs. As a result, the gas pressures in varanid blood tend to be maintained at relatively stable levels. Spontaneous activity can double the heart rate, with a 6-fold increase in oxygen consumption.

Varanid blood has oval erythrocytes (red blood cells), with a large centrally placed nucleus. Leucocytes number about 3700/mm^3 in males, 3300/mm^3 in females, while the haemoglobin content is 10–14g/100cm^3 blood in males and 8–14g/100cm^3 blood in females.

In at least some species, the erythrocyte number and haemoglobin content of the blood rises just before the breeding season, when the animals are particularly active and vigorous, with a high metabolic rate, and then fall during the winter months. In male Bengal monitors *(Varanus bengalensis)*, the highest red blood cell count occurs just before and during the breeding season in India, e.g. April–August, with an August peak of 1.25 million/mm^3 of blood, the female rise occurring from June to August with an August peak of 1.39 million/mm^3 of blood. In February, the figures for males and females respectively are 0.85 and 0.86 million/mm^3 of blood. The haemoglobin concentration remains almost uniform in males from January to March (about 10.2g/100cm^3 of blood), then increases significantly from April through August, with an August peak of 14.0g/100cm^3 of blood, followed by a slow decrease until December. Females show a similarly uniform haemoglobin level from the turn of the year until March (about 11.2g/100cm^3 of blood), rising to an August peak of 13.8g/100cm^3 of blood, and then decreasing to a constant September–December value.

THERMOREGULATION

Varanids are reptiles and, as such, possess a 'cold-blooded' physiology. Monitor lizards have an optimum internal temperature of about 35°C (95°F) but are far less able than 'warm-blooded' mammals to regulate their own body heat; they lack any sort of insulation, are incapable of shivering and there is no efficient separation of the pulmonary and systemic blood flow in the ventricle of the heart. In the morning, they depend on the sun's warmth to raise their temperature to a comfortable level, often basking on a convenient rock or branch; they take refuge from the excessive heat of the mid-day tropical sun and the chill of the night in burrows or similar shelter and, in markedly seasonal areas, hibernation occurs.

The skin of varanids, with body scales arranged in transverse and longitudinal rows, is a poor insulator, the peripheral body muscles being few and thin, while dorsal and lateral fat deposits are largely absent, although some ventral fat is present. Transmission of solar radiation through the keratinous layer of the skin amounts to less than 10 per cent of visible and infra-red light in the case of the Komodo monitor, which has exuvia 50μm thick (compared with 10μm in other lizards, whose skins transmit 40–60 per cent of light in these wave bands). Lizard skin, including that of monitors, provides virtually complete protection from ultra-violet light (wavelength 270–280μm).

The parietal 'eye' in the centre of the upper surface of the skull appears to be a thermoregulatory aid. When masked by felt in laboratory experiments to exclude ambient heat stimulus, there is a significant rise in cloacal temperature.

At their optimum body temperature (35°C/95°F), varanids exhibit faster growth, greater food intake and superior efficiency of conversion than they do at 24°C (75.2°F). At higher temperatures, the animals also exhibit a greater metabolic rate and increased thyroid activity – there is a close association between thyroid hormone and metabolism in general, increased thyroid activity contributing significantly to the superior growth, food intake and conversion efficiency of animals maintained at higher temperatures. In the warm-blooded mammals, administration of thyroxine and noradrenaline augments heat production and oxygen consumption. When administered to a Cape monitor *(Varanus exanthematicus albigularis)*, thyroxine produced a 27 per cent increase in resting metabolic rate and a 63 per cent increase in thermal gradient between core and ambient temperature at the preferred body temperature. Hence, the thyroid presumably plays a significant role in varanid thermoregulation. On the other hand, noradrenaline reduced the heart rate but, at the recommended dosage, had no effect on metabolic rate at either 35°C (95°F) or 15°C (59°F), indicating that non-shivering thermogenesis is absent in varanids. (In at least some cold-acclimatized mammals, noradrenaline administration increases heat production.)

At lower temperatures, varanids lose proportionately more energy via respiration than at higher temperatures. There appears to be little or no water uptake through the skin, water only being imbibed by drinking, and there is a high rate of water loss through transpiration (i.e. via the lungs) compared to tropical skinks and geckos. A Nile monitor *(Varanus niloticus)* lost some 6 per cent of its weight in this manner in 24 hours when kept in dry still air at 34°C (93.2°F), while a Gould's monitor *(Varanus gouldi)* lost only 0.3 per cent of body weight per day in dry air at 30°C (86°F) but 0.9 per cent at 37.5°C (99.5°F); at 43.5°C (110.3°F) the animal succumbed. This would account in part for the affinity many species have for water.

Varanids evidently have some control over heating, warming up faster than they cool down (resembling crocodiles in this respect) and being capable of elevating their body temperature some 2°C (3.6°F) above the ambient figure. Endogenous heat production is apparently more important than changes in heat transport by the circulatory system. Nonetheless, during cooling, the blood is apparently shunted from the tail and limbs to minimize heat loss. Experiments demonstrate that, when monitors are subjected to controlled cooling, the temperature of the tail and legs falls relatively quickly while the deep body temperature requires more than 6 hours to stabilize at a lower figure. When subjected to excessive heat, the head is maintained at a temperature about 2°C (3.6°F) below that of the body, thus deferring the adverse effects of heat on the brain.

Monitors can maintain a comparatively high level of sustained activity by reptilian standards and, in this respect, are almost intermediate between typical reptiles and the more energy-efficient mammals. Heart rate and weight-relative oxygen consumption are inversely related to body weight, a 10g (⅓oz) varanid having a heart rate of 60 beats/minute at 30°C (86°F), while a 1kg (2.2lb) specimen has a heart rate of only 20 beats/minute. Oxygen consumption of a 10g (⅓oz) varanid is 0.4cm^3 oxygen/g/hour, compared with 0.06cm^3 oxygen/g/hour for a 1kg (2.2lb) specimen and 0.045cm^3 oxygen/g/hour for a 10kg (22lb) specimen. The metabolic scope for activity increases continuously between 20° and 40°C (68° and 104°F). At 37°C (98.6°F) the minimum metabolism (i.e. oxygen consumption) of a 700g (1½lb) varanid is about one-third the basal rate of a similar-sized mammal but its maximum rate of metabolism will equal or even exceed the mammal's basal rate.

HIBERNATION

Many varanids hibernate during the winter if they live in areas with a seasonal climate. During this period, augmentation of muscle electrolytes has been reported, with sodium increasing by up to 100 per cent, potassium by 25 per cent, magnesium by 80 per cent, chloride by 20 per cent and phosphorus by about 40 per cent (calcium does not seem to increase significantly). Magnesium, it may be noted, is a depressive and hypermagnesaemia is manifested by depression of the central nervous system and cardiovascular system, with depressed blood pressure. On the other hand, the level of blood sodium shows a drop of up to 30 per cent compared with summer figures, while blood calcium falls by about 12 per cent. However, blood potassium increases by 25 per cent during hibernation, approximately compen-

◀ Transverse and longitudinal scale rows of a monitor lizard's skin.

sating for the reduced sodium figure, as does magnesium (up 50 per cent or more). Blood sugar levels fall by 60 per cent but glycogen in skeletal and cardiac muscles rises by about 40 per cent. In the cortex of the brain, glutamic acid (GA) decreases, probably because of its transformation to glutamine for the detoxication of ammonia in the brain and its role in the synthesis of the neuro-transmitter, gamma-amino-butyric acid (GABA), which functions by depressing activity in the cerebral cortex. The enzyme glutamic acid decarboxylase (GAD) is also possibly active in the brain during hibernation.

The endocrine cells of the pancreas become quiescent, as does the thyroid, and the red blood cells become enlarged in at least some species, e.g. *Varanus bengalensis*. Indications of seasonal growth rings have been detected in sections of varanid bone, taken across the borders of the alveolar groove in the dentary and across the limb bones, which suggest that growth also slows or ceases during hibernation.

DIGESTIVE SYSTEM

The varanid digestive tract (Fig. 2.7) incorporates a very long oesophagus that displaces the stomach and intestines posteriorly, enabling monitors to swallow consecutively several smaller lizards or similar prey, engulfing them whole, head first. Internally, the funnel-shaped oesophagus is lined anteriorly by a mucosa incorporating parallel, low, longitudinal folds (including some of relatively large size) separated by shallow grooves. There are no oesophageal glands, but cells of ciliated, calciferous and goblet types are present. The posterior third of the oesophagus becomes very narrow, with high mucosal folds projecting into its narrow lumen.

The stomach is wide and elongate with a mucosa exhibiting low but well-defined folds which incorporate gastric glands of several different types. A strongly muscled pyloric sphincter guards the entrance to the rather short small intestine, which initially forms a coiled tube; its mucosal walls are thrown into longitudinal folds (about 1.3–1.8mm / 1⁄16in across and 2.9–4.8mm / 1⁄8–1⁄4in high in an average-sized species), separated by narrow grooves and covered in finger-like villi, about 0.45mm (1⁄32in) long and 0.15mm (about 1⁄100in) in diameter, which overlap each other within the grooves. Absorptive and goblet cells have been reported in the epithelium of this region. The short, straight ileum has a relatively small number of large, thick internal folds and the epithelial lining contains columnar absorptive cells and numerous goblet cells. There are no intestinal glands of the type found in herbivorous reptiles.

▼ Fig. 2.7 Internal organs of *Varanus*.

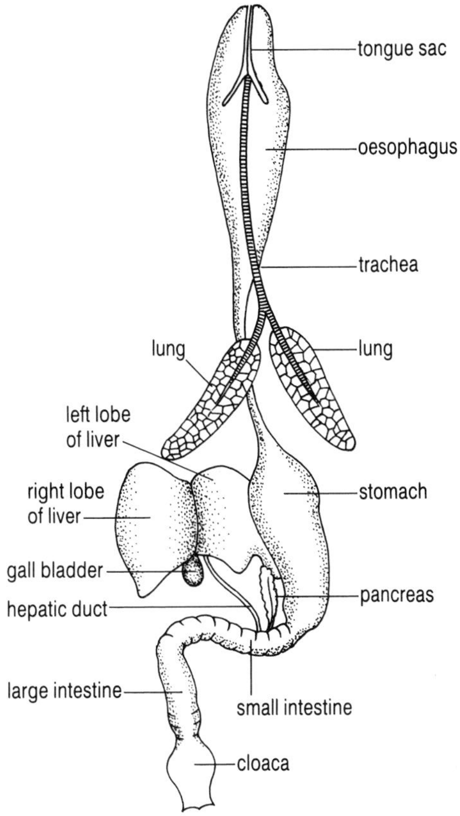

The digestive processes of *Varanus* were studied, in 1969, by R. Stuart Mackay of Boston University, using a specimen of *Varanus flavescens* weighing 510g (18oz) and measuring 31cm (12in) from snout to vent. Temperature transmitters were surgically implanted in the animal's abdomen and the subject was then fed a mouse containing an ingestible radio-transmitter. To aid X-ray monitoring of the progress of the meal through the digestive tract, the fur of the mouse was rubbed with barium sulphate. The monitor was kept in a room, the temperature of which could be regulated, in a box large enough to permit movement and illuminated by two spotlamps generating temperatures of 43° and 82°C (109.4° and 179.6°F) respectively. During the night, the lamps were extinguished and the room temperature was adjusted to 20°C (68°F). In the morning, when the lamps were switched on, the monitor invariably warmed itself under the 82°C (179.6°F) spotlamp until its body temperature reached between 28° and 35°C (82.4° and 95°F) – the maximum recorded temperature was 39°C/102.2°F – after which it moved to the periphery of the field of illumination, often curling itself around the outer edge.

Mackay fed the mouse to the reptile at a room temperature of 20°C (68°F) and found that, at this temperature, there was a delay of up to 8 hours before variations in peristaltic pressure, measured by the ingested radio-transmitter, indicated that digestion had commenced. Pressure changes, indicating contractions, occurred at a rate of 8–9 per hour for a period of about 4 hours. At 27°C (80.6°F), peristalsis began immediately after feeding and, after 3 hours, reached a rate of 24 pressure changes per hour. Cooling the animal reduced this rate, with the occurrence of paired pressure waves (not seen in human subjects), and rewarming did not immediately restore the previous level of activity. Peristaltic contractions seemed to be less intermittent than in humans.

Some gastro-intestinal activity continued at night when the room temperature fell to as low as 18°C (66.2°F), below the level at which feeding normally takes place, but a daily frequency rhythm was observed that matched the cycle of temperature and gross activity. Four days after feeding, there was a reduction in the amplitude and regularity of peristalsis, the ingested transmitter being finally passed out on the tenth day.

LIVER

The liver consists of two approximately hexagonal lobes, fused in the mid-region and connected to the dorsal body wall by the falciform ligament. From the left lobe, a long hepatic bile duct passes to the pyloric region of the duodenum, where a cystic bile duct from the thin-walled gall bladder also discharges, along with a pancreatic duct. The beta-cells of the pancreas secrete insulin.

EXCRETORY SYSTEM

The kidneys of *Varanus* are fan-shaped, lobulate and separate, whereas, in lizards generally, they usually join posteriorly to form a V-shaped structure. There is no urinary bladder and the cloaca is a three-chambered structure comprising the coprodaeum (at the front), the urodaeum and the proctodaeum. In males, these three divisions are disposed linearly but, in females, the urodaeal chamber is dorsal to the coprodaeum. The paired ureters open into the urodaeum; those of the males join with the vasa deferentia on each side to terminate on a prominent urinogenital papilla, while those of the females open on separate urinary papillae. The urine contains up to 90 per cent uric acid. Other constituents comprise creatine (2 per cent), creatinine (traces), ash (5 per cent, including traces of sodium chloride, sodium carbonate and calcium), moisture (2 per cent) and allantoin (3 per cent).

Excess sodium or potassium is probably excreted by the nasal salt glands; the kidneys seem to be rather inefficient where this function is concerned. Specimens of the rusty monitor *(Varanus semiremex)* from Queensland mangrove forests, exposed to sea water of oceanic salinity, with no source of water in the dry season except their food (crabs, fish, small mammals) and sea water, were found to excrete sodium and potassium from their nasal glands. Monitors can use their nasal glands to adjust the sodium: potassium ratio over a wide range. The sand goanna *(Varanus gouldi)* secretes nasal fluid containing more sodium than potassium, but the sodium : potassium ratio of this fluid is labile, varying in experimental procedures with the type of salt load injected or with the ionic composition of food. The maximum sodium excretion rate of the rusty monitor is very high for a lizard, exceeded, as far as is known, only by the marine iguana.

REPRODUCTIVE SYSTEM

Like most reptiles, all living varanoids lay eggs and, in the absence of evidence to the contrary, it seems likely that the extinct mosasaurs did too. Monitors are notoriously difficult to sex from external characteristics but, generally speaking, males grow faster than females, attain a larger size and, in at least some species, tend to be much more active.

The oviducts of the females are divided histologically into two regions: the oviduct proper (the glandular albumen-secreting area) and the uterus (or incubating chamber), where shell deposition occurs. The male reproductive system includes paired testes, each transmitting sperm via an epididymis to the two urogenital papillae in the cloaca. There are paired male intromittent organs (the hemipenes), in the form of pockets lying in the skin either side of the cloaca. During copulation, one of the pair is extruded and inserted into the female's cloaca to guide the sperm.

The structure of the hemipenes varies considerably and may be a significant guide to the relationship between species, with a flounced ornamentation present towards the distal end. In *Lanthanotus* and most species of *Varanus*, each hemipenis terminates in a pair of hard horns which are an extension of the main retractor muscle and apparently constructed around either fibrous cartilage or bone. These horns may pierce the dorsal apical tissues of each hemipenis and lie in the central lumen of the organ when it is retracted. They are not themselves capable of eversion.

In small species, e.g. members of the Australian subgenus *Odatria*, the hemipenis is about 1cm (½in) in length but in the very large Komodo dragon this organ attains a length of 11cm (4½in). When everted, the hemipenis twists so that the sulcal surface is directed dorsally and the sulcus runs around the side of the naked proximal region that faces the tail.

Interspecific hemipenal variation within *Varanus* is found in the ornamentation of the dorsal flounces and the shape and size of the horns. Primitive species tend to have symmetrical hemipenes, with undivided dorsal sulcal ornamentation, a simple sulcus and simple, paired horns. More specialized species develop asymmetry in the size and ornamentation of the horns, bifurcation of the sulcus, lateral cups surrounding the horns and variations in the number, arrangement and structure of the distal sulcal flounces; occasionally, secondary reduction of these features is observed. *Heloderma* differs from *Varanus* and *Lanthanotus* in having no horns on its hemipenes, which are about 2cm (¾in) long when everted.

Ritualized combat between rival males during the breeding season is common among monitor lizards and usually takes the form of wrestling matches, frequently with the adversaries adopting a bipedal stance. The prime objective is for one contestant to overthrow the other, demonstrating superiority by mounting its back and pinning it to the ground. Sometimes, when the wrestling pair, on their hind legs, have collapsed on top of each other, they may disentangle themselves and start all over again but eventually one or other emerges as the victor. Injuries seem to be minimal, although biting does occur and occasionally a vanquished lizard will limp away as if it has incurred some physical damage from the wrestling throws. Most other lizard groups engage in posturing and head bobbing during their intraspecific ritualized confrontations, but varanids, it seems, do not; the grappling indulged in by monitors and helodermas rarely occurs in other lacertilian families.

In seasonal climates, the oval, soft-shelled white eggs, which sometimes form an adherent mass, are usually laid at a time that will ensure the young emerge in spring, when temperatures are moderate and food abundant. Nesting sites vary, from simple holes in the ground to cavities in trees and the inside of termites' nests. Some species may excavate their eggs when the young are near term, notably those that deposit eggs inside termites' nests and seal them within the structure, but no parental care of hatchlings has been observed. The usually brightly marked young are on their own from the outset and have to be entirely self-reliant. Juveniles of most species head straight for the comparative safety of the nearest water, where food will be most readily obtained and relief can be found from tropical mid-day temperatures. Incubation times seem to be very much temperature dependent, with periods as short as 3 months and as long as 11 months being recorded.

LONGEVITY

Quite how long varanids can live, should they escape premature death from injury, predation or disease, is not certainly known. The larger monitors have survived for about 30 years in captivity but smaller species probably have a shorter potential life span. *Heloderma* is known to live for 40 years but the longevity of *Lanthanotus* has not been determined, and the durability of individual mosasaurs will presumably forever remain a matter for speculation, although such reptiles can be assumed to have lived for a half-century.

DISEASE

What level of disease occurs in varanids in their natural habitats is difficult to assess. Captive specimens are subject to a normal range of pathogenic bacterial infections, as well as neoplasms, while parasitic infestations include trematodes (found in the liver and gall bladder), cestodes in the small intestine and nematodes attached to the stomach and intestinal walls.

Tapeworms, when mature, secure themselves by four suckers to the internal surface of the intestine, just beyond the stomach, favouring the protected spaces between the villi at the bottom of the grooves separating the epithelial folds. The first host is probably a copepod, subsequently swallowed by a frog (perhaps as a tadpole) in whose viscera or body cavity it develops to become a pherocercoid. If the frog is subsequently eaten by a varanid, the digestive juices will release the encysted tapeworm, which then becomes an adult in the monitor's intestine.

Enteric bacteria commonly occurring in monitor lizards include *Enterobacter, Pseudomonas* and *Citrobacter,* but *Escherichia coli* – ubiquitous in mammals – seems to be rare or absent from the gut of these lizards, its place having been taken by *Citrobacter.* Haemogregarine blood parasites also commonly occur, mosquitoes being the probable vector, while ticks and mites are almost invariably present as ectoparasites.

ADAPTABILITY

Although monitor lizards have died out in North America, probably never reached South America and failed, not surprisingly, to withstand the cool climate of present-day Europe (although their fossil remains occur there), they have been a remarkably successful family in Africa, across southern Asia and through the Indonesian islands to the western Pacific and Australia. While some species live largely in watery habitats, such as rivers, lakes and mangrove swamps, at the other extreme even the inhospitable wastes of central Australia's Great Sandy Desert have been successfully colonized by monitors.

Extending for some 1300km (800 miles) westwards from Alice Springs to the Oakover River, the Great Sandy Desert is so arid that even camels cannot exist there without access to native wells, and agricultural stock has never become established. Yet several species of *Varanus* make it their home, including *Varanus gouldi, Varanus gilleni, Varanus eremius* and *Varanus acanthurus.* Probably the fat deposits that these lizards accumulate are an important adaptation, varying seasonally and allowing varanids to survive in desert areas, despite droughts and food shortages.

As a whole, monitors seem to display an unusually high level of behavioural plasticity that enables them to adapt very readily to a wide range of conditions or habitats. With lungs proportionately twice the size of those in other lizards and blood capable of becoming more saturated with oxygen than reptiles in general, they are capable of traversing large areas in search of prey and engaging in active pursuit of victims. The sensory specializations of varanids probably exceed those of other lizards as well, so that this dynamic group must be regarded as amongst the most successful of living reptiles.

Heloderma, on the contrary, is something of a relic, left over in North America from ancient stock that had specialized only in the development of tooth-associated poison glands. *Lanthanotus* is intermediate between monitors and *Heloderma* in its level of specialization, but seems to have achieved survival by extreme self-effacement. The great mosasaurs were unquestionably the most spectacular manifestation of varanoid evolution, but the very magnitude of their size and power rendered them vulnerable to extinction when the world around them changed and their specialized ecological niche vanished.

CHAPTER 3

The Greatest Living Dragon

No one knows how long the dragons of Komodo have reigned over their tiny island kingdom in the Flores sea and we can only guess at what their ancestors were and where they came from. But for long before humans came to the Indonesian archipelago, countless generations of these huge lizards have hunted the hills and valleys of Komodo and the adjacent islands, living out their lives undisturbed in the isolation of this remote tropical wilderness.

Native settlers who eventually stumbled on the lost prehistoric world of Komodo called its massive scaly ruler the *ora.* The biggest males may reach as much as 3.5m (11ft) in length, which is quite large enough to make these creatures exceedingly dangerous, even if travellers' tales of monsters 7m (23ft) or more in length are clearly gross exaggerations. A fully grown Komodo dragon in prime condition may weigh as much as 250kg (550lb), although a relatively lean specimen might weigh as little as 102kg (225lb).

The Komodo dragon *(Varanus komodoensis)* has a massive, broad-snouted skull of the mesokinetic type, i.e. with no movement between the parietal bones and the frontal bones, and the supraoccipitals fused to the parietals. The jaws are powerfully constructed and the maxillary bones, which carry all but the most anterior upper teeth, are capable of considerable outward movement, which effectively widens the mouth at this point. (Nile monitors, *Varanus niloticus,* exhibit some flexibility of these bones, but in other monitors, such as *Varanus salvator,* they appear to be rigidly fixed.) The quadrate bone, to the bottom end of which the mandible articulates, is more or less vertical, apparently to maximize the gape.

The pointed teeth are some 2cm (¾in) long, laterally compressed, posteriorly curved and aligned at an angle to the jaw margin so that, as they slice into a victim's flesh and the monitor draws back its head, the sliced meat is forced inwards into the mouth cavity and does not bind between the teeth. To aid in this surgical butchery, the rear margins of most of the teeth are serrated; the front edge, however, is smooth and the most anterior teeth are unserrated. There are seven teeth in the premaxillary bones at the front of the upper jaw, all inwardly curving, 13 pairs in the maxillary elements and 12 pairs in the lower jaw, but as many as four or five replacement teeth may be forming beneath every functional tooth. Some 200–250 teeth are replaced each year, individual teeth being shed after about 3 months' wear.

The body becomes more massive with maturity and acquires an increasingly flattened profile, while the tail constitutes a smaller percentage of the overall length in old individuals than it does in juveniles. For example, a Komodo dragon with a body 25cm (10in) long will have a tail measuring nearly 40cm (16in), whereas a creature with a body 125cm (48in) long will have a tail of only about the same length. Komodo monitors seem to have a rather high tail carriage, with a bulky caudo-femoral muscle complex that apparently supports it.

By the time adulthood is reached, the hind legs of Komodo dragons are stoutly constructed and proportionately rather short, having initially been quite long and slender at the juvenile stage. The forelegs are even more powerful than the hind ones and are used for seizing and holding down the prey or a carcass while the teeth tear at the flesh, as well as aiding the reptile to scramble about in mountainous areas. The toes of the fore- and hind feet have short but very sharp, recurved claws that are formidable weapons.

Fully grown Komodo dragons are of a nearly uniform clay colour, females having a slightly deeper reddish tinge to their flanks than males, which tend to exhibit a greater abundance of yellowish green spots on their snouts than females. Juveniles are speckled and multi-hued on emergence from the egg.

The scales of the Komodo dragon are underlain in many areas (e.g. the top of the head, the front of the legs, on the neck and belly and at the base of the tail) by small osteoderms. There is sometimes more than one beneath each scale, particularly on the head, where they form a network of small bones. Males can be distinguished by the presence, just in front of the vent, of small paired rosettes of scales; in the centre of each rosette is a scale incorporating a small depression. Females lack these features.

Komodo dragons are found not only on Komodo but also on the western end of Flores, on Rintja, and on the adjacent islets of Padar and Nusa Mbarapu. In addition, the islets of Oewada Sami, off Rintja, and Gili Mota, off the southwestern tip of Flores, are, or have been, home to small populations of these reptiles.

The area where the Komodo dragon lives is one of the driest regions in Indonesia. As they follow their southerly tracks, the monsoon storms of December to March have already dropped most of their rain on Java, Bali and other islands to the northwest of Komodo before they reach the land of the dragons and no rain at all falls there from the June monsoon. Nonetheless, there are heavy cloudbursts at the turn of the year and western Flores receives a total of over 800mm (32in) of rain every 12 months, Komodo itself rather less. Humidity on Komodo is about 75 per cent in October, rising to 85 per cent in February, while temperature ranges from 17°C (62.6°F) to a maximum of about 43°C (109.4°F). Komodo dragons can apparently manage for long spells without water during the dry season but, when it is available, they dip their snouts into pools or streams and drink deeply, raising the head to permit the water to flow back down the throat.

Most of Komodo, Padar and Rintja are completely covered in tropical savannah forests with adjacent woodland. This is the chosen habitat of the Komodo dragons, which have a population density there of about 15 individuals per km^2 / 0.4 mile. They spend much of the day hunting and foraging on the *Zizyphus* savannah but at night retreat beneath the woodland trees, where nocturnal heat loss is mitigated by the overhanging vegetation. During daylight, temperatures beneath the leafy canopy become too high for the dragon's comfort. Above 500–700m (1650–2300ft), there is quasi-cloud forest, but dragons are rarely found there, nor do they favour the deciduous monsoon forest that is present in some dry, hot regions below 500m (1650ft).

When seeking shelter, Komodo dragons commonly employ burrows, sometimes those of rodents or civet cats, occasionally the hollows excavated by wild boar in overhanging banks and, on Flores, the long, straight holes attributable to porcupines. Generally speaking, however, the Komodo dragon will dig its own burrow, usually on open hillsides or along dry creek beds. These refuges vary in shape: some are straight, some straight but angled off from the entrance, some taper, some expand to form a capacious inner chamber, some are U-shaped with a double entrance/exit and a few are little more than embayments. Komodo dragon burrows are normally only about 1.5m (5ft) long, just sufficient to accommodate the monitor if its tail is curled back round beside it. Burrows frequently occur in groups of up to 18 at a time, often, it seems, because the soil in particular areas is especially suitable for excavation.

There are so many Komodo dragon holes within this reptile's range that they cannot possibly all be in use. In fact, the amount of time that Komodo dragons spend in burrows is relatively limited. In the wet season, the burrows may provide a warm refuge when ambient temperatures fall, while in the dry season they probably enable the dragon to limit its moisture loss, keep cool during the hot days, or restrict heat loss during very cool nights. Hillside burrows tend to be used more than those along creek beds, occupancy peaking in the June–November dry season, with more limited usage in the wet season and virtually no resort to burrows during the equable climatic regime of March to May. Usually only one Komodo dragon will take up residence in a burrow but occasionally two will share.

The Komodo dragon has no nocturnal specializations and is not normally seen abroad after dark. By day, however, these monitors emerge to seek food and are active to some extent even during the heavy downpours of the wet season. Komodo dragons normally walk quadrupedally, with the soles of the feet placed flat on the ground and the head, body and tail undulating from side to side, in concert with the diagonal advancement of the limbs. If alarmed, the animals run with the body and tail in a relatively rigid pose, while the legs (especially the hind ones) are swung in wide lateral arcs. Speeds of up to 18km/h (11mph) can be briefly achieved, compared with a normal walking pace of some 5km/h (3mph).

Adults range on average about 2km (1¼ miles) a day, encompassing an area of some 4km^2 (1½ sq. miles), with a maximum of about 10km (6¼ miles) a day. They explore virtually every habitat in the region up to 500m (1650ft) above sea level – even mangrove swamps, beaches, offshore islets, sand-bars and reefs – but clearly prefer rolling areas of savannah. The scavenging areas of individual Komodo dragons frequently overlap but with no apparent conflict. Carrion is a prime source of food for these monitors and they can scent a carcass up to 11km (7 miles) away. Prospecting along game trails, dry river beds and their own established trails, they seek out the remains of large mammals, such as deer, wild boar, feral horses, goats and water buffalo that have for one reason or another met their deaths.

With the exception of turtles, monitor lizards are the only living reptiles that break up a carcass on which they are feeding with their teeth and swallow the meat in separate mouthfuls. Their knife-like, serrated dentition and kinetic skull and jaw structure are pre-eminently adapted for this task. When a Komodo dragon encounters a carcass, it will usually first tear open the body, then drag out the stomach and intestines so that they can be shaken violently from side to side, thus emptying them of vegetable matter, which is unpalatable to a dragon. Next the diaphragm is torn out and eaten, the lizard then plunging its head deep into the body cavity to devour the lungs and heart. The viscera is then bolted down and the monitor turns its attention to the body wall itself, bracing its legs against the carcass and rocking backwards and forwards, with its jaws fastened in the flesh, until a chunk of meat is abstracted by the sawing and cutting action of the teeth. In the case of smaller, goat-sized carcasses, the entire hindquarters or the head and shoulders may be swallowed at a gulp, the mouthful usually being oriented for swallowing in such a way that the lie of the hair does not impede the passage of the food down the throat. Practically nothing is wasted: Komodo dragons will eat 90 per cent of a carcass, finishing off their meal by swallowing the legs, haunches, shoulders and head. Even the bones are swallowed – components which most other scavengers (vultures, hyaenas) leave, satisfying themselves merely by crushing the shafts to extract marrow.

Komodo dragons not only consume virtually an entire carcass with extraordinary thoroughness, they do it with great speed. Walter Auffenberg, an American biologist who published a comprehensive study of Komodo dragons in 1981, saw a female *Varanus komodoensis*, weighing about 40kg (88lb), devour a 30kg (66lb) wild boar carcass in 17 minutes, leaving the scene only when she was totally bloated. A group of four large Komodo dragons were observed by other scientists to consume a large deer carcass in less than 4 hours.

These big monitors have acquired an unsavoury reputation for entering graveyards to dig up recently interred corpses and an even less attractive proclivity is their inclination to excavate camp or village latrines for faecal matter.

Although at one time regarded as essentially a carrion-eating scavenger, the Komodo dragon is a very efficient predator. Fully grown animals are capable of killing a domestic buffalo weighing about 600kg (1320lb), and deer, feral and domestic goats, and wild boar are regular victims.

The favourite ploy of Komodo dragons is to clear a small space beside a game trail in which they can lie in wait for a suitable victim. Smaller prey (sambar deer, goats) is ambushed from cover, seized in the monitor's jaws by the neck, throat, back or a leg, and thrown to the ground,

▲ **Komodo dragons *(Varanus komodoensis)* feeding at a carcass.**

where it is disembowelled by a slash of the formidable serrated dentition and dies within a minute or two from massive haemorrhage. Occasionally, the prey will struggle and a brief but inevitably one-sided contest will ensue before the monitor's teeth can be brought to bear on the victim's vulnerable belly. An attacking monitor sometimes drags or carries its prey into nearby thickets even before it is dead and will shake it with such violence that the neck is broken.

From an analysis of droppings, it is evident that the deer of Komodo and adjacent islands are the principal prey of Komodo dragons. They are a subspecies *(Cervus timorensis floriensis)* closely related to the Asiatic sambar and, in the case of stags, grow to 80cm (2.5ft) at the shoulder and weigh up to 200kg (440lb), although hinds only grow to about 50kg (110lb) in weight and are the preferred target of monitor attacks. Despite their size, even fully grown stags may sometimes be seized and disabled by a bite that severs the Achilles tendon, enabling the lizard to kill.

Although feral goats are regularly taken in areas where escaped domestic stock has established breeding populations, goats kept in native villages are the most frequent source of food for monitors on Komodo itself. Monitors raid the villages in broad daylight to secure a victim, in defiance of barking dogs and shouting, stick-wielding natives. Some local communities place flocks of goats on islets 350m (400yd) or so offshore, leaving them to breed and then, when numbers have multiplied sufficiently, harvesting the surplus. The dragons soon find these rich sources of food and will swim across the intervening sea, despite the swiftness of its currents, to eliminate a large proportion of the flocks, only leaving the islet when too few goats are left to support them. Komodo dragons swim with the legs held against their sides, propelling themselves by undulating movements of the body and tail. They can swim considerable distances underwater, will dive to depths of 4m (12ft) or more and have been observed resting on the bottom or searching coral beds along offshore sand-bars.

There are no wild boar on Padar, but on Komodo and Flores these animals are a regular source of food for the Komodo dragon. The local wild boar *(Sus scrofa vittatus)* weighs up to about 50kg (110lb) and stands some 60cm (24in) at the shoulder. The boars mostly feed in the early morning and late afternoon, on the savannah or along the edge of the monsoon forest. Komodo dragons apparently ambush them from beside game trails; once again the object of the attack is to throw the prey over so that it can be disembowelled. Many of the monitors exhibit the scars of puncture wounds that may have been inflicted by the tusks of wild boar, so these animals are by no means an easy option for hungry dragons.

▶ A somnolent Komodo dragon ***(Varanus komodoensis)*** that has gorged itself to repletion.

▼ The forked tongue of ***Varanus komodoensis*** is important for chemoreception, enabling carrion to be detected at a substantial distance. It also helps to establish the presence of rival Komodo dragons from their faeces.

Komodo, Rintja and Flores are home to quite substantial herds of feral water buffalo, apparently descended from animals brought to the islands by nineteenth-century settlers. In the Lesser Sunda islands, females grow to a weight of 400kg (880lb) and males to 600kg (1320lb), and they live in tall grass savannah with adjacent marshes or permanent pools. Even these rather small-sized island races (mainland animals weigh up to 900kg/1980lb or more) are formidable adversaries for a 250kg (550lb) dragon, but it seems they do, nonetheless, sometimes fall victim to the voracious monitors, although bulls in their prime are likely to be avoided.

Attacks by Komodo dragons on domestic buffalo in native villages or adjacent fields indicate that the method of subduing these animals is to seize them by the legs, severing the tendons and thus incapacitating the victim so that the belly can be ripped open. Some monitors seem to become habitual predators on buffalo, and one individual was well known to local villagers for its depredations over a period of 15 years. Other prey include feral and domestic dogs (quite a frequent source of food, to judge from the contents of faecal matter) and possibly the feral horses that occur on Rintja and Flores. These are small animals as horses go, but still stand about 1.2m (4ft) at the shoulder and weigh about 250kg (550lb), so adults are probably only attacked rarely. However, villagers say that Komodo dragons will gather around a foaling mare and tear the foetus from her as it emerges.

Slightly smaller prey, such as buffalo calves, deer fawns, piglets, or palm civets (which weigh about 0.7kg/1½lb and spend the day asleep in trees or rock piles, where they are presumably found by the prowling dragons) are manifestly easy victims for such voracious monitors and a large Komodo dragon is capable of ingesting a small piglet at a single gulp. In addition, snakes are regularly taken – even poisonous cobras *(Naja naja)* and vipers *(Vipera russelli, Trimeresurus albolabris)*, together with hawksbill turtles and their eggs (especially on Padar), and (notably on Flores) a small number of monkeys (crab-eating macaques) that are usually caught on game trails while seeking water, and porcupines. Crocodile eggs (laid by salt-water crocodiles) and hatchlings are welcome additions to the menu of *Varanus komodoensis* on Flores, but this species of crocodile apparently no longer occurs on Komodo.

Reptiles of such manifest power are clearly a potential hazard to people and evidence of attacks on human beings, some of which proved fatal, is available. An early report, dating back to 1931, concerns three men who were sitting in a small forest clearing on Komodo, cutting and trimming 'yellow wood' to equal lengths. A Komodo dragon about 2m (6ft) long moved into the glade and approached the trio, who decided, when it was about 15m (50ft) away, that it had come close enough, and took to their heels. One of them, a 14-year-old boy, ran into an overhanging vine and this enabled the monitor to reach him and bite out a huge piece of flesh from his buttock. The resultant massive haemorrhage caused death in less than half an hour.

In another incident on Komodo, one of a quartet out hunting water buffalo became ill and was left behind by his three companions, to be picked up on their return journey the next day. Unfortunately, 24 hours later, only the man's extensively mutilated remains were to be found. All the flesh from his arms and legs, as well as his viscera, had been eaten, clearly by Komodo dragons. Whether they had initially killed him or they had merely scavenged his already dead body is unknown, but certainly the monitors had made a substantial meal of his corpse.

There were unconfirmed reports of two tourists being killed on Komodo in the 1970s and, in 1947, a policeman who had been bitten by a Komodo dragon that was supposed to be securely tied up died a week later from severe infection (his right biceps muscle had been torn out). A villager at Nisar, on southeastern Flores, was allegedly killed and eaten by a large Komodo dragon in 1957, as a result of which these reptiles were subsequently killed on sight anywhere in the vicinity.

Komodo dragons have been known to rush from their burrows or from hiding places among undergrowth and try to bite at a passer-by's legs or ankles and, when apprehended on hunting forays into villages, they will turn on their pursuers in a very aggressive manner. One villager in western Flores sustained a severe bite in his calf when he tried to chase away a monitor that was seeking to make a meal of his chickens. Natives cutting grass or resting on the savannah have been the subject of stealthy attacks and, in one case, the victim died after 2 years of sickness following a severe monitor bite that tore out most of his right calf.

Generally speaking, Komodo dragons are inclined to avoid human beings and will shy away from them but occasional individuals unquestionably become excessively bold and aggressive, refusing to give way when encountering people on a game trail and exhibiting clear indications (open jaws, tail lashing) of willingness to attack. They have entered camps and even tents to rifle through equipment, causing apparently purposeless damage to clothing pulled from knapsacks and, on occasion, even driving the human occupants out of their quarters. Such seemingly rogue monitors are quite likely to attack a man, whether or not they are provoked.

Partially grown Komodo dragons could, of course, scavenge carcasses of any size, providing their larger brethren did not chase them away, but, as far as active predation is concerned, their prey would perforce have to be of a size they could readily overcome. As a result, rodents and birds are the main prey for immature monitors. Avian species taken include jungle fowl, Freycinet's megapode *(Megapodius freycineti)*, various small birds (e.g. doves), and eggs when available, especially megapode eggs. Megapodes, known locally as *wontongs*, nest on the ground in August–November, constructing mounds some 7m (23ft) across and 1m (3¼ft) high, into which the monitors dig with their forefeet to extract the eggs. Mice and black rats are the principal small mammals caught, and bats, skinks *(Sphenomorphus florense)*, small snakes, such as rat snakes *(Elaphe)* and whip snakes *(Dendrelaphis pictus)*, crabs and land molluscs *(Asperites)* are also taken. Because of a lack of larger prey on Padar, rodents and birds are a major feature of fully grown dragons'diet on this island, which does not support a wild boar population or any water buffalo.

Small Komodo dragons retain an ability to climb trees that larger, more mature individuals gradually lose. These youngsters hunt for prey under tree bark, in old logs and tree stumps, and seem to exist mostly on arboreal geckos during the first eight months of their lives. This diet is supplemented by insects during the May–December rainy season, when grasshoppers, caught on the ground, become a favourite meal, along with beetles. By the beginning of the first dry season of their lives, young komodo dragons are ready to graduate to killing rodents and birds, and also start to feed on carrion.

Although a fully grown Komodo dragon has virtually no natural enemies, small individuals suffer predation by civet cats, dogs, rats, birds of prey and probably snakes. They are also a regular food item in the diet of larger Komodo dragons – cannibal feasts of juvenile 'dragons' make up nearly 10 per cent of a fully grown monitor's diet in *Borassus* savannah areas, although only about 2 per cent elsewhere in the range.

Komodo dragons are essentially solitary animals, although groups of them will gather around a carcass to feed, with the establishment of a 'pecking order' that confirms the dominant status of the largest and most powerful lizards. Juveniles have a curious habit of rubbing their bellies and rolling in hair or intestinal contents at the site of a scavenged carcass. Since Komodo dragons will not eat either loose fur or the contents of the bowels, it has been surmised that this practice makes small monitors unappetizing to larger ones.

There appears to be no establishment of territories but smaller individuals evidently avoid their larger congeners, using the presence of excreta as an indication of which large monitors from the local population are currently hunting in any given area. Like all monitors (and lizards in general), Komodo dragons excrete nitrogenous wastes as a light-coloured semi-solid (uric acid), along with pellets of digestive waste. The voiding of faecal pellets usually occurs in the morning, when the lizard emerges prior to its hunting foray, often after it has basked briefly in the sunshine to warm itself. As a consequence, Komodo dragon faecal pellets occur in large numbers around hilltop basking sites, but they may also be found along game trails or in dry river beds. Digestion of a single large meal can take up to 5 days. Remains which have to be excreted because they cannot be broken down and absorbed by the gut include hair (often in large quantities), feathers, hooves, teeth, claws, the outer skin of reptiles' and birds' legs, skull fragments, accidentally ingested earth, presumably adhering to the carcass, and vegetable matter (including seeds) that was contained within the digestive tract of the dead animal.

In addition, Komodo dragons share with other monitors an ability to regurgitate gastric pellets. This practice usually seems to take place in the early morning, often along valley floors where the lizards are embarking on their day's hunting activities. Slightly larger than faecal pellets, and elongate in shape, they include substantial quantities of hair, along with bones (even complete skull and jaw bones of small wild boar), horns, claws, pig tusks, etc.

Faecal matter, casually deposited along trails and occurring in substantial concentrations at thermoregulatory basking sites frequented by Komodo dragons on their early morning emergence, enables individual lizards to ascertain who else is hunting the local patch. Small individuals can often be seen spending 10 minutes or more investigating varanid faecal matter, using the forked tongue as a tactile and chemoreceptive organ. Clearly it would be prudent for them to steer clear of larger dragons, although, if an encounter does take place, the less powerful lizard can usually make its escape, albeit often suffering bites, lacerations, or blows from a larger adversary's tail. If cornered, however, the possibility of being killed and eaten is real. Small Komodo dragons have been seen to exhibit appeasement behaviour or a submissive manner in the presence of large dragons in an effort to forestall aggression; inflation of the throat, compression of the body, and the assumption of a dignified or stately gait are all employed to try and defuse a potentially dangerous encounter.

Ritualized combat between Komodo dragons has been observed but actual intraspecific conflict between these vicious reptiles is a common occurrence and virtually all bear the scars of savage encounters. Males frequently attack females and are, in turn, often the victims of severe bites or tail blows from unreceptive females, especially if the would-be suitor is inferior in size to the object of his attentions. The breeding season in the wild seems to be June–August but courtship apparently takes place sporadically throughout almost the entire year; however, successful coitus is mostly restricted to the June/August period. This near-continuous sexual behaviour, declining or ceasing only in the months of October to December, may indicate some degree of pair bonding, and observation in the field tends to confirm that certain males and females occupying adjacent or overlapping activity ranges habitually consort together.

In these pairings, aggression between the partners is minimal and, in a brief courtship ritual, the male approaches the female from behind, touches her cheek and temporal region and the axil of her hind limbs with his tongue to achieve receptivity, proceeds to lick her back, and then scratches his claws across the scales of her dorsum, creating a scraping noise audible 27m (30yd) away. The female will frequently respond with a weak threat display (head lowered, throat inflated) but then usually submits when the male nudges the side of her face and her flanks with his snout and finally mounts her, clasping his forelegs around her body just behind her forelimbs. The female raises the base of her tail in response to tactile stimulation of this area by one of the male's hind legs and the male then rapidly twists his own tail to bring the vents of the mating pair into contact. Copulation takes about 12 minutes. Mating frequently occurs in the vicinity of carrion upon which a group of Komodo dragons are feeding, since this necessarily brings together a mixed group of males and females.

Eggs are evidently laid in nests excavated in sandy soil but detailed information is lacking. Captive Komodo dragons have been seen to dig U-shaped burrows in sandy substrates, presumably for the deposition of eggs, in the process heaving up a mound above ground level, which collapses when the monitor leaves the excavation and thus presumably buries the eggs. Specimens in zoological gardens have been recorded laying eggs from January to December but this probably reflects local climatic conditions rather than the natural reproductive cycle.

In Indonesia, August and September – the dry season – are the normal months for egg deposition. Weighing between 60 and 200g (2 and 7oz) or so, and measuring 6–11.5 × 4–6.5cm (2½–5 × 1½–3in), they have a smooth, soft shell of leathery texture and are laid a few each day over a period of anything up to 4 months, the total number sometimes being as many as 60 eggs in three separate clutches (a specimen in Surabaja Zoo). More usually, a female will lay only a single clutch each season, containing up to about 30 eggs, with a maximum of about 20 laid in any one day.

Whether Komodo dragons exhibit any maternal care is doubtful, although local Indonesian folklore claims that females do remain in the vicinity of the nest during the incubation period. On the other hand, when in captivity, these monitors have been seen to eat the eggs of their own kind, in the case of females even their own eggs.

Incubation in the wild takes about 8 months, with the young emerging in April/May, at the end of the short wet season, to take advantage of abundant insects as a food source. Hatchlings are about 20–55cm (8–22in) long and are agile, slenderly built little reptiles with a relatively long tail and proportionately elongate hind limbs. Their speckled patterning gradually fades to the uniformly hued adult coloration, sexual maturity being achieved around 5–7 years of age, when the lizard measures about 70cm (28in) from its snout to its venter.

Growth is rapid during the first few months of life, with a 60 per cent length increment, slowing slightly in the next 10 months (during which a further 50 per cent increase in length occurs). Size is then augmented by only 25 per cent in the ensuing 3 years and only 2 per cent during the 7 years thereafter. The skin of Komodo dragons is shed in patches over a 6-month period, beginning in September. The last epidermis to slough off is generally that of the dorsal surface (the top of the head, the back and the upper part of the tail), which usually comes away in February or March, when rainfall in the Komodo area is at its heaviest and the lizards can soak themselves in water-filled game wallows.

◀ **The apparently benign appearance of this Komodo dragon is misleading. In the wild these reptiles are voracious and have been known to kill and eat humans.**

The maximum life span of a Komodo dragon is probably about 50 years. A captive specimen at Frankfurt Zoo, which was received as a mature adult, lived for 16¾ years until it was killed during a Second World War air raid, and estimates of age based on seasonal growth rings in the bones or osteoderms of Komodo dragons support the conclusion that 20-year-old specimens are not uncommon. However, few individuals in the wild are likely to live to a great age. Accidents, disease or intraspecific conflict usually terminate the lives of even the most powerful individuals before senility occurs.

Despite its size, the Komodo dragon does not appear to be a particularly specialized monitor and is, indeed, regarded by some zoologists as quite primitive. Its origins are obscure but it seems likely that it evolved in or near its present Indonesian homeland. Komodo itself was probably not the actual centre where the 'dragon' which has made this obscure island famous actually arose; since the time, some 5 million years ago, when it seems likely that *Varanus komodoensis* first evolved, the Indonesian archipelago has probably undergone many geographical changes. It is an area of extensive volcanic activity, where many islands have in all likelihood arisen and then vanished again, only to rise once more above the waves in a fresh convulsion of lava. Krakatoa, further west along the island chain, between Java and Sumatra, is a notable example, having been almost totally destroyed in the famous volcanic eruption of 1883. Komodo dragons are quite capable of swimming across short stretches of sea and, as one island was swallowed up beneath the waves, they could easily have migrated to a more secure adjacent one. There is evidence for a more widespread distribution in earlier times, two fossil vertebrae from the Pleistocene of Indonesian Timor being probably referable to *V. komodoensis*, while other varanid bones of similar age from Timor and Java may also prove to be remains of this species.

The island region between Australia and Asia (known as Wallacea, after Alfred Russel Wallace, the British naturalist who surveyed the archipelago in 1854–62) supported a Pleistocene fauna that included elephants (both *Elephas* itself and the pygmy *Stegodon*), pig deer (*Babyrousa babyrussa*), endemic wild cattle (*Anoa depressicornis*) and a giant tortoise (*Geochelone atlas*). The large monitor lizards of the area presumably evolved in response to the presence of this appetizing range of potential prey; the pygmy elephants (*Stegodon*) have been suggested by some scientists as an especially likely source of protein for the lizards. The arrival of humans in Wallacea was possibly a significant factor in the demise of the pygmy elephant population but, fortunately for the dragon, the new invaders brought with them domestic animals which provided them with a convenient alternative prey.

CHAPTER 4

Dragons of Asia, Indonesia and the Western Pacific

Somewhere in southern Asia lies the probable ancestral home of today's monitor lizard population, an area which seems to have been the centre of an evolutionary expansion of varanids that began around 40 or 50 million years ago. From here they radiated westwards into Africa, northwestwards into Europe and southeastwards through Malaysia into the Pacific, where the domain of the dragons ultimately extended as far as Micronesia in the north and the Coral Sea in the south. Varanids probably reached Australia around 10 or 15 million years ago and a number of specialized forms evolved there, including some that were very large and others of truly diminutive size. Asiatic monitors, however, have remained relatively conservative to this day.

WATER MONITOR (*Varanus salvator*)

Ranging across southern Asia, from Bengal in the west to the Philippines and the Indo-Australian islands in the east, is the second largest living monitor and one of the most conservative species of the family. The water monitor *(Varanus salvator)* may well represent the basic stock from which most of the extant Asiatic monitor lizards are derived.

Known variously as the two-streaked lace lizard (a black temporal band edged with yellow extends back from each eye), two-banded monitor, land crocodile, lizard dragon, ring lizard (from the persistence of yellow rings on the hide even after tanning) or *kabaragoya,* this powerful reptile can attain a length of up to 3m (10ft), with males exceeding females in size and weight. A water-dependent species, it is found principally in humid forests and along river banks, favouring marshy localities but sometimes occupying drier areas if adequate cover can be found. The water monitor is a long-necked reptile with an elongate snout (depressed towards the tip), oval, valvular nostrils, located closer to the end of the nose than to the eyes, and a ventrally flattened but laterally compressed tail which is surmounted by a dorsal keel, formed from a strip of connective tissue, with a low, double-toothed crest.

The scales on top of the head are bigger than those covering the temple, with 4–10 large, transversely broad scales above each eye. Along the back, the scales are small, oval and keeled, while the similarly keeled abdominal scales comprise 74–102 transverse rows. The neck scales are smaller than those on the head but, along the top of the back, the scales are enlarged.

The water monitor is dark brown or blackish above, with yellow spots or ocelli and yellow underparts. The yellow-edged black temporal band sometimes extends down the neck from the eye and the snout is light-hued with black transverse bars (especially marked on the lips). The yellow markings are very conspicuous in young individuals but tend to fade with age, old adults being a dark olive colour with only indistinct yellow patterning.

The compressed, pointed teeth of the water monitor form a murderous battery of predatory weapons with which it secures its prey: birds and their eggs (among them, notoriously, domestic poultry), small mammals (especially rats), fish, lizards, frogs in large numbers, snakes, juvenile crocodiles, tortoises, crustaceans and molluscs (often sought along beaches at low tide), the eggs of turtles and crocodiles, and beetles. This varanid is a fierce and voracious feeder: a turtle *(Melanochelys trijuga)* with a carapace 16 × 10.5cm (6 × 4in) was found inside a water monitor 2m (6½ft) in length; a snake 1.3m (4½ft) long was observed being consumed by a specimen of *Varanus salvator* measuring only 1.2m (4ft); and an eel 1m (3¼ft) long has been witnessed disappearing head first down the throat of a hungry water monitor. Cannibalism is rare but not unknown. Unusual victims of water monitors include flying squirrels and mouse deer *(Tragulus)*, and these monitors also have a predilection for carrion.

They are notorious grave-robbers in native villages and the Kalabit tribe of Borneo build fences around graves to prevent water monitors from eating the dead. Other tribes cover graves with stones, place bodies in wooden receptacles and, in Mindanao, heap coral on graves to prevent desecration. In the Mergui archipelago, where bodies are disposed of by placing them in trees, water monitors will climb up into the branches to feed on putrefying corpses. On Bali, however, corpses are placed in a wicker basket with an opening just large enough for a water monitor to enter but too small for monkeys or dogs seeking access to the corpse. A family member watches and, when a water monitor enters the basket and begins to feed, it is believed that the human spirit has been carried off to the land of the dead.

The water monitor has its own enemies, notably large snakes, such as hamadryads, but usually seeks safety in water when threatened and can remain submerged for 30 minutes or more, swimming by undulations of the body. It will often climb 3–5m (10–15ft) onto branches overhanging the water and even quite large individuals are capable of running up trees to escape danger or raid birds' nests, taking a headlong leap into the water if the parent bird is large (e.g. a stork) and returns in time to drive the monitor away from the nest. When cornered, water monitors lash their tails and inflate themselves with air, expelling it in a threatening hiss.

Like monitor lizards in general, water monitors seem to be active only by day, emerging at dawn and regulating their daily routine to maintain a body temperature of about 30–35°C (86–95°F). They frequently rest on partially submerged stumps in shallow water, sitting motionless, with eyes open, or lying along branches to cool themselves in any gentle breeze that may be blowing. At nightfall, they seek shelter in dense thickets or bushes, or in water (which is warmer than the ambient air). The water monitor seems to be somewhat less active than the Bengal monitor *(Varanus bengalensis)*, possibly because it requires a much lower body temperature to fuel all of its metabolic requirements.

The aquatic life style of the water monitor, and its tolerance of salt water, readily explain its wide geographic range. In the Indian subcontinent, it probably originally occurred throughout the extreme northeast, Bengal, and the eastern Himalayas up to 1800m (6000ft), and was particularly abundant in the Sundarbans. It was also possibly once present in the mangroves in the extreme southwest of the Malabar coast (Kerala State), as well as in the deltas of the Krishna and Godavari Rivers in Andhra Pradesh, and perhaps in Tamil Nadu.

By 1980, there were only two breeding populations left on mainland India: in the mangrove swamps of the Bhitar Kanika sanctuary in Orissa and in the mangroves of the Sunderbans of western Bengal and Bangladesh. It is still probably the commonest reptile to be found in the Sundarbans Forest Reserve of Sugar Island. The last major populations in this area are in Sri Lanka and in the Andaman and Nicobar islands. Numbers have declined because of destruction of mangrove habitat for farming, timber and firewood, and overhunting for meat, fat and skins.

Varanus salvator salvator

In this most westerly region of the water monitor's range, the indigenous subspecies is *Varanus salvator salvator*, which can be distinguished from other members of the species by its coloration. Adults lack enlarged dorsal ocelli but have ventral yellow markings, forming a series of confluent diamond shapes, with black bands at the tail tip that are no more than twice as long as the yellow ones. Juveniles, however, do have ocellate

▲ **The beautifully marked skin of the water monitor *(Varanus salvator)* makes it the victim of extensive hunting for its hide.**

dorsal spots. The most brightly marked races are claimed to be from Thailand and Java; those from Ceylon are less distinctly patterned while animals from the Andaman islands have only weak patterns. Ventral scalation is in 80–95 transverse rows.

Varanus salvator salvator ranges eastwards from the Indian subcontinent through Assam, Burma, Thailand and Indo-China to Malaysia and Indonesia, occurring as far eastward as Halmahera, Sulawesi and Flores. It is not present in New Guinea and reports of its occurrence on Buru and Ambon, in the Torres Strait, and in northern Australia, are probably erroneous. (There is a water monitor in northern Australia but this is a separate and somewhat smaller species, *Varanus mertensi.*) Local names for this lizard include *biawak* (in Indonesia), *weri* (in the Mangarrai dialect) and *alu* (on Bali).

The breeding season of *Varanus salvator salvator* varies through different regions of its extensive range but generally coincides with the rainy season: in Orissa and Thailand, eggs are laid in June/July; in Malaysia they are laid in September/October. Ritualized fighting has been observed, presumably at least sometimes between rival males, although food rivalry also promotes conflict, irrespective of sex. This involves grappling in a bipedal posture, preceded by hissing, gaping and tail lashing, with one adversary seeking to overthrow the other. If a subordinate individual refuses to submit, its vanquisher will bite its neck, although the presence of enlarged dorsal neck scales is likely to prevent serious injury. Some 15 per cent of water monitors seem to be lacking their tail tips, however, possibly because of this intraspecific combat.

Clutches of up to 35 eggs, each up to 8 × 5cm (3 × 2in) and weighing about 90g (3oz), are laid in termite nests near water, in holes in trees adjacent to, or even overhanging, rivers and lakes, in excavations along the banks, in mounds of rotting vegetation and sometimes in the nests of megapode birds. When a termite nest is selected for the deposition of the eggs, an existing access hole is enlarged by digging with the fore- and hind feet and an egg chamber is excavated deep within the mound, measuring about 30 × 20cm (12 × 8in). Incubation of the elongated, bluntly tapered eggs takes 2½–10 months, depending on conditions.

Hatchlings are about 35cm (14in) long when they emerge (in March/April to the west of the subspecies' range) and they employ an egg tooth on the snout to slit open the soft, leathery white eggshell. The young are very active as soon as they are free of the shell and its membranes. They are black, with yellow spots arranged dorsally in transverse rows. When ready to hatch they make no noise (in the way that baby crocodiles do) and there appears to be no parental care, although the female will fill in the tunnel leading to the egg chamber after she has laid her eggs. In captivity, eggs have been incubated at 28–32°C (82.4–89.6°F) for as long as 327 days and some hatchlings have been observed to take 2–6 days to emerge fully from the egg.

Varanus salvator bivittatus
Sharing the more southerly portion of the range of *Varanus salvator salvator* are three other rather poorly known subspecies of somewhat uncertain status. *Varanus salvator bivittatus* occurs in Java, Bali, Lombok, Sumbawa, Flores, Alor, Wetar, and possibly Kalao and Saleyer, but, while some authorities consider it to be simply a geographical variant of *Varanus salvator salvator*, others regard it as meriting the status of a distinct species.

Varanus salvator andamanensis
The water monitor of the Andaman islands may be a small separate subspecies, *Varanus salvator andamanensis*, and is only about 1m (3¼ft) in length, with a notably pointed snout.

Varanus salvator togianus
In the Togian islands (Timotto) and northeastern Celebes, there is a dark brown form, *Varanus salvator togianus*, with rather large scales.

Varanus salvator cumingi
The Philippines have their own separate subspecies of water monitor, the most specialized being *Varanus salvator cumingi*, from Mindanao, Leyte, Bohol and Samar, ranging south into Celebes. With 77–85 transverse rows of ventral scales, large dorsal neck scales and fewer occipital scales than *Varanus salvator salvator*, this yellowish water monitor has black transverse bars across the head (which fail to reach the lips), the back, and around the tail (where they are interrupted ventrally). Black bars across the belly are present in juveniles but fade with age.

Varanus salvator nuchalis
Intermediate in specialization between *Varanus salvator salvator* and *Varanus salvator cumingi* is *Varanus salvator nuchalis* from Panay, Cebu, Masbate, Negros and Guimaras. This subspecies has 85–89 transverse rows of ventral scales and seems inclined to remain on the ground at night when seeking a place to sleep, rather than climbing trees, as seems to be the habit of *Varanus salvator marmoratus*.

Varanus salvator marmoratus
From Luzon, Mindoro, Palawan, and possibly Culion, *Varanus salvator marmoratus* grows to about 2m (6½ft) in length and is distinguished by the possession of 84–102 transverse rows of ventral scales; it is seemingly closely related to *Varanus salvator salvator.* It has been suggested that both *Varanus salvator marmoratus* and *Varanus salvator nuchalis* reached the Philippines from Borneo during the Pliocene period and occupied the northern, central and western regions of the archipelago, while *Varanus salvator cumingi* reached the southern and eastern islands from Sulawesi.

* * *

Varanus salvator has an innate adaptability which, combined with its swimming capacity and tolerance of salt water, has enabled it to exploit almost every available habitat from the eastern Indian Ocean to the western Pacific. These monitors have been seen swimming in the sea in the Gulf of Siam, between islands several kilometres apart, and occur on islands with no fresh water, except the rain that falls during the wet monsoon. Water monitors were among the first vertebrates to recolonize Krakatoa and its neighbouring islands after the 1883 eruption. A 1908 survey reported that monitor lizards were numerous on the island's shores (this expedition captured a young individual swimming off Lang Island) and, by 1929, water monitors were so numerous in the Krakatoa islands that local natives were poaching them for skins.

Adaptable and prolific it may be but, in many areas, the water monitor is holding its own with difficulty in the face of human competition and exploitation. The hide, traditionally used to make drums, is popular in international trade because of the animal's large size, while the persistence of the attractive yellow juvenile markings after tanning is another feature that places a premium value on water-monitor skins. The meat is palatable, although tending to be rather stringy and tough. It is widely exported from western Malaysia to markets in India and China and is a popular item of diet in Bengal and Andaman, where dogs are used to run the reptiles down. In Mindoro, the Mangyan tribe subsists largely on water-monitor flesh, eating it stewed, grilled, boiled, curried, fried or smoked. It is frequently served in restaurants (often as 'iguana'), usually as a soup (a few pieces of flesh and vegetables).

Semi-developed eggs from gravid females are regarded as a great delicacy (they have the consistency and flavour of an expensive liver paté) and the fat is alleged to have medicinal qualities, promoting strength and vigour when eaten and easing joint and muscle pains if applied topically.

In some parts of India, however, the brightly marked juveniles are considered to be venomous and, in Sri Lanka, the flesh of this species is regarded as poisonous. (The Singhalese hang dead water monitors by the tail and collect the dripping saliva, which is claimed to make a deadly poison.) The species is still very abundant in Ceylon, largely because of these taboos and because it is regarded as beneficial since it feeds on the freshwater crabs that damage rice terraces. Males up to 2.5m (8¼ft) long and weighing 18kg (39½lb) still occur on the island.

BENGAL MONITOR *(Varanus bengalensis)*

Nearly as large as the water monitor but of more terrestrial habits, the Bengal or common monitor *(Varanus bengalensis)* has an extreme westerly occurrence in southeastern Iran and then extends through Afghanistan, the Indian subcontinent, Ceylon, Assam, Burma, Thailand, southern Indo-China and Malaya to Java. Its absence from Sumatra is something of an anomaly; further eastward expansion into the western Pacific has presumably been curtailed because it lacks the aquatic adaptations that have so facilitated the spread of *Varanus salvator.*

Usually regarded as a distinct subgenus *(Indovaranus),* the Bengal monitor is up to 2m (6ft) in length and has a high-snouted skull with oblique, slit-like nostrils located closer to the eyes than to the end of the convexly contoured snout. The scales covering the skin are relatively small, those on the back being oval in shape, while the smoothly surfaced abdominal scales are arranged in 75–110 transverse rows. The feet have strong, moderately elongate toes and the compressed tail is keeled dorsally, with a low, double-toothed crest. The laterally compressed dentition includes 10–12 maxillary teeth, the crowns being blunt in large adults but pointed in immature individuals; replacement of individual teeth probably occurs about four times in any one year.

In colour, the Bengal monitor is yellowish, brownish or olive above, with blackish dots and a black streak on the temple, while the underparts are yellowish, sometimes dotted with black (especially on the throat). Juveniles have numerous white ocelli, frequently alternating with blackish transverse bands that persist after the ocelli have disappeared with the onset of maturity.

The Bengal monitor is able to function over a wide range of temperatures and can remain relatively free of energy-expenditure fluctuations due to minor changes in ambient temperature. The optimum daytime body temperature is about 34°C (93.2°F) and it has a lower cooling to heating ratio (0.63) than Australian monitors. At comparable body temperatures, its standard metabolic rate (the minimum metabolism of a fasting individual) is one-third that of an equal-sized mammal, but the maximum rate of metabolism exceeds the basal rate of a mammal by 30 per cent – an unusual phenomenon among reptiles. Despite this, a hibernating specimen can go without food for as long as 7 months.

A very active terrestrial form, largely independent of water although a capable enough swimmer when necessary, the Bengal monitor hunts by day for earthworms, beetles (scarabids, tenebrionids) and beetle larvae (dug out with the forefeet from under rocks or logs), ants and small lizards (sought by nosing through surface litter, a practice facilitated by the slit-like nostrils set well back from the tip of the snout), termites, caterpillars, spiders, snails, crabs, crayfish and even snakes. Fully grown adult animals will seek birds' eggs or nestlings (the species is quite capable of climbing trees although not habitually arboreal), fish, frogs, small mammals – such as squirrels, mice, shrews, bandicoots or hares – and carrion. Large Bengal monitors have been seen to consume a snake up to 1.2m (4ft) in length, first shaking and biting the serpent before swallowing it tail first, despite sustaining many small wounds from the struggling prey. Pythons, however, will kill monitors, although it may take as much as half a day to subdue even a half-grown specimen of *Varanus bengalensis*, while wild pigs allegedly kill young monitors and eat monitor eggs.

Sight and smell are the principal senses used to locate prey, the perceptual field having a mean reactive distance of 1.3m (4¼ft) and the mean active pursuit distance being 2.6m (8¼ft); prey is usually located within an arc of about 90 degrees to each side (mostly between 30 and 80 degrees). When the monitor is seeking food, tongue flicking is more rapid and regular than when it is simply moving from place to place, and greater lateral head and body movements result in convoluted or sinuous trackways. During searches for moving prey, the head is held high but the tongue is used only rarely, suggesting that vision is of primary importance; the demeanour is alert and tense, with the head turning quickly from side to side. Movement of potential prey leads to a rapid dash in its direction, followed by pursuit for a short distance. The smell of carrion can be detected from distances in excess of 2km (1¼ miles) and often attracts groups of Bengal monitors to a carcass.

Observation of captive animals suggests that the Bengal monitor shows both area- and object-concentrated foraging behaviour. The most common hunting mode is speculative, comprising walking over or tonguing a small area. Flushing may be either speculative or following a pursuit when the prey hides or freezes. Area-concentrated foraging habitually includes casting behaviour, with flush-pursuit the most common foraging behaviour, yielding success rates of 44–82 per cent, depending on prey type. Stalking or ambush is rare.

Because of its wide geographical range, the life habits of the Bengal monitor are necessarily diverse to accommodate varying habitats. Towards the western end of its range, in Pakistan, this species is common at elevations below 900m (3000ft) but it avoids large tracts of wind-blown sand and talus fans, favouring nullahs and cliffs in desert areas. In the Indus Valley, it abounds in dense vegetation bordering marshes and canals, and will often drop to the ground from the branches of trees 10 or 12m (30 or 40ft) high without injury. Occasionally, it occurs along the coast on the banks of tidal creeks or among dunes.

In the desert, it usually appears about 2 hours after sunrise and forages until heat drives it to seek shelter in burrows located among dense clumps of vegetation, clefts in rocks, hollow logs, crevices around bridges, or in old buildings; in marshland habitats, it is active all day. On land, it moves sinuously and carefully unless alarmed. Bengal monitors are very strong and can be pulled from their burrows only with difficulty.

In Pakistan, semi-hibernation occurs from late November until early March, greatest activity taking place during and after the monsoon, which coincides with the breeding season and is also a period of abundant prey (notably insects); this provides an opportunity for the animal to accumulate fat reserves to see it through the ensuing dry season.

In the central provinces of India, Bengal monitors live in burrows and cracks in the ground, from which they emerge to bask in the sun during winter, retreating quickly if disturbed. On the hot, dusty plains they either dig their own burrows or take over and enlarge rodent holes or natural crevices, as well as hiding out in dense vegetation, derelict buildings or (at certain seasons) in hollow tree limbs and trunks. They are rarely found in ponds or pools.

When the Bengal monitor digs its own burrow, it usually chooses to do so in earthen mounds, in near-vertical earth faces, under exposed tree roots, or beneath large stones; high sandy embankments surrounding agricultural plots on terraces are a favourite choice. In cross-section, these burrows are usually flat floored, with a convex roof at the mouth, becoming cylindrical and evenly tapered, sometimes with a slight terminal enlargement. Each time the animal enters the burrow, it undertakes additional excavation, using the forefeet alternately. None of the burrows is forked (although the smaller burrows of other animals often connect with them) and they usually run straight unless they encounter roots

or stones. Normally, they are about 1m (3¼ft) long and slightly inclined if dug from ground level, more steeply inclined if among tree roots.

Abandoned termitaria are also employed as a refuge, with natural breaks in the surface being used to gain access, after which the tunnels within the mound are then widened and enlarged by the monitor digging down at an angle of about 45 degrees (several Bengal monitors may use a single termite complex).

A resting Bengal monitor will lie curved in a U-shape in its burrow, with both the head and tail facing the opening. If threatened, however, the body is oriented towards the rear, with the tail curled laterally against the burrow wall and then back to the other side before passing forwards, parallel to the body or over the back. The thick tail base blocks the burrow lumen and, if the tail is seized, it is pulled back quickly; the spikes on the caudal scales can draw blood from a hand.

Burrows are used mostly at night and Bengal monitors often occupy each other's burrows, spending different nights in different burrows; sometimes more than one animal occupies a single burrow. In India, during the cold months of January and February, a Bengal monitor will emerge for only a few hours each day and keeps to a single burrow (males seem rather more active than females at this time, as indeed they do for most of the year). Burrows usually occur in aggregates and it is noteworthy that young Bengal monitors appear to stay in clusters for some months after hatching – the species seems to be to some degree sociable.

In Ceylon, the Bengal monitor becomes active towards noon and forages until late afternoon, often after basking on ant hills or other exposed habitats to raise its body temperature. During the night, it rests in burrows or hollows in trees, where it usually takes refuge by late evening, the body temperature dropping below air temperature by morning.

In Burma, this species is known as the *phut-mwe* (land monitor or grey monitor) and is regarded as a denizen of drier areas, especially well-forested regions, although it is also encountered on the outskirts of urban settlements.

◀ Bengal, or common, monitors *(Varanus bengalensis)* are supremely adaptable, equally at home climbing trees or in the water.

If threatened, Bengal monitors will try to escape down a hole or up a tree, gripping the bark with their sharp claws and frequently disappearing into a hole at the top. Alternatively, they may freeze and are then very difficult to discern against the ground or the tree bark.

Bengal monitors can run extremely fast, with the tail held at an angle of 45 degrees to the ground, and, when cornered or angry, will raise themselves on their forelegs, inflating themselves with air and then sharply expelling it with a noise described as 'resembling that made by drawing a tarpaulin or tent along the ground'. 'Gaping' is a defensive gesture and the tail may be used as an offensive weapon, lashing at an opponent. The bite is powerful and the backwardly directed teeth can leave a severe wound if the victim tries to pull away. Despite this, natives fearlessly pull these monitors from their burrows, claiming that, because the animal always enters head first, it cannot then turn round to bite.

Males are larger than females, with a greater percentage of overall length represented by the tail and a small percentage contributed by the head. Males also have black dots, occurring in greater numbers near the throat, yellowish ventral surfaces with uniformly scattered red spots, and pink scales in the cloacal region which females lack. In males there is a patch of scales just posterior to each lateral corner of the vent (the post-anal flap) while in females, the scales of the axillary, post-cloacal and inguinal regions lack micropores (males have one or two micropores per scale in these areas). Around the hind and forelimbs of the females, the scales have one or two micropores; in males, there are usually three micropores per scale.

All ages and both sexes of *Varanus bengalensis* have been observed to fight but only females and subadults seem intent on inflicting physical damage on a rival. In these non-ritualized contests, the females commonly seek to bite the dorsum, neck or head of an antagonist (more rarely the legs or tail) in energetic prosecution of an attack. They do not adopt a bipedal pose and the tail is often used to deliver a swift sharp blow to the side of the opponent's body, or sometimes the head, often preceded by coiling of the tail in a horizontal plane. The loser offers appeasement gestures, including dropping the head below the level of the trunk axis, facing away from an adversary, closing the eye facing an antagonist and pressing the body (and sometimes the head and neck) to the substrate. The successful animal assumes a dominant pose, with the head raised above the trunk axis, and may place one foot on the back of the loser, straddle it, or climb on it and maintain its tenure even when the defeated animal seeks to run away.

Intraspecific combats of this nature are usually preceded by agonistic behaviour (not the case in ritualized male/male combats), which includes gaping of the mouth to display the teeth, laterally compressing the trunk to make it look deeper, with concomitant lateral presentation to the opponent, arching of the body, expansion of the gular region, and hissing or huffing vocalization.

When two males come to blows, they begin by hissing and panting, then rush together, rearing up on their hind legs to embrace and seek to topple each other (Fig. 4.1). If one is successful, it will pin its antagonist to the ground by throwing the fore- and hind limb of one side over the recumbent animal's back. Biting is common but the teeth seem to do no serious damage, although both reptiles may suffer bleeding scratches on their backs as they pull away from each other's clawed grasp.

Eventually, after about 10 or 15 minutes, one of the monitors generally breaks away and scuttles off into the undergrowth, often briefly pursued by the victor. Despite these conflicts, Bengal monitors do not seem to be territorial animals and have not been observed to defend their home ranges (about 7 hectares/17 acres in extent in the case of males, 6 hectares/15 acres in the case of females) with any degree of resolution.

The breeding season of the Bengal monitor tends to vary across the animal's extensive range so that it coincides with the hot season. In northwestern India, for example, there is a regressive phase in the female's reproductive cycle from September/October to February/March, during which the number of ova progressively increases, but without deposition of yolk in the eggs, followed by a recrudescent phase (late March/April–June), marked by rapid deposition of yolk in the ova. By late June, the ovaries contain eight to ten mature follicles (up to five per ovary, measuring up to 8mm/⅜in in diameter), as well as a number of small follicles. The ovulatory/post-ovulatory phase extends from late June through July, with simultaneous rupture of mature follicles from both ovaries and development of a transient corpus luteum at each rupture site. Mating occurs at this time and a clutch of up to 30 eggs is laid each year, sometimes followed by a second clutch. By September or October, the corpora lutea have disappeared and the monitor re-enters its sexually regressed phase. The glandular mucosa of the oviduct regresses and hypertrophies in concert with the ovaries during

▶ Fig. 4.1 Male Bengal monitors engaged in bipedal combat, seeking to wrestle each other to the ground.

this annual cycle; in males spermatogenesis ceases during the infertile period. Elsewhere breeding activity takes place at other times: in Burma, it occurs in March/April; in Uttar Pradesh, in mid-April to late July.

The females can be aggressive when males attempt to mate with them and, apparently to avoid injury, the male habitually pacifies and immobilizes the female by holding her with his feet and claws. Courtship and intromission only last about 2 minutes. The outer hind toe in males is separated from the other toes by a considerable distance and is used during coition, in opposition to the other toes, to adjust the position of the female's tail.

Clutches consist of up to about 30 eggs (older females lay most eggs, of larger size), individual eggs being about 5 × 4cm (2 × 1½in) and weighing about 11.5g (⅓oz). A hole may be dug to receive them, the clutch being covered with excavated earth and other debris so that it is difficult to locate, but sometimes eggs are simply laid under thick vegetation, in ruined buildings or in abandoned termite nests. When a burrow is excavated in a steep-sided site, it may slope upwards at about 15 degrees, with an egg chamber some 10cm (4in) in diameter and 30–60cm (12–24in) long; the opening is sealed with earth from the roof and walls. Hatchlings escape by digging through this obstruction near the roof with the first clutch to emerge excavating a passageway that is often used as an exit route by its siblings. Rodent burrows, and possibly the nesting holes of cliff swallows, are also remodelled by nesting Bengal monitors. Nest chambers often occur in groups.

A Bengal monitor in Ceylon was observed to excavate an oblique, goblet-shaped nesting pit, working in daylight and using the forelimbs alternately. She then spent 2½ hours laying 24 eggs at a depth of 28cm (11in), subsequently covering them with earth by breaking down the sides of the pit using the forelimbs and employing her snout in an up and down manner. Sometimes she walked around the rim of the excavation to collapse the walls before climbing down into the nest to tamp down loose earth onto the eggs, which were completely covered after about an hour's work. Finally a number of shallow 'false pits' were made (perhaps to mislead would-be predators), some of which were above the eggs and others nearby.

Eggs hatch after about 5 months, the hatchlings being about 20cm (8in) long. In nearly full-term embryos, numerous scales, that each incorporate a large pore, are arranged in rows anterior and posterior to the vent or cloacal aperture and along the hind border of the thighs.

Small juveniles are probably completely insectivorous; specimens of up to 29cm (11in) snout to vent length feed mostly on coleopterans, but beetles (tenebrionids) also form a significant component of the diet, together with lesser quantities of termites, orthopterans, etc. With increasing size, they progress to fish and eggs, and scavenging at the kills of larger predators.

Bengal monitors are regarded as a nuisance in many areas because of their predilection for domestic poultry. In addition, in India, they are hunted for their flesh, which is used for food or medicine, while the skin is employed to make small drums *(khanjeries)* and fiddles *(chikara).* Parties of three or more men with dogs seek out burrows with footprints outside, guard the main exit and find the secondary exit, over which a guard is also mounted; they then dig in between to find the lizard.

Varanus bengalensis bengalensis

Two regional subspecies of *Varanus bengalensis* have been described. The typical form, *Varanus bengalensis bengalensis*, is found from southwestern Iran, through Afghanistan and extreme southeastern Uzbekistan, to Pakistan, India (north to Nepal, Bigrani and Darjeeling), Ceylon, Assam and Burma, and is distinguished by a count of 88–110 transverse rows of ventral scales.

Varanus bengalensis nebulosus

A dark-coloured subspecies, with a conspicuous, banded skin-patterning and 75–77 transverse rows of belly scales, *Varanus bengalensis nebulosus* occurs from Bengal through Thailand, Burma (where it is known as the *kon-phut* and is found as far up-country as Ye, 15°N), South Vietnam, Malaya and Java (but not Sumatra).

◀ **Fig. 4.2 Butaan (*Varanus olivaceus*) in a fig tree.**

GRAY'S MONITOR *(Varanus olivaceus)*

Conventionally, monitor lizards are generally regarded as ruthless predators and voracious scavengers, their prey varying from cattle or even human beings to insects, depending on the size of the lizard. There is one exception to this generalization, however. Living in the Philippine islands is a monitor that subsists almost entirely on molluscs (which is not unusual for these reptiles) and fruit – a wholly unexpected item of diet for a varanid.

Gray's monitor *(Varanus olivaceus)*, known locally as the *butaan* or *batua* (Fig. 4.2), occurs only in the Bicol area of southeastern Luzon and on the adjacent island of Catanduanes, where it lives in heavily forested, hilly or mountainous country with an annual rainfall of about 3000mm (117in) and temperatures annually averaging 30°C (86°F), with a maximum of 35°C (95°F) during the southwest monsoon in May and a minimum of 16°C (60.8°F) when the northeast monsoon blows from October to January.

Male butaans attain a length of up to 1.75m (5¾ft) and weigh as much as 9kg (20lb) (females 1.5m / 5ft and 2.5kg / 13¾lb), so this rather slender monitor is one of the larger members of the family. As with all varanids, the relative proportions of the butaan's body, limbs and tail change as it grows to adulthood, but fully grown specimens have a quite large head and a long, laterally compressed tail bearing a double row of strongly keeled scutes along its crest. On the top of the head, the scales are relatively large, with up to 14 conspicuous supraocular elements above each eye. The nostrils are slit-like, with a short passage leading more or less directly to the internal nares, and the ear opening is rather small.

Coloration is greenish grey, relieved by dark transverse bands across the neck, back and tail, with greyish green to yellowish grey ventral surfaces bearing three or four brown or black longitudinal stripes down the throat. The butaan is an arboreal species and the coloration provides a very effective camouflage when it is climbing up tree trunks or along branches. The black, yellow and cream spots, randomly superimposed on the basal banded coloration, make the lizard very hard to pick out against the bark of forest trees.

Its preferred habitat is dipterocarp forest growing at altitudes of up to 1000m (3300ft) on limestone soils or volcanic rocks, with tall, slender trees supporting a dense canopy that gives heavy shade to a shrub layer which includes abundant ferns. Much of the primary forest in the Philippines has been cleared for agriculture or felled for timber and it has been replaced by secondary growth, typified by small trees and shrubs. The butaan has adapted to this replacement flora and lives quite happily in such areas, using deep rocky fissures as a refuge. (These also provide a source of water in the limited March–April dry season.)

Agility in the forest trees is facilitated by the laterally compressed tail – a feature that is usually regarded as an aquatic specialization but, in the case of the butaan, is employed as a climbing aid and endowed with keeled ventral scutes to give grip – and large, hooked claws that flex through a substantial angle. The feet can be turned backwards to slow a rapid descent through the foliage of tall trees, and an anatomical sliding lock-joint between each claw and the toe bone behind it provides such a strong articulation that a butaan can hang from a branch suspended by just a single claw.

The extensive reliance on fruit as a source of food makes the butaan unique among monitor lizards. In the tropical forests where it lives, plants that are collectively available for most of the year include: *dao (Dracontomelum)*, *parong (Grewia)* and *lubas (Spondias)*, all of which have sugar-rich fruits, and *pili (Canarium)*, *bagsang (Caryota)*, *pandan*, *ollano* and *karagumoi (Pandanus)*, and *matobato (Aglaia)*, which are oil-rich, together with figs *(Ficus)* of the strangler type. *Pandanus* fruits, for example, are eaten during the early (drier) months of the year, while *Canarium* is to be found at all times except during the wettest (December) and driest (March–April) periods. It seems that the butaan does not normally take fruit from the forest canopy itself but only collects fallen fruit, which must be of perfect ripeness, yet never over-ripe or rotten. Very often, this tumbles into holes or crevices, from which the butaan is obliged to retrieve it, evidently relying principally on its sense of smell to detect suitable food items. Many of these fruits are very hard shelled and although some (notably *Canarium* fruits, which have a waxy rind) may be punctured or crushed before ingestion, the butaan customarily swallows most fruits whole.

To facilitate this, the bones of the palate (like those of the skull in general) are unusually robust, with the palato-pterygoid complex projecting downwards at the point where these two bones articulate in such a manner that a hard fruit pressed back beyond this point is squeezed into the opening of the oesophagus.This is aided by the wider than usual posterior half of the lower jaw (the two rami spread further apart in the articular region than is the case in non-frugivorous varanids) and a heavily ossified, uniquely shaped hyoid apparatus, which is first pulled forwards to 'cup' the fruit and then retracted, carrying the hard-shelled food item into the narrower region of the oesophagus. Peristaltic action then moves it into the stomach for digestion.

Less unusual is the butaan's taste for slugs and snails, which are taken all the year round, forming about half the food intake of adult animals. The most favoured is *Lepidotrichia* but others which meet with approval include *Trochomorpha*, *Obba*, *Geophocus*, huge land snails *(Ryssota)* and the slugs *Hemiglypta* and *Cyclophorus*. Most of these molluscs occur in rocky, forested situations and hide up during the day in litter-filled holes or crevices in the rock, where the butaan seeks them out with its snout and well-developed sense of smell (the slit-like external nostrils, set back from the end of the nose, are presumably adaptations to this method of foraging). Some, however, are to be found on vertical rock faces or tree trunks, and others may have to be dug out from beneath rotten fallen branches or from under leaf litter.

The teeth and jaws of the butaan are specially adapted for crushing the shells of molluscs, with strong muscles attached to robustly proportioned skull bones, and a thick, deep lower jaw; these modifications maximize the pressure which can be exerted by the bluntly pointed posterior teeth. The largest food particle that can pass down the butaan's gullet is about 5cm (2in) in diameter, so the shells of snails much larger than this have to be crushed, the jaws being capable of exerting the remarkable pressure of 1180kg/cm^2 (16 783lb/sq. in). Juveniles do not, it seems, feed much, if at all, on snails, since the teeth do not acquire the blunt-crowned conformation for shell-crushing until adulthood is attained. Two other monitor lizards – the Nile monitor *(Varanus niloticus)* and the African steppe monitor *(Varanus exanthematicus)* – also feed regularly on molluscs and exhibit cranial and dental specializations similar to those of the butaan.

Also consumed with relish by the butaan are the legs of hermit crabs (apparently bitten off the living animal), together with the occasional spider, beetles and insects (eaten more especially by juveniles which consume a rather smaller proportion of vegetable material than adults). There is some limited evidence for predation on birds and their eggs, but these favourites of other monitor lizards seem not to be a significant item in the butaan's diet.

It takes at least 2–3 days for the butaan to void undigestible residues (mostly pieces of snail shell and the hard seeds of fruit) in the faeces, which it does along with a whitish pink faecal cap of semi-solid nitrogenous waste (uric acid). The butaan is unusual for a varanid in possessing a quite conspicuous caecum just beyond the beginning of the large intestine (Fig. 4.3). This structure is a common feature of the digestive tract in herbivores and contains a bacterial flora that assists in the breakdown of cellulose. Clearly only a proportion of food material passing along the gut is shunted into the butaan's caecum, which normally accommodates no more than two or three fruits at a time. An additional specialization found in the butaan is a well-developed small intestine lined with long, absorptive villi – also an adaptation to its partly frugivorous diet. (Varanids in general have a shorter small intestine, with much smaller villi.)

After a particularly large meal, the butaan may void gastric pellets orally. This has principally been observed in captive zoo specimens, which will eat rodents and birds and egest the fur or feathers as odiferous mucus-covered pellets.

Despite claims by local people that the butaan prowls at night, there is no scientific evidence of nocturnal habits. It is a shy and timid creature, even in daylight, usually trying to escape by fleeing into a hole or up a tree if threatened and freezing, motionless, if escape is impractical. Its vision is sharp enough to discern an approaching person 100m (110yd) away and, if danger is perceived from this distance while the monitor is scrambling up a tree, it will surreptitiously move around the far side of the trunk to conceal itself. Attempts to reach a butaan hiding in a hole result in the animal shrinking away, with its tail coiled in a curious figure-of-eight configuration, the reason for which is unclear. Only if cornered and actively threatened will the butaan leap, mouth agape, at an aggressor, if necessary inflicting a painful crushing bite that may be maintained for a substantial period. The hissing that is common among monitors in general is a rare occurrence, however. Butaans have been witnessed throwing themselves as much as 30m (100ft) from the high branches of trees if capture seems imminent.

Butaans sleep at night in hollow trees, rock crevices or, more especially, the tangled arboreal thickets of vines, scandent shrubs and epiphytes that occur anywhere from 3 to 40m (10 to 130ft) up the larger forest trees. They usually emerge between about 08.00 and 10.00 hours, and bask for half an hour or so (often draped over a branch near the top of the forest canopy) to raise the body temperature to the optimum 30–32°C (86–89.6°F); the night-time low is about 20°C (68°F), while 42°C (107.6°F) is about the maximum tolerable. Rain seems to make little difference to their foraging activities, unless it is accompanied by storm-force winds, but, in dry seasons, butaans descend from their preferred hilltop environment and seek out water in the sink holes, ponds, mangrove swamps and rivers at lower elevations.

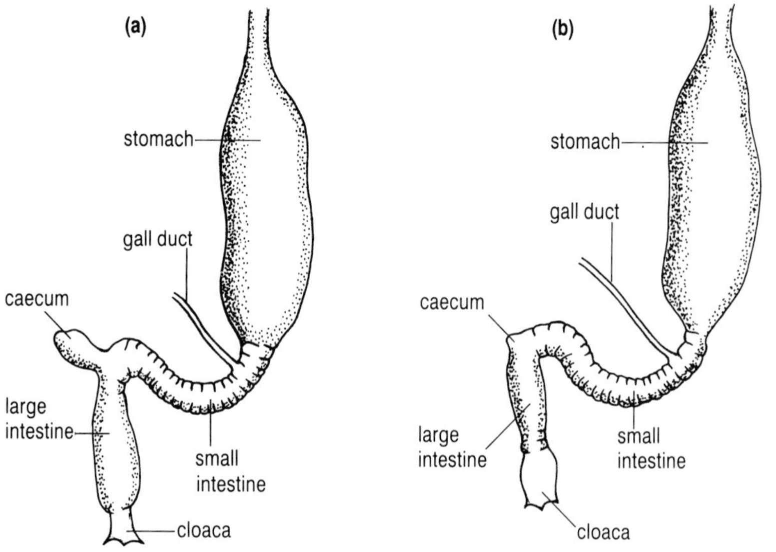

▶ Fig. 4.3 Digestive tract of: (a) the butaan (*Varanus olivaceus*); (b) the water monitor (*Varanus salvator*). Note how the caecum is prominent in the partially vegetarian butaan but inconspicuous in the wholly carnivorous water monitor.

Each butaan seems to have a normal home range area of about 21 hectares (52 acres), territories of different individuals often overlapping.

On some days a well-fed butaan will not emerge until as late as noon, or may not bestir itself at all. Such lethargy belies its capacity for quite rapid movement on occasion, the average quadrupedal walking pace being about 13m/minute (14yd/minute); a similar speed can be attained when scrambling vertically up a tree trunk. Bipedal locomotion has not been observed, nor does the butaan seem to engage in any digging activity.

Sexual maturity in the butaan occurs at about 3 years of age, when males measure approximately 1.2m (4ft) overall and weigh 1.5kg (3¼lb); females are smaller at 1m (3¼ft) and 1kg (2.2lb). In males, the testes begin to increase in weight in March and reach maximum size in May–July, with ritualized combat between males starting in April as a prelude to breeding. In these encounters, two antagonists will approach, extending their tongues to sense chemical odours (probably pheromones) emanating from the rival. Rearing on their hind legs, they will seize each other with the forelimbs in an embrace, trying suddenly to twist one another to the ground. The loser may indicate submission by such actions as hiding, lowering or turning away the head, or closing the eyes. Little actual physical injury is inflicted, although the tail is sometimes coiled up and may then be used as a lash, or there may be some biting of the well-protected back of the neck.

Courtship, from June through September, is normally initiated by a male approaching a female and passing his tongue over her neck and head. He then mounts the female, grasping her in an embrace with his forelimbs, raises his tail (in response to which the female moves her tail to one side), and then inserts one of his hemipenes in her cloaca. Females, not surprisingly, tend to breed with the largest males, which are most successful in ritualized combat.

Ovulation usually occurs in July/August, and 4–11 eggs, measuring about 7 × 3.5cm (3 × 1½in) and weighing 40–50g (1½–1¾oz), are deposited in a single clutch, the nest apparently being located in hollow tree trunks or branches, or inside the rotten structure of fallen timber. Normally each female lays only one clutch per year, depositing all the eggs in a single 24-hour period (occasionally the laying process may extend over several days). Incubation lasts from 6 to nearly 12 months, depending on the laying date. The hatchlings, about 35cm (14in) long and 25g (1oz) in weight, always emerge at the beginning of the southwest monsoon, and it seems likely that, in eggs laid early in the breeding season (i.e. in June), the embryos, once fully developed, remain dormant to await the next year's June rains. Some large females may lay a second clutch in October or November, but these too will hatch the following May or June. The wet season, of course, is calculated to provide an abundance of food for the newly emergent juveniles. Adults also prosper amid the rich and varied gastronomic fare of the rainy months and, while fully grown butaans tend to be lean during June and July, when breeding activity is at a maximum, by the time the northeast monsoon is in full spate in November they may be carrying fat deposits representing 10 or 12 per cent of their total weight.

Although one or two specimens of the butaan reached Western scientists in the middle of the nineteenth century, its apparent rarity led zoologists to assume that it was a scarce species inhabiting some remote island. In 1845, John E. Gray of London's Natural History Museum proposed the name *Uaranus armatus* for what was clearly a juvenile specimen collected in the Philippines by Hugh Cuming – who supplied a great deal of material from these islands to this famous museum during the years 1836–40, unfortunately usually without adequate location details. A skin of what was in fact the same species, although no one realized it at the time, turned up in the Academy of Natural Sciences in Philadelphia and a description of the species, under the name *Varanus olivaceus*, was published in 1856 by Edward Hallowell. After George Albert Boulenger, the Belgian-born, naturalized British biologist, who worked at London's Natural History Museum from 1880 until 1920, pointed out that John Gray's name *(armatus)* had previously been used for a monitor from Africa (in fact an example of the Nile monitor) and so was zoologically inadmissable, another name, *Varanus grayi*, appeared in 1885. However, Edward Hallowell's name clearly has priority.

A butaan skull discovered in the Munich Museum in the 1940s was placed in a separate subgenus, *(Philippinosaurus)*, by Robert Mertens, the dedicated German student of monitor lizards. Many authorities believed that this apparently obscure form must be extinct, since no other specimens had materialized, but American varanid specialist Walter Auffenberg located a further specimen of *Varanus olivaceus* in the US National Museum of Natural History: a stuffed skin, with a skull, that for the first time gave a precise location – Pasacao, in Luzon.

Aided by funds from what was then the World Wildlife Fund (subsequently the Worldwide Fund for Nature) and the New York Zoological Society, Auffenberg set out for the Philippines to try and discover whether the butaan still existed. It did. No one had thought to look for it among the treetops of mountain forests, which is where it makes its principal home, and its secretive habits, excellent camouflage and propensity for freezing motionless (thus remaining unnoticed by passers-by) meant that it had contrived to escape attention, despite the fact that it occurred in some numbers only an hour's drive from Manila, the largest city of the Philippines.

Where it originally evolved, and how such a specialized monitor came to be domiciled in the Philippine islands, is a matter for speculation. Derivation from a subspecies of the Bengal monitor *(Varanus bengalensis nebulosus)* is considered to be probable. This quite large lizard ranges from Assam and Bengal through Burma, Thailand, South Vietnam and Malaya to Java and is the likely progenitor not only of *Varanus olivaceus*, but also of the rough-necked monitor *(Varanus rudicollis)*, Dumeril's monitor *(Varanus dumerili)* and the yellow monitor *(Varanus flavescens)*, all of which have distributions centred on the Indian subcontinent, Thailand and Indonesia. Furthermore, all of these forms are to some extent arboreal and prefer a tropical forest habitat.

The plants on which the butaan feeds are part of a rather distinctive lowland flora occurring up to altitudes of 500m (1650ft) that is found not only in the Philippines but also in Malaysia, Borneo and Celebes. The butaan's likely descent from a varanid stock of Indo-Malaysian origin, and association with a plant population of similar provenance, strongly suggests that it, too, came from this part of the world.

The Philippine islands have probably not been in existence for more than about 70 million years and, throughout this, geologically speaking, relatively short time, were never connected with any of the adjacent continents. Tectonic activity between the Asiatic plate and the Philippine plate produced a fault line through the eastern Philippine islands and, during the Miocene, some 30 million years ago, this led to the appearance of a continuous narrow strip of terrain that extended from Luzon southwards through Mindanao to Celebes. This, presumably, must be the route by which the butaan and its associated dipterocarp forest travelled from Indonesia to reach its present toehold in southeastern Luzon. The land connection between Mindanao and Celebes was broken during the Pliocene as sea levels rose, and a breach also appeared between Mindanao and what are now the northern islands of the Philippine archipelago, Somar being largely or completely submerged. Bicolandia, where the butaan population is currently centred, became cut off from the rest of Luzon by a seaway that became a freshwater swamp in the Pleistocene and eventually dry land again, enabling the monitor to move northwards into Luzon proper. The island of Catanduanes was temporarily joined to Bicolandia during the worldwide Pleistocene oceanic regression, enabling butaans to colonize it, but, with the subsequent rise in sea levels, Catanduanes again became an island, on which the butaan population was now marooned.

DUMERIL'S MONITOR *(Varanus dumerili)*

From Thailand to the eastern end of the Indo-Australian archipelago, the mangrove swamps and dense evergreen coastal forests are home to Dumeril's monitor *(Varanus dumerili)* (Fig. 4.4). Also known as the *uaran*, this monitor, 1.5m (5ft) in length, with a small flat head and prominent elongate nostrils located much nearer to the eyes

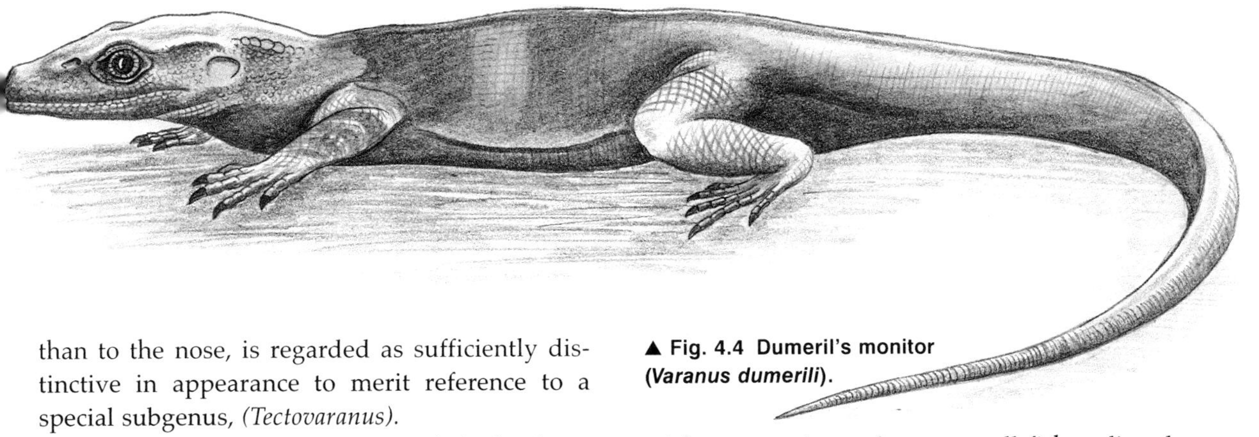

▲ **Fig. 4.4 Dumeril's monitor (*Varanus dumerili*).**

than to the nose, is regarded as sufficiently distinctive in appearance to merit reference to a special subgenus, *(Tectovaranus)*.

The skull is relatively long and fairly deep, with a straight profile. The cranial scales are of unequal size and the supraoculars above the eyes are slightly enlarged transversely. On the top of the neck, there are prominent, oval, protective scales that have a smooth, flat surface; there are similar but usually keeled scales present on the back and the upper surface of the limbs. Weakly keeled abdominal scales occur in 37–41 transverse rows. The tail is muscular, strongly compressed and dorsally keeled, with a low, double-toothed crest.

In colour, Dumeril's monitor is a light brownish yellow above, with a dark temporal streak from eye to ear that is generally confluent with a dark U-shaped marking on the neck. The back bears very broad, dark transverse bars, which are broader than the interspaces between them, and the limbs are dark brown spotted with yellow. Moderately distinct, dark vertical bars are present on the lips, and the belly is yellowish with dark transverse bands.

This species spends quite a lot of time in the water and exhibits obvious aquatic specializations, such as valvular nostrils that can be sealed via an interior scale operated through a sphincter muscle. It is a good swimmer and will forage underwater for short periods, forcefully expelling air from its lungs as it dives, to reduce its buoyancy, and pulling itself along stream beds by means of its claws. On the other hand, it is also entirely at home on land and will readily climb trees if alarmed.

Its prey, effectively anything that it is big enough to overpower and swallow, includes crickets, ants, insect larvae, small fish or lizards, crabs, eggs, mice and (in captivity) hamsters. As would be expected in a predator, the teeth are pointed and laterally compressed, although they lack serrated edges and attain only a small size. Seven are present in the premaxilla at the front of the upper jaw, about eight in the maxilla, and eight to ten in each side of the lower jaw.

Primarily a diurnal species, Dumeril's monitor is most active from mid-morning to late afternoon. It is a slow, methodical forager, exploring any object it comes across for food and digging beneath material too large to move. When a relatively large prey victim is seized, such as an 8cm (3in) mouse, it is usually grasped by the head, neck or shoulders, shaken, and then taken by the head for ingestion. Swallowing is not accompanied by the low vertical undulations of the neck and head seen in *Varanus salvator* and *Varanus bengalensis*. Instead, the snout is angled upward, air is forcibly expelled from the glottis, the body is flattened horizontally and the anterior of the body and neck is raised, air being exhaled slowly. Anything from 45–90 seconds is required to swallow a large mouse.

When no longer hungry, this species finds a retreat and may sleep for up to 14 hours, although, if it feeds in the morning, it may become active again late in the afternoon. (Otherwise it will sleep through the rest of the day and the ensuing night.) Burrows are dug by dislodging soil with the snout and then using the forelimbs (alternately in rocky or dry soil) to move the spoil, kicking back the accumulating pile occasionally with the hind limbs.

Intraspecific ritualized combat has been witnessed, bipedal wrestling being combined with head crossing and snout thrusting, each antagonist trying to topple the other. When threatened, responses include raising the body, hissing and lashing the tail, but the animal adopts a rigid bodily response if handled.

Varanus dumerili dumerili
and *Varanus dumerili heteropholis*

Dumeril's monitor is especially common in the Mergui archipelago, notably in the mangrove swamps along the Mergui coast, where it is to be seen lying on mangrove roots uncovered by the tide. Two subspecies are recognized, *Varanus dumerili dumerili* being the principal one, occurring throughout the known range of the species except for northern and northwestern Borneo. There it is replaced by *Varanus dumerili heteropholis,* which can be distinguished from the more common form by the possession of varying shaped scales, those on the neck being moderately keeled.

ROUGH-NECKED MONITOR
(Varanus rudicollis)

A rather small, almost black monitor, with essentially arboreal habits, occurs from Burma and Thailand, down through peninsular Malaysia, to Sumatra, the Riouw archipelago, Banka, Sarawak and Borneo. Known as the rough-necked monitor because the upper surface of the long neck is protected by 10 or 12 longitudinal series of very large scales bearing prominent keels, *Varanus rudicollis* only attains about 1m (3¼ft) in length and is generally assigned to the separate subgenus, *Dendrovaranus.*

The head is slender and elongate, although the snout is proportionately short, with slit-like nostrils located nearer to the eyes than to the end of the nose. Above the eyes, the supraocular scales include a posterior central series of half-a-dozen elements that are transversely widened. The toes are short, with long, curved claws, and the compressed, dorsally keeled tail has a low, double-toothed crest. Abdominal scales are keeled and arranged in 79–90 transverse rows.

The very dark coloration is relieved by a yellowish tinge on the neck and foreparts of the body, yellowish ocelli on the flanks and the rear part of the trunk, and yellowish spots on the limbs. Three longitudinal black stripes occur along the back and there are two broad, black transverse bands across the anterior trunk.

The dentition includes 15 or more pointed, compressed maxillary teeth and about 15 pairs of lower teeth in the elongate mandible. The diet consists of small mammals, frogs, insects and sometimes fish (when these tree-dwelling reptiles descend to the ground, as they quite often do).

YELLOW MONITOR *(Varanus flavescens)*

Once common across northern India but now rather rare, the yellow monitor or Indian empagusa *(Varanus flavescens)* grows to about 1m (3¼ft) in length (males are slightly larger than females) and is distinguished by its olive or yellowish brown coloration, with irregular darker markings that usually become confluent broad cross-bars. There is a blackish temporal streak and the ventral surfaces are yellowish with indistinct brown cross-bars (better defined on the throat). During the rainy season, broad red cross-bands become visible.

The head is quite wide, with rather slit-like nostrils located slightly nearer to the end of the nose than to the eyes. The cranial scales are small and subequal, with the median row of the supraocular series slightly dilated transversely. The tail is weakly compressed laterally and keeled dorsally, with a low, double-toothed crest. The toes are short and rather straight, the hind legs not being particularly elongate. There are oval, keeled dorsal scales and 67–73 transverse rows of abdominal scales.

A terrestrial monitor that prefers a marshland habitat in low-lying sandy areas bordering rivers or lakes and subject to annual flooding, the yellow monitor includes frogs as a major feature (perhaps 40 per cent) of its diet, together with smaller quantities of toads, small mammals, birds, insects, earthworms and the eggs of amphibians, lizards, turtles, crocodiles and birds. During the night, this species will resort to burrows which it has excavated for winter protection and possibly also aestivates in these refuges at the onset of the dry season.

Courtship generally occurs in May–July and clutches of 4–30 cylindrical, leathery-shelled eggs with tapering ends, measuring about 3.7 × 2.1cm (1½ × ¾in) and weighing some 10.5g (⅓oz), are laid in the ground, often in deserted white ants' nests, from May to September. Incubation, at 30°C (86°F), takes about 150 days, the emergence of hatchlings being co-ordinated with the occurrence of the monsoon, i.e. from March in West Bengal to July in Uttar Pradesh.

Newly emergent juveniles measure about 14cm (5½in) in length and are more brightly coloured than adults, the undersurfaces being dark brown with yellow spots confluent into cross-bars and the lower surfaces yellow with dark brown cross-bars that are continuous below the neck but not under the chest, abdomen or tail.

Beyond its Indian homeland (from Sind in Pakistan to West Bengal), the yellow monitor also apparently occurs through Burma (where it is known as the *phut-gya*) and, according to some records, also in Thailand, peninsular Malaysia and Indo-China. However, the encroachment of rice paddies or the desertification of its wetland habitat, allied with it being hunted for food in Thailand, for medicinal oil in India, and for skins generally, have severely restricted both its numbers and range. In the Indian subcontinent, it is now found only in the Indo-Gangetic plains south of the Himalayas, from Pakistan east to the Brahmaputra River, south to Kutch (Gujarat) in the west and northeastern Orissa in the east.

Varanus flavescens is sometimes placed with an African monitor *(Varanus exanthematicus)* in the subgenus *Empagusia*, but it is becoming increasingly evident that these two geographically disparate forms are not, in fact, closely related at all. Chromosomal studies have disclosed numerous significant differences in their respective karyotypes, but there are strong similarities between the chromosomes of *Varanus flavescens* and the water monitor *(Varanus salvator)*. The yellow monitor occurs sympatrically with both the water monitor and the Bengal monitor *(Varanus bengalensis)*, and is very probably a descendant of the *Varanus bengalensis nebulosus* lineage, along with the rough-necked monitor *(Varanus rudicollis)* and Dumeril's monitor *(Varanus dumerili)*. An additional distinctive feature of *Varanus flavescens* is the unusual forked horns on the hemipenes of male individuals which are of similar size and shape; in the African *Varanus exanthematicus*, the hemipenal horns are of differing proportions.

DESERT MONITOR *(Varanus griseus)*

Possibly derived from either the Bengal monitor or the yellow monitor, the desert monitor *(Varanus griseus)*, also known as the grey monitor, has acquired an ability to live in much more arid environments than either of its presumed close relatives. Measuring about 1.5m (5ft) in length, with a long flat head, a narrow snout and a greyish yellow coloration, sometimes with more or less distinct brown cross-bars on the back and tail, this monitor occurs in dry, sandy areas rather than in the moist rainforest environments favoured by other Asiatic dragons. In fact, the desert monitor occurs not only through Asia Minor and southern Asia as far east as central India, but has also spread westwards into the arid terrain of Arabia and northern Africa.

The desert monitor is regarded as an elusive, reticent creature that is in consequence difficult to study, but this reputation stems largely from its need to seek shelter from desert temperature extremes during burning hot days and freezing nights. Very often it digs its own burrow in which to take refuge, the slit-like, obliquely oriented nostrils being set back closer to the eyes than to the nose, as is commonly the case in burrowing lizards. The toes are quite short and the uncrested tail is rounded or only slightly compressed. Desert monitors can swim and are also able to climb trees, but clearly neither activity is likely to be a premium requirement in a desert, so adaptations for swimming or climbing are not evident. The scales are of small size, particularly those of the head. On the sides of the neck they may be weakly keeled and those on the abdomen occur in 110–125 transverse rows.

Life habits vary according to the dictates of the inhospitable environment in which desert monitors live. In Morocco, for example, they live in sandy wadis, hiding beneath large rocky slabs; juveniles are frequently found under partially buried stones. The prey includes other lizards,

▲ The slender, elongate head of the rough-necked monitor *(Varanus rudicollis)* – a small largely arboreal monitor occurring from Burma and Thailand to Sarawak and Borneo.

▲ Sought by hide hunters for its attractive skin, the yellow monitor *(Varanus flavescens)* nonetheless seems to be maintaining its numbers by colonizing agricultural habitats such as rice paddies and fish farm parks.

▶ Entirely at home in the most arid of desert regions, *Varanus griseus* prowls in the early morning and the evening, but seeks shelter from the mid-day heat.

▶ Inset: The desert monitor (*Varanus griseus*) has a narrow snout, with the oblique, slit-like nostrils closer to the eyes than to the end of the nose.

snakes, jerboas, rodents, birds and birds' eggs. These are swallowed whole, the pointed, laterally compressed, serrated teeth, numbering ten in the upper jaw and nine to ten in the lower, being unsuitable for chewing. The long neck enables them to engulf large prey and also enables the head to be cast forward, in typical monitor fashion, to seize victims.

In the Rajasthan Desert, the desert monitor digs a burrow, using its snout and forelimbs, in compact sand near bushes. It emerges during the day, notably in the morning and at evening, often resting with the head just outside the burrow as it makes its morning debut, presumably to warm the head region. The subterranean temperature in these burrows is lower than the surface temperature in summer, but higher in winter.

The thermal niche of this species in the Sahara is limited. Sand heats quicker and cools faster than rock and the desert monitor is a sand-dweller. In April in this part of the world, the night sand temperature is only 16°C (60.8°F) when the air temperature is 25°C (77°F); at sun-up, it rises rapidly to reach 64°C (147.2°F) at 14.00 hours (air temperature 41°C/105.8°F). The desert monitor becomes active when the temperature of the sand reaches 30°C (86°F) and usually continues to be active throughout the rest of the day – about 5 hours of activity. In June, however, the monitor retreats to shelter at mid-day, activity being limited to 2 hours in the morning, when the sand is warming from 30 to 39°C (86 to 102.2°F), and 2 hours in the evening, when the sand cools down from 49 to 32°C (120.2 to 89.6°F). There is no evidence of nocturnal emergence. The maximum activity occurs at a temperature range of 32–50°C (89.6–122°F), with an optimum of 30–44°C (86–111.2°F). The critical thermal maximum cloacal temperature is 43°C (109.4°F), with a lethal maximum of 44–47°C (111.2–116.6°F), while the critical thermal minimum cloacal temperature (including hibernation) is 17–20°C (62.6–68°F), an optimum cloacal temperature being 35–38°C (95–100.4°F).

In northern Africa, this species hibernates from October to April. During this period it has been found that the level of blood sodium present in summer is decreased by nearly 30 per cent, while the summer potassium level is increased by 25 per cent, thus compensating for the sodium figure. There is also a decrease of about 10 per cent in blood calcium during hibernation and a marked winter increase of over 50 per cent in blood magnesium (magnesium has an anaesthetic effect on reptiles and mammals and may affect hibernation). Blood sugar levels fall by about 60 per cent during hibernation but glycogen in skeletal and cardiac muscles rises by about 40 per cent. In the cortex of the brain, glutamic acid (GA) decreases, probably due to its transformation to glutamine for the detoxication of ammonia in the brain and also because it is used to synthesize gamma-amino-butyric acid (GABA), which depresses activity in the cerebral cortex. During hibernation, the thyroid is inactive. This gland is composed of large numbers of follicles held together by loose connective tissue: the intracellular colloid droplets which are found apparently demonstrate regular seasonal changes.

On the southern coastal plain of Israel, the desert monitor is active only during the months of March through November, hibernating below ground for the rest of the year, often in a crude burrow it has dug itself, using the forefeet alternately. These burrows, normally dug in light soils, are on average 1.25m (4ft) long and 30–40cm (12–16in) deep, usually with a single entrance and a small chamber at the end. Because of low population density (less than two individuals per km^2/0.4 sq miles in inhospitable stony areas, about 6 per km^2/0.4 sq miles in irrigated wadis), a high level of mobility, and an elusive character, the Israeli population of this species is especially difficult to study, but peak activity appears to occur in May/June (the breeding season), with males ceasing activity as early as July. After egg laying, females feed intensively, their very rapid weight increase compensating for a nearly 50 per cent loss in weight immediately after oviposition.

There is a marked home range (about $1km^2$/0.4 sq miles for males, about $0.25km^2$/0.1 sq miles for females) but the species is not territorial – there is overlap of ranges between the sexes and between individuals of the same sex. The estimated population density is four adults per

km^2/0.4 sq miles but foraging distances of 2km (1¼miles) or more have been recorded, extending through varied habitats (e.g. unstabilized dunes, dense vegetation, construction areas, garbage dumps). Females use most of their home range each day, while males forage in just one specific area of their personal patch.

The diet of the desert monitor in Israel includes jerbils, jirds *(Meriones)*, partridge eggs and chicks, skinks *(Chalcides)*, fringe-toed lizards *(Acanthodactylus)*, chameleons, elegant geckos *(Stenodactylus)*, tortoises *(Testudo graece)*, snakes (even poisonous ones, such as horned vipers), hedgehogs (the spines are eaten), leverets, shrews, toads and jerboas. Other prey includes ants, hemipterans, coleopterans, gastropods, ticks, spiders, scorpions, roaches, wasps, mantids, lepidopteran pupae, neuropterans, siphonapterans and arthropod eggs.

When cornered, desert monitors rise up on their legs, flatten the body and tilt the back towards the enemy, inflating the throat and hissing loudly with open mouth and protruding forked tongue. They may lash their tail, or flatten the ribs to depress the body, but seldom bite. Alternatively, these monitors may stand broadside, inflate the throat, pull the tail to one side, preparatory to delivering a blow, and hold the head low and the back arched in a threatening posture. The desert monitor is said to be capable of jumping up to 90cm (36in) and allegedly attacks horses, asses and dromedaries by leaping up and biting them in the belly.

Breeding maturity is reached at 2–5 years, when a length of 47–75cm (19–30in) is attained. Mating occurs in or around June and 10–20 leathery-shelled eggs are laid in July and buried in sand. Incubation takes 10 months. Young desert monitors are seen in August and September in at least some regions of the range, exhibiting bright juvenile coloration that comprises yellow spots and dark brown cross-bars, with temporal and cervical streaks.

Desert monitors are hunted locally for their skins, which are used to make shoes and drums, and for oil from visceral fat (employed as a treatment for failing eyesight in the elderly). Folk legends include the belief that a man should keep his mouth shut if a *gho* or *gho-pard* (a local vernacular name for monitor lizards) is watching him because, if the lizard sees his teeth, disaster will befall him. It has frequently been claimed that the bite of the desert monitor is toxic, with effects lasting some hours, and there is some evidence for this, since injections of saliva into sparrows and laboratory rats cause paralysis.

Varanus griseus griseus

The most westerly subspecies of the desert monitor, *Varanus griseus griseus*, is found across northern Africa from Rio de Oro to the Sudan and Egypt, into Syria, Lebanon, Israel, Jordan, Iraq and the Arabian peninsula.

Varanus griseus caspius

Towards the eastern end of this range, *Varanus griseus griseus* intergrades with the Trans-Caspian desert monitor *(Varanus griseus caspius)*, which lives in the deserts of Trans-Caspia, from southern Kazakhstan, Iran and Afghanistan to northern Baluchistan.

Varanus griseus koniecznyi

The most easterly representative of *Varanus griseus*, the Indian desert monitor *(Varanus griseus koniecznyi)* is a rather smaller form, measuring only about 1.3m (4¼ft), that ranges from Sind and the Punjab across central India, sharing much of this area with the Bengal monitor.

* * *

The versatility and adaptability of *Varanus griseus* is demonstrated by the way in which the various subspecies have adapted their life styles to differing climatic regimes. In the Indian subcontinent, for example, *Varanus griseus koniecznyi* is active all year round but, in Pakistan, it hibernates during the winter months, as does the sympatric *Varanus griseus caspius*, which also hibernates in Turkmenistan and Iran. The Iraq population of *Varanus griseus griseus*, however, is to be found foraging throughout the year.

CHAPTER 5

African Dragons

From the southern shores of the Mediterranean right down to the Cape of Good Hope, monitor lizards are an abundant feature of the African fauna. Desert species occur across the sand dunes of the north, while the savannah and veldt of the tropical belt provide an abundance of suitable habitats. Only the most dense rainforests have proved uncongenial to the dragons of Africa.

NILE MONITOR *(Varanus niloticus)*

The second largest reptile in Africa, surpassed in size only by the huge Nile crocodile, is the Nile monitor *(Varanus niloticus)*. Usually referred to a separate subgenus, *Polydaedalus*, this powerful lizard attains 1.5m (5ft) in length and occurred originally throughout most of Africa, except in the arid regions of the north and the southwest.

It is an aggressive predator, taking frogs, toads (even poisonous ones such as *Breviceps*), rodents, fish, lizards, small turtles, birds and their eggs, beetles, orthopterans, crabs, caterpillars, spiders, millipedes, earthworms and slugs with indiscriminate relish, as well as being an inveterate robber of crocodile nests for eggs. Even after hatching, newly emergent crocodiles are not safe from the Nile monitor, which regards them as a tasty addition to its diet, but eventually, of course, the tables are turned and even a half-grown Nile crocodile will soon see off a marauding monitor.

In addition, hard-shelled molluscs are a conspicuous feature of the Nile monitor's menu and cranial specializations designed to facilitate the consumption of these invertebrates include a deep, stoutly constructed skull, blunt, crushing posterior teeth and a bowed lower jaw. The geometry of the biting equipment is designed to impart maximum leverage towards the back of the gape in order to aid the crushing of snail shells (*Achatina* is a favourite prey). The actual biting action, however, is somewhat slower than the rapid snap-like closure possessed by, for instance, the water monitor *(Varanus salvator)*.

◀ Robbing crocodile nests for eggs is a favourite foraging practice of Nile monitors, but demands constant alertness in case an angry crocodile rushes to defend its brood.

Scavenging is also a common Nile monitor strategy and these reptiles are often to be seen at lion kills, where they will try to swallow bones and quantities of flesh that are far too large for their gullets, resorting to breaking bones against hard objects and tearing at meat with their teeth and claws. Fully grown Nile monitors have no scruples when it comes to robbing smaller specimens of their species of their food if the opportunity presents itself.

Known in Arab countries as the *ouran* or *varan*, from which the scientific name *Varanus* was derived, the Nile monitor is misleadingly referred to as the iguana, *lagavaan* or water *leguaan* in Afrikaans-speaking areas of southern Africa, while Zulus know it as the *qamu*. The Greek author and historian Herodotus, who visited Egypt in the fifth century BC, referred to the Nile monitor as a 'land crocodile', which is a fair reflection on its impressively powerful physique. The bones of the heavily constructed skull are thickened and the rounded nostrils are located slightly nearer to the eye than to the rather depressed termination of the snout. The toes are strong and moderately long and the tail is markedly compressed, with a dorsal keel and a very low, double-toothed crest. Cranial scales, including the supraoculars, are subequal in size and larger than those of the temple region, while the dorsal scales are small, oval and of tectiform (roof-like) configuration. Abdominal scales are smooth and arranged in from 75 to nearly 100 transverse rows.

The adult coloration is brownish or greenish grey above, with darker reticulation and yellowish spots or stripes on the back and limbs and yellowish green spots on the head; ventral surfaces are yellowish with blackish cross-bands. Juveniles are black above, the head bearing yellow cross-lines with black and yellow vertical bars on the lips, while the neck exhibits posteriorly directed, chevron-shaped yellow lines; a transverse series of yellow spots or ocelli is present on the back, and yellow spots also occur on the limbs. Black reticulation overlies the yellow underparts of immature individuals, with black transverse bands under the head and body; the tail of juveniles exhibits alternating black and yellow bars.

There is probably only a single form of Nile monitor, with a huge pan-African range, although it has been suggested that a forest subspecies *(Varanus niloticus ornatus)* may exist in western Africa that has fewer (three to five) yellow cross-bars or series of spots between the fore- and hind limbs than *Varanus niloticus niloticus*, which has six to nine such yellow cross-bars.

Nile monitors are stealthy hunters, concluding their predatory quests by pouncing with lightning speed on their prey. The teeth can administer a painful crushing bite, although this is likely to be lethal only to relatively small victims. However, while holding an adversary in its jaws, a Nile monitor can cause severe injuries with its claws and, if these are fastened upon the victim's back, the snout will be bent downwards between the firmly implanted feet so that the powerful shoulders and forelimbs can break the prey's spine, or at least inflict massive lacerations.

When digging out the eggs of crocodiles, a Nile monitor will use its forefeet. As soon as an egg is exposed, the lizard warily looks into the excavation and then around at the adjacent forest several times before summoning the courage to take the egg and retreating into the bush a couple of metres (around 6ft) or so away. It then turns the egg in its mouth, with its head slightly raised to puncture the shell and allow the liquid contents to run down its throat. One specimen was observed to take five eggs from a nest in this manner while the parent crocodile watched from the water. Nile monitors seem able to wander among basking crocodiles with impunity, sometimes rising on their hind legs to survey the surrounding area while supported by their tails; the crocodiles appear largely to disregard them.

The voraciousness of the Nile monitor is almost legendary. One young female held captive in Tanzania attempted to swallow a female stripe-bellied sand snake *(Psammophis subtaeniatus sudanensis)*. The victim was seized head first and half-ingested, but then had to be disgorged. The snake died soon afterwards, whereupon the monitor made another attempt to swallow it, stretching herself to try to accommodate the serpent and endeavouring to break off the unconsumed half of its huge meal by rubbing the dead snake against the wooden sides or the wire netting of the confining box. Eventually the monitor was obliged to admit defeat and had to disgorge its putative meal. Slightly over 2 weeks later, the monitor was itself swallowed by a vine snake *(Thelotornis kirtlandi capensis)*. Another captive specimen, fed on hens' eggs, was observed to take a drink of water before breaking an egg in its mouth, the crushed shell being swallowed along with the contents.

Nile monitors are usually found near water, especially rivers, but will habitually rest on a cliff ledge or up a tree. Juveniles often lie on branches overhanging rivers or pools and, when disturbed, will simply drop into the water, sometimes from a considerable height. If alarmed, they readily scale trees when water is not immediately available, using the sharp claws and strongly muscled legs to swarm up to a height of 5–6m (15 or 20ft), whence smaller specimens in particular are prepared to jump down if further pursued. However, Nile monitors apparently find it impractical to climb smooth-barked trees. Alternatively, these monitors may flee down a hole or rocky crevice, or into a termite nest.

When running quadrupedally, the body is flexed from side to side but, at slow gaits, the tail is left to drag while the tongue flicks continually in and out. If angry, a Nile monitor will arch its back and stand at full stretch on its legs, hissing as the body inflates and flicking the tail sideways. As a last resort, a cornered Nile monitor will eject foul-smelling matter from the cloaca to deter attack or throw off a pursuer. The back is strongly protected by scales and will resist a spear thrust.

Enemies from which the Nile monitor needs to protect itself include pythons: a newly caught python, 9ft (2.5m) in length, at Fitzsimons Snake Park, Durban, was reported in 1962 to have regurgitated the skin, feet and claws, and a few large bones, of a 45–60cm (18–24in) specimen of *Varanus niloticus*, and a 4.5m (14ft) specimen of *Python sebae* has been seen to seize a 1.4m (4½ft) Nile monitor by its head, throw four coils around it, and subdue it in 45 minutes. (The snake then released its coils and swallowed the dead monitor head first, a feat requiring about half an hour.)

The deep-body temperature of *Varanus niloticus* has been measured using radiometric techniques, including a transmitter in a small fish that was fed to a captive animal. In basking and activity periods, this temperature varied from 26 to 37°C (78.8–98.6°F), falling to 20°C (68°F) at night (21.00 to 07.00 hours), when the monitor was resting in water whose temperature declined steadily from 20 to 17.6°C (68 to 63.5°F); the night-time core temperature proved to be 0.4°C (0.72°F) above that of the air and 3°C (5.4°F) above that of the water. Compared to tropical skinks or geckos, the species loses water rapidly (6 per cent per 24 hours) in dry conditions and is clearly not fully adapted to xeric environments.

To maintain an optimum body temperature of 34–35°C (93.2–95°F), the Nile monitor employs a variety of strategies. In Uganda, for instance, it habitually basks in the morning (07.00–09.30 hours) and afternoon (14.30–15.15 hours) during February–June, with smaller animals basking for a shorter time than large ones. Holes or crevices are used as refuges, individuals in this population apparently being disinclined to dig their own burrows. Further south, in Natal, it seemingly goes into partial hibernation (e.g. in cracks in cliffs) from April to August, appearing only occasionally on warm days to bask in the sun close to the hole or termite nest in which the den has been established. In September–March in this region, *Varanus niloticus* is usually found near streams or other bodies of water, favouring thick brush or reed-grown water courses. During December–February in particular, it is to be found basking along streamsides, often on driftwood or on overhanging rocks and branches (from which it can quickly drop into the water if alarmed). Steep mud banks or the pressed-down reeds overhanging streams are other favoured basking spots. The creatures are, in fact, excellent swimmers, propelling themselves with horizontal strokes of the tail and undulations of the body, the limbs being folded against the sides. The head is held clear of the surface, which sometimes leads to it being mistaken for a snake but obviates any chance of it being misidentified as a crocodile.

Studies of Nile monitors in Senegal have indicated varying levels of thyroid activity associated with seasonal climatic variation and winter hibernation. In this area, the thyroid is active in the rainy season, which begins in July, with a maximum of activity in November–December, preceded by a brief interval of quiescence in October. During December–June (the essentially dry season) the thyroid is inactive, although March and April see some reactivation of this gland, which subsides again in May. The function of the thyroid in monitors seems to be primarily temperature control. This is linked to the nutritional process and is possibly also geared to increased food requirements during the mating season. In the Senegal population of *Varanus niloticus*, sexual activity is initiated at the beginning of the hot season in June and the monitor remains sexually active until October. This correlates with the development of the gonads, the testicles of males being enlarged from June until September, while females are being sought. Regression of the gonads subsequently occurs until January and the cycle recommences. Evidence of intraspecific conflict in the Nile monitor is limited but fighting between rival males does seem to occur.

In the more northerly part of its range, the Nile monitor lays its eggs in the ground, preferably in sandy loam, buried 75cm (30in) deep; holes scraped in the mud banks of irrigation canals are used in the Sudan and, in many areas, nests are dug on the same sandy shores where crocodiles nest. In southern Africa, this species lays its eggs in termite nests. These mounds are dome-shaped, cellular clay structures up to 1.2m (4ft) high and 2.2m (7ft) or more across at the base, with an even larger subterranean component, narrowing down to a cone-like termination well below the surface. Internally, termite nests comprise a large number of small chambers with thin cell walls. Nile monitors choose ant hills at most only a few hundred metres from water as surrogate nests, preferring those located in warm, sunny spots surrounded by tall grass, reeds, brush or bush. The outside bakes hard in the dry season but, when the rains come in December–February, female monitors can dig through the softened wall and enter the nest to lay their eggs. Sometimes they are covered up but, on other occasions, no attempt at concealment is apparently made and, after the lizard has left the nest, the diligent termites speedily repair the hole in its wall.

Nile monitor eggs are approximately 6 × 3.5cm (2½ × 1½in), with an average of about 35 in a clutch, although much larger numbers have been reported – in some instances perhaps the result of two females using the same nesting site. The integument is leathery or parchment-like, becoming brittle as it dries, the original white coloration staining browny-buff from surrounding mud when a termite nest is used as a repository. The eggs weigh about 40g (1½oz) each and, if laid in an ant hill, are integrated into its structure so that their surfaces form part of the divisions separating the chambers within the termites' nest. Many eggs are positioned vertically and they are frequently either touching or separated only by a thin layer of dried mud.

Access to a termites' nest is gained at ground level and a tunnel of 10–12cm (4–5in) diameter is dug to approximately the centre of the nest, where the eggs are deposited in an enlarged egg

▼ Only one reptile in Africa exceeds the Nile monitor *(Varanus niloticus)* in size, and that is the notorious Nile crocodile.

chamber. Several thousand small chambers surround the clutch, providing a very efficient insulating system that keeps the eggs cool in hot weather and warm when it is cool outside. Nest temperatures vary from as little as 19°C (66.2°F), when the ambient air temperature is only 13°C (55.4°F), to 30.5°C (86.9°F) in the 36.5°C (97.7°F) late afternoon heat. On average, the temperature of the egg chamber is about 26.5°C (79.7°F).

Incubation in a termite nest apparently requires 10 months, although eggs incubated artifically at 30°C (86°F) will hatch in 130 days. The hatchlings escape via a vertical 'chimney', about 2.5cm (1in) in diameter, running up through the ant hill. Within the eggs, the embryos are coiled head uppermost, the snout being forced against the shell wall to rupture the integument; emergence takes from 15 minutes to 7 hours. When the shell breaks, there is a flow of liquid which softens the surrounding nest structure; the emergent young, also covered in this fluid, quickly enlarge the egg chamber and then start to dig upwards.

An entire clutch will require up to 4 days to hatch and several more days to reach the summit of the nest. They do not immediately vacate the ant hill but remain near the chimney's exit and scuttle back inside if alarmed. It is impossible for the termites to repair the damage to their home until the brood has finally left because the mud-covered young monitors effectively plaster up the walls of the chimney. Once the hatchlings eventually depart, the termites not only repair the structure but also apparently destroy any eggshell left lying in the former egg chamber. Clutches of monitor eggs are at risk during incubation from the depredations of the ant-bear (aardvark) but otherwise enjoy almost total security in their commandeered refuge.

On emergence, hatchling Nile monitors are about 30cm (12in) long and weigh about 26g (1oz), having grown just over 2mm (1/16in) per day during the last 120 days spent in the egg; 2 months before hatching, they are 14cm (5½in) long and already have some adult markings. As soon as they are out of the egg, they exhibit very aggressive behaviour, scuttling actively about, adopting the threatening stance typical of adults, lashing their tails and biting fiercely. Their conspicuous black and yellow markings are good camouflage when they reach the safety of nearby water (for which they head as soon as they leave the vicinity of the nest site), but render them conspicuous on land, although a covering of mud derived from the termite nest assists concealment. They often feed on termites streaming out of the damaged nest.

Juveniles lack the crushing teeth and bowed lower jaw of adults but, during post-embryonic ontogeny, the lower jaw of this species exhibits development of a crushing dentition with concomitant shortening of the proportional length of the tooth row and increased ventral curvature of the mandible; recent hatchlings possess a relatively straight jaw with pointed, recurved, laterally compressed teeth. The changes probably reflect a shift from an insectivorous to a molluscivorous diet and they result in a slower but stronger bite.

Nile monitors are adaptable and hardy reptiles, as their extensive geographical occurrence across the African continent demonstrates. They are even bold enough to enter human habitations and steal fish from camp-site fires. However, human persecution has made considerable inroads into populations, while habitat destruction now permanently excludes the Nile monitor from some former parts of its range, e.g. the Nile delta (the species has become rare north of Cairo). In certain areas, they are hunted to obtain fat from the reproductive organs, which, when melted down, is believed to be a cure for ear ache, as well as a protection against lightning. There is no truth in the belief that Nile monitors will suckle from domestic cattle.

SAVANNAH MONITOR
(Varanus exanthematicus)

A rather more variable species of monitor lizard than the Nile monitor is found throughout Africa south of the Sahara. The savannah monitor *(Varanus exanthematicus)* is stockily proportioned, with a wide and relatively high head, a short neck and an abruptly tapering, weakly compressed tail bearing a very low, double-toothed crest. It attains a length of about 1.5m (5ft) and is represented by five regional subspecies.

In this species, the snout is convex, with the obliquely slitted nostrils located closer to the eye than to the end of the nose and small subequal scales covering the cranial region. On the dorsal surface the scales are small, smooth and oval; the abdominal scale rows number 60–110, and the caudal scales are keeled.

In colour, the savannah monitor is greyish brown above, with large, round, dark-edged yellow spots in rows across the back. A dark temporal streak extends along the side of the neck and the tail is ringed with alternating brown and yellowish annuli, while the lower surfaces are yellowish in colour.

As its common name suggests, *Varanus exanthematicus* is essentially a savannah-dwelling lizard but can adapt to such diverse habitats as rocky desert areas on the one hand or open forest and woodland on the other. It often occurs many kilometres from the nearest water, although it is, in fact, a capable swimmer and, in times of drought, will readily enter any rivers that are still running. It is absent from the dense forests of western Africa, however, and tends to avoid highland areas.

Primarily terrestrial and generally rather slow moving, it can nonetheless briefly exhibit considerable speed and immature specimens will readily run up trees if alarmed. A cornered savannah monitor adopts a menacing attitude, hissing loudly and coiling the tail ready to strike but, as a last resort, will simply play dead. The savannah monitor is active only by day and, even then, seeks shelter in burrows or hollows between tree roots during the hottest noon hours. When a pronounced seasonal climate is present, this monitor hibernates during the dry season. In the Sahel, for example, this lasts from November to June and the savannah monitor appears to fast throughout this period, living on fat reserves by metabolizing intra-abdominal adipose bodies and ultimately emerging distinctly emaciated, with the normally thick, rounded tail markedly concave-sided. As in the Nile monitor, the thyroid gland of the savannah monitor is largely quiescent during hibernation, the period of maximum thyroid activity coinciding with mating and breeding, which takes place in the wet months of the year from July onwards.

The diet of adults includes small mammals and birds, snakes, lizards and toads, together with large quantities of snails, the shells of which are cracked open so that the flesh can be extracted. To facilitate this process, the teeth of fully grown savannah monitors are quite blunt and the bite is adapted to afford maximum leverage towards the back of the jaws, with concomitant bowing of the mandible (paralleling the similar modifications for the same purpose seen in Nile monitors and the butaan). Carrion is also readily consumed and the eggs of birds and reptiles are favourite items of food.

Immature savannah monitors lack masticatory specializations and subsist principally on locusts, millipedes, caterpillars, orthopterans and the eggs of other lizards, graduating to small snails as they mature (and their jaws and teeth slowly acquire the adult conformation), until they are large enough to overcome the bigger prey which adults take. Even fully grown savannah monitors will still eat insects and the like, however, and exhibit a curious and unexplained practice when endeavouring to consume a millipede. The monitor rubs its chin on the millipede when it tries to escape, often for 15 minutes or more, and it has been surmised that this habit is in some way connected with the supposedly distasteful protective fluid that millipedes are believed to exude.

Tongue flicking in the savannah monitor is significantly increased after prey has actually been struck at with the jaws, rising from 20–40 flicks every two minutes, which is normal during general sampling of the surrounding environment, to as many as 160 flicks in the two minutes immediately after the victim has been bitten for the first time but is no longer held in the lizard's jaws. So-called Strike Induced Chemosensory Searching (SICS) is quite well known in snakes and presumably helps the hunter to follow odour trails left by a wounded victim trying to escape. Varanids no doubt use it for exactly the same purpose; although devoid of taste buds, the flicking tongue of a monitor lizard can sample an area of air comparable to or even greater than that which is sampled by advanced species of snakes employing similar repeated rapid extension movements of the tongue.

The savannah monitor is customarily placed in the subgenus *Empagusia* but this assignment has usually been in conjunction with the yellow monitor *(Varanus flavescens)* and it seems doubtful whether combining an African form with an Asiatic one in a single subgenus is appropriate, particularly as there are conspicuous chromosomal distinctions between the two taxa.

Cape monitor
(Varanus exanthematicus albigularis)

The most southerly, and the largest, subspecies of *Varanus exanthematicus* is the Cape monitor *(Varanus exanthematicus albigularis)*, also known as the rock monitor, veld leguaan, white-throated leguaan, tree leguaan or bush leguaan. Occurring almost throughout southern Africa as far north as Malawi, Angola and Mozambique, living in rocky areas of plains, and usually becoming dormant in the winter months, it is a rather cumbersome, sluggish monitor, grey-brown in colour, with yellow spots forming transverse bands on the back, a yellowish, brown-spotted belly and 85–110 transverse rows of ventral scales.

Between 15 and 40 eggs usually constitute a clutch, each egg measuring about 6.5 × 3.5cm (2½ × 1½in) and weighing about 40g (1½oz). Sometimes a hole dug beneath tree roots is used as a repository, but hollow trees may also be employed in some areas. The Cape monitor has been successfully bred in captivity, and artificial incubation of eggs at an ambient temperature of 25–30°C (77–86°F) in San Diego Zoo, with water added when wrinkling of the shells indicated incipient dessication, led to hatching after an incubation period of 170 days (10 or 12 months is more likely in the wild, so that hatching coincides with the wet season). After the appearance of longitudinal indentations in the eggs, which the addition of water failed to eliminate, the eggs began to split along their exposed surface. Each embryo initially punctured the shell with the egg tooth on the end of its nose, then protruded the snout and head, often resting for 2–3 hours at this stage, with the head reposing on the sand of the enclosure floor. Sporadic wriggling and pushing, combined with convulsive gulping of air, achieved emergence in about six hours, the juvenile initially dragging with it the remains of the yolk sac, which dried and dropped off in a few hours.

Even when only the head had emerged from the shell, the hatchlings would bite fiercely if threatened. On emergence, they were about 20cm (8in) long and weighed nearly 30g (1oz), attaining almost 23cm (9in) and 40g (1½oz) after a month. When danger appeared, they would either become limp and apparently feign death, or else lower their bodies to the sand surface and expand the rib cage with quick inhalations, simultaneously hissing and cocking their tails to strike. They had a habit of suddenly pausing abruptly with one forefoot off the ground, the cupped foot pointing to the rear.

Initially, the young of the Cape monitor have the top of the head black, fading to purple on the neck, with jet black and orange bars on the body and wide yellow bars down the tail. Although the Latin name *albigularis* means 'white-throated', this area is in fact black; the underparts are light yellow and there is fine black reticulation on the belly. Hatchlings begin to eat insects after 2 days and captive specimens have been found to thrive on a diet of fish, ground raw shrimp, young geckos, and crickets; the curling bodies of cut worms seem difficult to manage and roaches have awkward wings, but moths and beetles are taken. The prey is habitually seized, shaken, dropped, shaken again, then grabbed by the head and bolted down with a series of body jerks.

Angolan monitor
(Varanus exanthematicus angolensis)

Slightly further north than the domain of *Varanus exanthematicus albigularis*, the savannah monitor is represented by *Varanus exanthematicus angolensis*, with 74–92 transverse rows of ventral scales and an overall length of about 1.4m (4⅔ft) – slightly smaller than the more southerly subspecies. *Varanus exanthematicus angolensis* is not restricted to Angola, as its name might suggest, but also occurs in the Congo Republic, southeastern Zaire and Zambia.

Varanus exanthematicus exanthematicus

The western African subspecies, *Varanus exanthematicus exanthematicus*, is present from Guinea to

▲ **Regarded as essentially a savannah dweller, *Varanus exanthematicus* is also found in rocky deserts or open forest and woodland.**

the northern Congo and has 59–77 transverse rows of ventral scales. This form seems to subsist largely on invertebrates, especially insects (coleopterans, sphingid caterpillars, orthopterans), mantids and myriapods, with occasional scorpions and gastropods, and eggs of other lizards (even those of its own kind) if they can be found.

Varanus exanthematicus microstictus

In eastern Africa, there is a rather small savannah monitor, *Varanus exanthematicus microstictus*, with 88–94 transverse rows of ventral scales and relatively large scales on the nape of the neck. From a southerly boundary in Mozambique, the range of this subspecies extends northwards to Ethiopia and Somalia and westwards through areas of wooded terrain.

Varanus exanthematicus ionidesi

The presence of a separate subspecies closely related to *Varanus exanthematicus microstictus* has been reported from Tanzania. *Varanus exanthematicus ionidesi* is distinguished by a lighter and less contrasting juvenile coloration, exhibiting fewer (four or five) transverse series of larger light spots with black borders crossing the back than is the case in *Varanus exanthematicus microstictus*, and only six to eight caudal cross-bars (compared with nine to ten in *Varanus exanthematicus microstictus*).

YEMEN MONITOR ***(Varanus yemenensis)***
A rather unspecialized member of the African monitor community seems to be the geographically isolated *Varanus yemenensis* (Fig. 5.1). Restricted to western Saudi Arabia, this lizard is evidently closely related to *Varanus exanthematicus* and may even prove to be another subspecies of that wide-ranging form.

Compared to the typical savannah monitor, the Yemen monitor has the elongate, slit-like nostril located closer to the eye, smaller head and body scales (especially on the neck), a uniformly yellow termination to the tail and a broad yellowish band across the snout. *Varanus yemenensis* can only really be distinguished from *Varanus exanthematicus microstictus* by features of the hemipenis, which has reduced and less symmetrical horns and eight rows of paryphasma (hemipenal ornamentation) in the Saudi subspecies. *Varanus yemenensis* has no pale spots or ocelli on the dorsum, a brownish ground colour with dark crossbars in the sacral area and on the tail, and yellow forelimbs, with the upper part of the head dark hued. Large supraocular scales are absent and the nuchal scales are only slightly larger than those on the upper side of the head, with roundish, strongly convex centres. The tail is markedly compressed, with a double keel.

Observation suggests that the Yemen monitor is relatively common in the eastern foot-hills of the southwestern Arabian mountains (the Tihama range), occurring at altitudes of 300–1350m (1000–4500ft). This is an area of basaltic rocks, partially covered by a dense *Euphorbia* vegetation, with cultivated maize and millet fields surrounded by thick shrubs and bushes, and loose groups of acacia trees. Yemen monitors seem to appear only in the daytime (local claims that they raid chicken runs at night are unsubstantiated) and forage beneath stones and dead vegetation along the margins of water courses and pools for insects (especially beetles) and snails. They may occasionally take young hares, which are locally abundant, and captive specimens eat mice, chickens and other birds, fish, crickets and large cockroaches.

▼ **Fig. 5.1 Yemen monitor *(Varanus yemenensis)***

CHAPTER 6

Australian Giants and their Kin

Some 70 million years ago, at the end of the Age of Dinosaurs, Australia was part of a huge southern supercontinent, called Gondwanaland, that also included South America, Africa, India and Antarctica. Towards the end of the Mesozoic era, this huge landmass began to fragment. Australia became cut off from the rest of the southern continents by sea-ways and, eventually, by oceanic barriers and drifted off into biological isolation, carrying with it a bizarre relict population of animals and plants.

Today, there are more than twice as many species of monitor lizards in Australia as there are in the rest of the world put together but, although varanids had been fairly widespread during and just after the Age of Dinosaurs, it seems unlikely that there were any in Australia when this island continent became separated from the rest of Gondwanaland. A single, broken fossil vertebra of Middle Miocene age apparently indicates that, 10 or 15 million years ago, this adaptable group of lizards had somehow managed to reach Australia, where they quickly established themselves. The only possible route must have been from the north, and as Australia was then considerably further south than it is today this necessarily entailed them crossing a substantial oceanic gap – no mean feat, even bearing in mind the swimming capabilities of monitor lizards and the tolerance of salt water that is manifested by at least some living species. Later on, when sea levels fell during the Pleistocene ice age, there was evidently a secondary transit of varanids across land bridges connecting New Guinea and Australia, but it was the primary (mid-Cenozoic) invasion of monitor lizards that was to result in their most spectacular evolutionary development.

MEGALANIA

Alone on their island continent, with no other major predators to challenge them, Australian varanids grew in size and variety until they ultimately evolved the giant *Megalania,* some 7m (23ft) in length and effectively the undisputed ruler of prehistoric Australia (Fig. 6.1). In its day, this huge varanid was challenged only by the crocodiles (some of which exhibited markedly terrestrial specializations and evidently spent more time on land than their modern relatives), the somewhat problematical 'marsupial lion' *(Thylacoleo,* an animal about the size of a leopard that seems to have been carnivorous, since it had enlarged stabbing incisor teeth, shearing blade-like premolars and heavy claws), and perhaps a few very large pythons *(Wonambi).*

For reasons still not clearly understood, much of the unique indigenous Australian fauna died out some 20 000 years ago. Perhaps the expansion of human settlement was to blame, with hunting and environmental impoverishment becoming significant factors in antipodean ecology, or possibly climatic change was the catalyst. Conceivably they together tipped the balance.

In any event, the huge herbivorous marsupials on which the giant monitor preyed all vanished. Deprived of its food supply, and possibly harried by the human newcomers, who may have first reached Australian shores as long as 60 000 years ago, the biggest of the antipodean varanids also quickly became extinct.

Remains of *Megalania* have been found in Queensland, New South Wales and South

Australia, a distribution that probably reflects the occurrence of fossiliferous sites rather than actual geographical range and, considering it was clearly a dominant predator, this huge monitor has left remarkably few fossil bones for scientists to find. Such apparent scarcity is difficult to explain. There is no known complete skeleton, or even a complete skull.

The first evidence of the creature's existence was three vertebrae unearthed in Queensland during the middle of the nineteenth century and described in 1858 by the celebrated British anatomist, Richard Owen, as a new genus and species of 'gigantic land-lizard', *Megalania prisca*. Over 20 years later, in 1880, Owen reported further remains of this enigmatic reptile from Australia (an occipital fragment and vertebrae), along with a horned skull that he mistakenly assumed must belong to the same animal as the other bones. In fact, the skull later proved to be that of a turtle called *Meiolania*. In 1884, Owen described a varanid tooth fragment from New South Wales and called it *Notiosaurus dentatus*, correctly deducing that it could not belong to the animal with the edentulous horned skull.

The confusion caused by the mistaken association of huge varanid bones with the horned turtle skull was eventually resolved, but further discoveries of *Megalania* bones were only scrappy. They included a maxilla (upper jaw bone) with 10 dental sockets and a single implanted tooth, skull bones (frontals, parietals), a lower jaw with 11 teeth in it, isolated teeth, a number of vertebrae from different sections of the spine (cervical, thoracic, lumbar, sacral and caudal), ribs, pectoral girdle elements, a pelvis, and limb and foot bones. Latterly, some massive skull bones (two frontals with a sagittal crest and a matching parietal) have come to light but not a single complete skeleton exists, although one or two may in fact have been discovered at the famous Darling Downs locality during the nineteenth-century heyday of fossil collecting there. (Very little material has been found at this site in the twentieth century.) Unfortunately, these comprehensive Darling Downs specimens of *Megalania* were apparently regarded simply as collections of assorted bones and the individual components were sold or distributed to about a dozen different museums around the world. This scanty evidence is known to date from 19 000 to about 26 000 years ago, with some of the bones being perhaps a bit older than this.

Despite having so little to go on, scientists have nonetheless managed a fairly comprehensive restoration of *Megalania*, using the extant Komodo dragon as a basis. The massive proportions of the vertebrae, and the presence of a prominent ridge for muscle attachment on the supraoccipital bone of the skull, testify to a reptile of formidable power. Skull kinesis seems to have been largely eliminated to enhance the strength of the bite, with no evidence of the sliding joint between the supraoccipital and parietal bones seen in the living *Varanus*. Large, slightly recurved teeth, nearly 2.5cm (1in) in length, furnished the jaws with a ferocious array of weaponry. Typical varanid teeth either have anterior and posterior cutting edges, with or without serrations on both surfaces, or rounded edges on both sides of the teeth but, in *Megalania*, there is a rounded front cutting edge bearing serrations only towards the point, while the back edge is a thin blade bearing serrations throughout its

▲ **Fig. 6.1** ***Megalania*, the extinct giant Australian monitor.**

length. Wear facets are visible on *Megalania* teeth, a feature which does not normally occur on the regularly shed teeth of living monitor lizards, from which it may be inferred that tooth replacement was a much slower process in the extinct Australian giant.

The humerus (upper arm bone) is remarkable for its very short shaft, presumably an adaptation to compensate for the sheer bulk of an animal estimated to have weighed over 600kg (1320lb). Among various isolated claw bones from different localities, there is a specimen obtained in the eastern Lake Eyre basin (Cooper Creek) that measures no less than 84.5mm (3¼in) in maximum length and 33.4mm (1½in) in height, which suggests it belonged to an animal with a body length (excluding the tail) of 4–5m (12–15ft). The tail of *Megalania* is presumed to have been proportionately rather short, since in general small varanids have long tails and large varanids possess relatively short tails. For example, the Komodo dragon has a 1 : 1 body : tail length ratio but, in small members of the group, the body : tail length ratio may be 1 : 2 or even more. *Megalania* tail vertebrae are few and far between, only about a dozen being known, of which possibly only two are from the distal region.

Reconstruction of the complete skeleton has been undertaken at the National Museum of Victoria in Melbourne, employing scaled-up bones based on those of living varanids as a substitute for the still unknown *Megalania* elements, with due allowance being computed for the changes in overall proportions which a reptile twice the size of a Komodo dragon and eight times its mass would inevitably have displayed. The result is the imposing skeleton of an immensely powerful reptile with a stoutly constructed skull, short stocky limbs, a barrel-like body and a rather short deep tail.

So what manner of beast was this Pleistocene monster from the Antipodes? Like the Komodo dragon, it was almost certainly an ambush predator, waiting in scrub along game trails, probably in the vicinity of waterholes, and rushing out initially to cripple its prey by severing the ham strings if the victim was too large to kill quickly, even with the giant monitor's formidable teeth and claws. Bones of *Megalania* regularly occur in association with remains of uniquely Australian herbivorous marsupials that are now extinct. Particularly abundant are skeletons of wombat-like diprotodonts, which were as big as a large rhinoceros with a length of about 3.5m (11ft); some (palorchestids) may have had trunks and attained the size of a large bull (they were perhaps Australia's equivalent of elephants). Pleistocene kangaroos also achieved huge dimensions and probably represented a regular source of meals for *Megalania,* with some of them possibly standing 3m (10ft) tall, a third as large again as the living grey kangaroos. Rat kangaroos, now reduced to diminutive creatures weighing only 500g (18oz), equalled the largest modern-day kangaroos in size, and very large kangaroos with single-toed hind feet *(Sthenurus)* were a common element in the temperate zone faunas of southern Australia. There were also enormous flightless birds *(Genyornis)* which would have formed a welcome repast for a hungry giant monitor.

Evidently these were the key prey animals for fully grown specimens of *Megalania,* although juveniles doubtless made do with lesser victims, such as the smaller species of contemporary kangaroos, wallabies and wombats. Carrion would undoubtedly have been avidly sought and consumed, and a Pleistocene picnic of 25 000 years ago, with a group of slavering *Megalania* tearing flesh from the carcass of a diprotodont, disputing with each other for the best of the spoils and chasing off hungry juveniles trying to snatch a few crumbs from the adults' table, must have been a fearsome sight. A meat-eating reptile as big as *Megalania* would have been a significant threat to any people living in Australia at the time and there were probably some human victims.

It has been suggested that *Megalania* is really only a bizarrely overgrown species of *Varanus* but the consensus of scientific opinion suggests that it is, in fact, a separate genus, distinguished by such significant features as: tooth structure and the slow rate of dental replacement (with occlusal wear facets developing); the massive trunk vertebrae; the structure of the ilium, with a horizontally oriented posterior dorsal protuberance for attachment of the ilio-pubic ligament (this bony

projection is acutely angled in *Varanus*) and a thick, prominent external ridge for the origin of the gluteal muscles that run down to the femur (thin and rather blade-like or even absent altogether in the ilium of living monitors); the short humeral shaft; and the supraoccipital bone of the skull forming a 90-degree angle with the occipital condyle.

How *Megalania* evolved, or where it came from, is unknown. The presence of the Komodo dragon in the Lesser Sunda islands today, and the occurrence of large varanid bones on Timor, on Java and in New Caledonia, suggests that large monitor lizards were a significant feature of the East Indies/southern Pacific region in the Late Cenozoic. Isolated fossil bones of varanids intermediate in size between *Megalania* and the Komodo dragon occur in the Pliocene of Australia and it seems likely that large representatives of the group must have somehow reached Australia about 10–15 million years ago and then acquired giant size in response to the presence of very large potential prey – the huge marsupials and the massive flightless birds.

▲ Active and powerful, the gigantic lace lizard *(Varanus giganteus)* may be 2.5m (8½ft) in length. It will range considerable distances in search of such prey as snakes, small mammals and other lizards; carrion is also readily consumed, along with bird and reptile eggs.

GIGANTIC LACE LIZARD *(Varanus giganteus)*

There are still large monitor lizards in Australia, although none of them even approach the dimensions of *Megalania*. The appropriately named gigantic lace lizard *(Varanus giganteus)* grows up to 2.5m (8¼ft) in length and lives in arid areas of central Australia, where it either digs burrows, 7–8m (22–25ft) long and over 1m (3¼ft) deep, to escape the intense heat of the desert environment or else hides out in deep rock crevices or under slabs (the animal keeps its body temperature at about 38°C/100.4°F). To search for food, it will range considerable distances along dry creek beds or adjacent flats, hunting lizards, snakes, birds or small mammals (including rabbits), scavenging carrion and digging out the eggs of birds or reptiles. It has been reported to kill young kangaroos and will readily catch and eat juveniles of its own species – a 2m (6½ft) long specimen was observed to sprint 30m (100ft) to seize a 1.5m (5ft) relative that had become caught in a fence. On Barrow Island, off Western Australia, these monitors search along the edge of the sea during December–February for hatchling green turtles and have been seen to catch seagulls by hiding under vehicles and executing a short sprint to seize victims.

Also known as the perentic (perentie, perenty, perinthic, perenthie) in the Lake Eyre region, and as the *echunpa* in the Arunta aboriginal language, the gigantic lace lizard is a slender, elongate species with a proportionately large head, a long, narrow, parallel-sided snout and oval nostrils situated about twice as far from the eye sockets as from the nose. The teeth are compressed and acutely pointed, and the head scales are small, with diminutive, granular supraocular elements. The dorsal body scales are small, oval and keeled, while the abdominal scales are smooth and arranged in up to 155 transverse rows. Marked lateral compression is present in the tail, which has a very low, double-toothed crest.

Coloration on the dorsal surfaces is brown or blackish, with large, round, light-coloured spots or ocelli in transverse rows across the back and tail. Smaller round spots are present on the limbs and large black reticulations occur on the ivory-coloured neck. Undersurfaces bear dark reticulated markings and the chest may have about four black, irregular, zigzag cross-bars.

The range extends from the coast of Western Australia (Pilbara south to Yalgoo and the Menzies District), through the southern part of Northern Territory (as far north as Hann's Range) and northern South Australia, to extreme western Queensland (Fig. 6.2).

Although normally a burrow-dweller, customarily preferring areas around rocky outcrops, the gigantic lace lizard will climb trees if hard pressed and, in panic, has been alleged even to run up a horse or a man (some supposed cases of attacks on natives may be attributable to this aberration). It is able to grip a branch with its hind claws and reach out with the forefeet for a fresh purchase, using the tail as a lever. The quadrupedal gait can be quite fast, with the body and tail carried clear of the ground, but the animal is said to resort to bipedalism when extreme speed is required. The long muscular tail is an effective weapon of offence, its use being preceded by flexing to one side with only the midsection touching the ground; a single blow is sufficient to break the forelegs of a dog. When excited or provoked, the large head may be held stiffly at an angle to the neck, the throat is inflated and the animal emits a hissing sound, simultaneously flicking the tongue in and out with great rapidity and lunging open-mouthed.

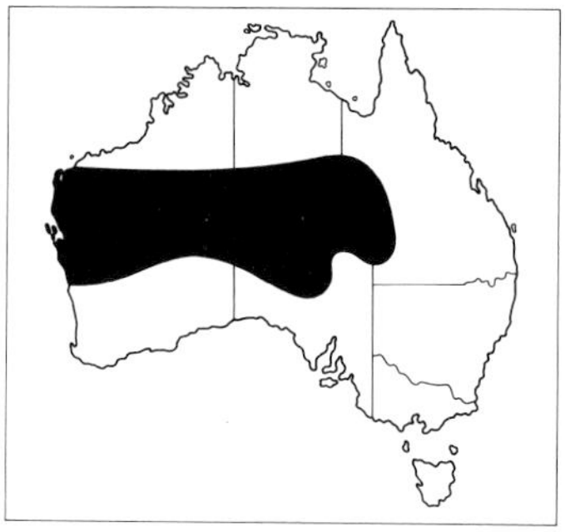

◀ **Fig. 6.2 Distribution of *Varanus giganteus.***

Gigantic lace lizards hibernate from May to August, either singly or in male/female pairs. The eggs measure about 5 × 8cm (2 × 3in) and weigh about 80g (3oz). Incubation takes approximately 230 days and emergent hatchlings measure 38cm (15in) in length.

SAND GOANNA or GOULD'S MONITOR (*Varanus gouldi*)

The most familiar and widespread member of Australia's extensive galaxy of monitor lizards is the sand goanna, or Gould's monitor *(Varanus gouldi)*. About 1.5–2m (5–6½ft) in length, this ground-dweller favours sandy locations and is seldom found far from cover, relying on its speed and agility for safety, although it will climb trees as a last resort, ascending as high as 15m (50ft). It occurs throughout the continent, except for southeastern Victoria and Tasmania, northern Arnhem Land and a small area in the eastern part of the Great Sandy Desert (Fig. 6.3), adapting to forests, woodlands, humid to semi-arid heathlands, seashores and even offshore islands, as well as the arid central deserts and the wet sclerophyll forests in the far southwestern corner

◀ **Fig. 6.3 Distribution of *Varanus gouldi.***

of its range. In such inhospitable wastelands as the Nullarbor Plain and the Great Victoria Desert, it has perforce to hibernate during the winter months (March–August), hiding away underground and emerging in September, usually in an emaciated condition that is quickly transformed by intensive foraging for food.

The sand goanna has a long snout with rounded nostrils located nearer to the end of the muzzle than to the eyes. The feet have moderately elongate, strongly proportioned toes and the laterally compressed tail bears a dorsal keel with a very low, double-toothed crest. The cranial scales, including the supraoculars, are small and subequal, while the dorsal scalation is oval and tectiform; the smooth abdominal scales occur in about 120–150 transverse rows.

Coloration of the sand goanna varies considerably across its extensive range but the basic pattern is dark brown to almost black above, with round yellow spots or ocelli on the back (in transverse rows) and limbs, and yellow annuli round the tail. On the temple, there are two yellow streaks, separated by a distinctive black band, that extend along the sides of the neck. Lower surfaces are yellowish, sometimes with small blackish spots, and the tail tip is habitually white or yellowish. Juveniles have more accentuated spotting than adults.

The compressed, acutely pointed teeth are the hallmark of a predator and the sand goanna will kill other lizards (including smaller varanids), snakes, nestling birds, small mammals (e.g. mice, bandicoots), centipedes, scorpions, wasps, cockroaches, moths, caterpillars and an abundance of beetles and grasshoppers. Seashore populations take fish and crabs, and eggs from birds' nests or crocodile breeding sites are a favourite dish (along some rivers it has been estimated that sand goannas take 5 per cent of the eggs laid by the Australian freshwater crocodile, *Crocodylus johnsoni*). Carrion is avidly consumed and sand goannas can frequently be seen feeding on dead sheep and the carcasses of animals killed by road vehicles (e.g. kangaroos).

Foraging and general mobility is restricted to times when environmental conditions are suitable by maintaining different activity patterns. This behavioural flexibility and use of thermal refuges (e.g. burrows) accounts for the ability of the species to live in a wide range of thermal regimes, its extensive geographical occurrence probably being determined by rate of water loss in xeric conditions. It pants at elevated ambient temperatures but, while the head temperature is maintained at a lower figure than that of the ambient, the cloacal temperature may rise above the ambient. Sand goannas often live in hollow logs or in rabbit burrows (derelict or occupied), but may also excavate their own subterranean lair, with an enlarged, terminal living space. Sometimes a single individual may have several burrows or refuges at its disposal.

Before emerging in the morning from its nighttime retreat, the sand goanna often sits with just its head in the entrance, sometimes for as much as an hour. It then crawls onto the mound of earth just outside, where it basks by flattening the body to the ground. Sometimes these monitors seek an adjacent pile of dead branches on which to bask and, occasionally, they raise the front of the body by placing the forefeet and head on small humps in the ground. In winter the cloacal temperature eventually rises to about 23°C (73.4°F), in summer to 35.5°C (95.9°F); the preferred body temperature seems to be about 35–38°C (95–100.4°F). If heavy cloud or rain causes the cloacal temperature to fall, the lizard returns to its burrow and rarely re-emerges that day. It is seemingly strongly territorial, with a permanent home-site, and has apparently been seen abroad by night as well as by day, which is unusual for a monitor. The daily activity range is probably just under 1 hectare (2.5 acres) but overall home ranges of 40 hectares (100 acres) or more have been reported.

▲ **The most common and widespread of Australia's many monitor lizards, the sand goanna *(Varanus gouldi)* is beautifully marked. Coloration varies considerably within its extensive range, which includes almost the whole continent except for Tasmania, the extreme southeast and a few other isolated areas.**

A voracious feeder, with an especially keen sense of smell, the sand goanna will dig out scorpions from burrows 40cm (16in) deep, using each forefoot in turn for about five 'digs' before pausing to stand on its hind legs, propped on its tail, to survey the surrounding area. A 1.2m (4ft) specimen was seen to seize a tiger snake of similar size by clamping its jaws on the snake's neck. After some 30 minutes wrestling, the snake weakened and was gulped down by the goanna until only the end of its tail remained visible, but was then regurgitated. The goanna returned 20 minutes later, seized the still living snake by the head, and this time swallowed it successfully, although it required half an hour for the operation. Among the other varanids upon which sand goannas are known to prey, *Varanus caudolineatus*, the diminutive *Varanus brevicauda* and *Varanus gilleni* are notably frequent victims; a large captive male specimen was observed to devour a half-grown juvenile of its own species.

Sand goannas are usually wary of pedestrians and, if approached, seek cover (running anything up to 100m/110yd to reach the sanctuary of a burrow or fallen log) or flatten themselves against the ground with the forelimbs folded at the sides, to give the lowest possible profile, but with the hind limbs normally oriented to facilitate escape. When directly threatened, they elevate the head, raise the body and arch the back, hissing loudly while inflating the throat and neck. The 22cm (9in) tongue is flicked rapidly in and out as the animal becomes more agitated, the body is rapidly inflated, and the animal finally adopts a bipedal stance and lunges towards its antagonist. If grabbed, it will claw, bite and discharge its cloacal contents. Sand goannas are almost impossible to drag from their burrows by the tail because of the strength with which they cling to the ground with their foreclaws. The speed that an alarmed sand goanna is capable of generating when trying to escape has led to them being referred to as 'racehorse monitors'.

The sand goanna lays its eggs during November–February, usually in termite nests; clutch sizes generally varying from 4 to 19. Incubation of the 6 × 3cm (2½ × 1¼in) eggs takes about 170–200 days, depending on nest

▲ **Although most at home in arid areas, the sand goanna *(Varanus gouldi)* is often encountered among spinifex grass and dry, stunted woodlands**

temperature, with the young emerging from January/February onwards. Males are up to three times the weight of females.

There is a good deal of geographical colour variation within the species, which, except for the darker and less patterned Kimberley population, tends to intergrade. In the northwest of Australia, the head and neck are reddish brown; in the south they are blackish brown or dark olive, peppered with yellowish brown; and in desert areas of Western Australia, Northern Territory and northern South Australia, the coloration is similar to animals from the northwest but brighter hued.

Varanus gouldi gouldi

Three subspecies are in consequence usually recognized. The most widespread is *Varanus gouldi gouldi*, which is present in arid areas of western, northern and eastern Australia, where it hibernates below ground during the winter season.

Varanus gouldi flavirufus

The inland subspecies is *Varanus gouldi flavirufus*, from semi-arid and desert areas of Northern Territory and Western Australia, occurring in the inhospitable wastes of the Great Sandy Desert, as well as extending into Arnhem Land and out to the Monte Bello Islands. Distinguished by a yellow ground coloration, *Varanus gouldi flavirufus* prefers semi-arid country sparsely covered with spinifex and stunted trees. It is a wide-ranging forager, often stopping in its journeyings to dig up prey (the diggings are a common occurrence in desert areas, readily identified by their kidney-shaped cross-section). They leave very light footprints and do not drag their tails. The average volume of individual prey items – consisting mostly of lizards, grasshoppers, insects, beetles and reptile eggs – is 1.5cm^3 ($^9/_{10}$ cu. in) per item. *Varanus gouldi flavirufus* has been seen to attack a specimen of *Varanus gilleni* that measured 15cm (6in) from snout to venter, and another specimen contained two baby birds of about 6g ($^1/_4$oz) each. Lizards are an important prey and have been found to include arboreal species, such as *Varanus caudolineatus* and the gecko, *Diplodactylus ciliaris*, but it is not known whether these are caught in trees or dug up from the ground. *Varanus gouldi flavirufus* remains underground during the winter and is active in the early morning and late afternoon from September through February. Mating takes place in September and October.

Rosenberg's monitor
(Varanus gouldi rosenbergi)

Occurring across southern Australia is a large, dark-coloured ground monitor up to about 2m (6½ft) in length, with a laterally compressed tail, that was originally described as a subspecies of *Varanus gouldi* (Rosenberg's monitor, *Varanus gouldi rosenbergi)* but is now regarded by many authorities as a species in its own right, since no hybridization has been observed between this form and the typical widespread sand goannas, despite the fact that *Varanus gouldi* and Rosenberg's monitor have overlapping geographical ranges on the Swan coastal plain and through the southern wheatbelt.

Rosenberg's monitor is especially well established in the Stirling Range of southwestern Australia but also extends as far north as Perth (Mussel Pool), across the southern region of Western Australia, and additionally occurs in isolated areas from southeastern South Australia to Big Desert (Victoria), and Goulburn, Nowra and the Sydney area in New South Wales. There is a population on Kangaroo Island, off the South Australia coast, which includes individuals of notably large size.

These island residents seem to have a slightly later breeding season than sand goanna populations in central Australia, males having maximum testicular development from late November to February. Females on Kangaroo Island contain oviducal eggs with a mean length of about 3cm (1¼in) in February, the passage of eggs through the oviduct probably being rapid. Mating in all likelihood occurs during the ovulatory and post-ovulatory phase; coupling of *Varanus gouldi rosenbergi* was observed on 4 and 5 January one year between animals that sheltered separately overnight in burrows 5m (15ft) apart, copulation occurring several times during the 2 days. A female was seen preparing a nest chamber in a termite nest on 21 February, in which a clutch of 12 eggs was laid (the nest chamber was found to be at a temperature of 27°C/75.2°F). Hatching takes place in September, after an incubation period of 6–7 months. The newly emergent young weigh about 15g (½oz). After February, the testes of male Rosenberg's monitors on Kangaroo Island decrease in size and the animals are largely or totally inactive from May through August. The diet of this population includes mammals (especially rats), birds, reptiles and their eggs, amphibians and invertebrates.

The coloration of Rosenberg's monitor incorporates black bands on the neck and back, a dark tail with a banded or dark-coloured tip, and dark reticulation or banding on the lower surfaces. The black head is occasionally peppered with yellowish or greyish white and the black (rarely bluish grey) of the neck and back is spotted with sulphur yellow, greenish yellow, yellowish white or greyish white; dots on the back and at the base of the tail sometimes cluster to form small spots. Three or four narrow black bands on the neck curve downwards and forwards along the sides, the front one being parallel to the pale-edged, black temporal stripe. The back has about 12 narrow black cross-bands, a little narrower or wider than the interspaces, while the tail is proximally black, ringed with dull yellow, becoming blackish brown narrowly banded with yellowish brown. The legs and toes are black, with dots and small spots of brownish or yellowish white. Ventral surfaces are yellowish or whitish, the black or grey reticulation extending from chin to abdomen (and occasionally under the legs), sometimes forming bands or chevrons on the chin and throat.

ARGUS MONITOR *(Varanus panoptes)*

Clearly a member of the general sand goanna assemblage (and in the view of some authorities warranting inclusion in *Varanus gouldi* itself), the Argus monitor (*Varanus panoptes)* extends the range of this group into New Guinea, with an Australian occurrence that embraces the arid interior of Western Australia and the dry northern region of the continent from the Kimberley

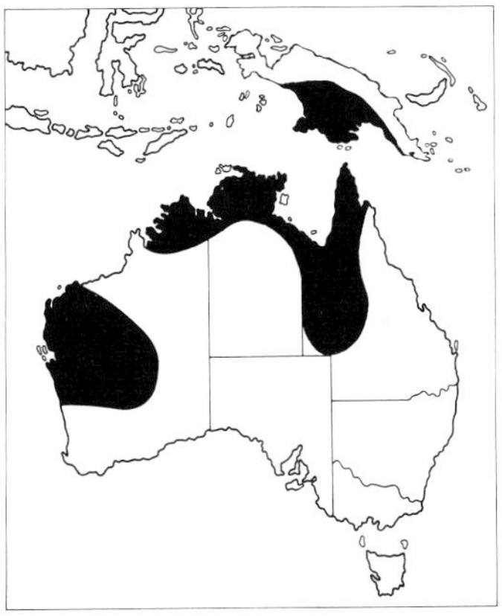

◀ **Fig. 6.4 Distribution of *Varanus panoptes*.**

district of Western Australia, through Northern Territory, to northern and interior Queensland, extending just south of the tropic of Capricorn in the Thompson River region (Fig. 6.4).

A robustly proportioned reptile, about 1.5m (5ft) long, with a double-crested, strongly compressed tail and a blackish brown to dull reddish brown ground colour, the Argus monitor (Fig. 6.5) differs from the typical sand goanna in possessing a strongly spotted dorsal surface with transverse rows of large dark spots alternating with rows of small pale spots. In 1980, when this monitor was first described by G.M. Storr of the West Australian Museum in Perth, the unusual skin patterning reminded him of Argus Panoptes, the 100-eyed guardian of Princess Io in Greek mythology, so he chose to name it *Varanus panoptes*. Small dark ventral spots, aligned with large dark spots, occur on the back and flanks and, compared to *Varanus gouldi*, there are more numerous mid-body scale rows and also smaller inter-orbital scales.

The Argus monitor seems to be found mainly in riparian habitats and preys extensively on aquatic creatures (e.g. crabs, fish, frogs), as well as taking scorpions (which it digs out of burrows), beetles,

▲ **Fig. 6.5. The Argus monitor *(Varanus panoptes)*.**

▲ **A penguin chick falls victim to a prowling Rosenberg's monitor *(Varanus gouldi rosenbergi).***

orthopterans, agamids, ants, lepidopteran larvae and pupae, spiders, centipedes, roaches, hemipterans, trichopterans, skinks, other (smaller) varanids, snakes, rodents, bandicoots, echidnas, reptile eggs and birds. It is active all year round, breeding in the wet season. The males are three times the weight of females. Courtship takes place in July and there are about 12 eggs per clutch. Hatchlings measure some 10cm (4in) in length.

Varanus panoptes panoptes

Three subspecies have been described. In *Varanus panoptes panoptes,* from the northern part of Australia, the skin patterning varies from prominent to (in old individuals) relatively obscure, with transverse rows of black or blackish brown spots over the neck, body, limbs and proximal region of the tail (sometimes these spots are pale edged and alternate with rows of dark-edged white to pale yellow spots). A pale-edged dark streak extends through the eye along the side of the neck, with another dark, often broken line extending from the lip. The end of the tail varies from yellow to pale brown, banded with dark brown; terminal banding of the caudal extremity persists even in aged animals.

Varanus panoptes rubidus

Restricted mainly to the arid western plateaux of Western Australia, from the southern Pilbara south to Fields Find and Mount Linden, *Varanus panoptes rubidus* also occurs on Dolphin Island in the Dampier archipelago. It is distinguishable from *Varanus panoptes panoptes* by the reddish (rather than brown) ground colour and the end of the tail, which becomes completely yellowish with age (as in *Varanus gouldi).*

Varanus panoptes horni
New Guinea populations of the Argus monitor are assigned to *Varanus panoptes horni*. These representatives of the species presumably crossed northwards out of Australia, via a land bridge, when sea levels fell during the Pleistocene ice age. Subsequently isolated from the parent stock when sea levels rose again, *Varanus panoptes horni* is now firmly established as a geographically distinct subspecies.

MANGROVE MONITOR *(Varanus indicus)*

A very peripheral member of the Australian varanid assemblage, and in fact an evident immigrant from points north via New Guinea, the mangrove monitor (*Varanus indicus*) occurs only along the northern coastal strip of Australia (the northeastern coast of Northern Territory, the northern Cape York Peninsula and islands in the Torres Strait). Its origin is clearly to be sought somewhere in the western Pacific or the Indo-Malaysian archipelago, which is still its principal home today. Its range extends through Celebes and Timor to the Moluccas, the Palaus, the Marshalls, the Marianas, the Carolines, the Solomons, New Guinea and northern Australia (Fig. 6.6 below).

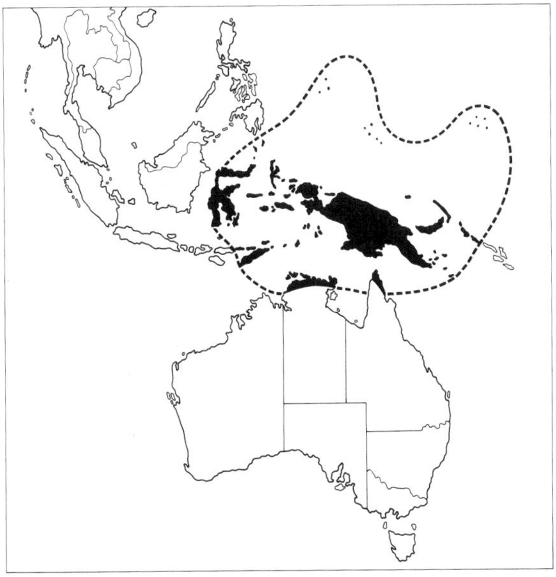

▲ Fig. 6.6 Distribution of *Varanus indicus* (within the dashed circle).

Something over 1m (3¼ft) in length, this water-dependent, powerful swimmer is nonetheless a competent terrestrial forager and is frequently found in trees, where it will often lie basking on branches overhanging rivers or lakes, sheltering at other times in hollow limbs and trunks.

The head is proportionately large, with an elongate snout (depressed at the tip), the rounded nostrils being located rather nearer to the end of the snout than to the eye. The toes are long, ending in sharp claws, and the strongly compressed tail is dorsally keeled, bearing a low, double-toothed crest. There are large cranial scales with a series of 4–6 prominent, transversely broadened scales in the supraocular region. The small dorsal scales are oval and keeled, and smooth, almost square abdominal scales are arranged in 76–110 transverse rows.

Ground coloration is olive, brown or blackish above, dotted all over with yellow or greenish blue spots, the ventral surfaces being yellowish. In young individuals, the spots are larger than in adults, sometimes forming ocelli, and the belly exhibits anastomosing blackish lines.

The customary catholic monitor diet is evident, with giant snails and crabs featuring prominently as food items: large specimens of the snail *Achatina* are apparently removed from their shell but small specimens may be ingested only partially crushed, as are crabs.

Mangrove monitors were introduced onto Japtan in the Marshall Islands before World War 2 and also occur on Aur atoll in this archipelago, as well as on Agiguan, Tinian and Sarigan in the Marianas, Kusaie, Mortlock and Woleai in the Carolines, and Angaur, Koror, Babelthaup and Kayangel in the Palaus. Toxic toads *(Bufo marinus)* were introduced on Kayangel and Kusaie to kill these monitors because they were taking domestic chickens. Many monitors were found dead, sometimes with toads in their mouths, but the islands became over-run with rats and the toads had to be killed off so that the monitor population could revive and control the rats. The numerical decline of the mangrove monitor in several parts of its range may be due to the introduction of this poisonous amphibian, as it is toxic enough to kill any monitor trying to eat it.

The mangrove monitor will take crocodile eggs when they are available and, on Campbell Island, in the Torres Strait, mangrove monitors take the eggs of the hawksbill turtle *(Eretmochelys imbricata)* during the December–March nesting season. A monitor will return on several successive mornings to complete the consumption of an entire clutch when it has once excavated a nest, and also digs into nests from which hatchlings have already emerged, probably to eat unhatched eggs. Turtle hatchlings crossing the beach to the sea are not apparently touched.

Attempts to use the mangrove monitor as a biological control of rats on the atoll of Ifaluk, in the western Caroline Islands, were not entirely successful. The atoll comprises the islets of Ella, Falarik and Falalap and is infested by two species of rats, the Polynesian rat and the roof rat, which gnaw holes in growing coconuts; in addition to despoiling the coconuts this also provides a recess in which the larvae of mosquitoes will grow. The Japanese introduced monitors onto Falalap in about 1939 and they subsequently spread to Falarik, but were still rare there in 1953. Eventually, however, they swam to Ella and thus became well established throughout the atoll. Captive mangrove monitors will eat rats, seizing them head first when they are offered alive and taking 5–7 minutes to swallow them, accomplishing this by turning their heads from side to side without chewing (the monitor will not eat again for 3–5 days after consuming a rat).

Wild mangrove monitors, however, to judge from their stomach contents, subsist mostly on small lizards, land crabs and hermit crabs, the Caroline islanders alleging that they also take coconut crabs, wild birds, chickens and the eggs of both wild birds and domestic poultry. (Certainly the crab density on Ella islet was substantially reduced after the monitors arrived.) The local people bred dogs for keeping down the monitors because of their poultry depredations, and it was finally concluded that varanids are not a good proposition for rat control.

Adult male mangrove monitors are larger than adult females and, in at least some parts of the range (e.g. Guam), sexually active males have testicular sperm present all year round, with the male fat body increasing slightly in size in the latter part of the wet season (mid-July to mid-November) – the fat is probably used for energy generation connected with reproductive behaviour rather than spermatogenesis. In the females, the ovary mass is larger in the dry season (January–April), with corpora lutea present early on. Reproduction is in the dry season, with mating at the end of the wet season or beginning of the dry months. Clutches of about eight eggs are laid in mounds of rotting vegetation.

Varanus indicus indicus, Varanus indicus spinulosus and *Varanus indicus kalabeck*

Three subspecies have been identified, the principal one being *Varanus indicus indicus* from the Solomon Islands and the Pacific islands to the north and west of New Guinea, with smooth, closely apposed neck scales. *Varanus indicus spinulosus*, from the Solomons, possesses fine, spike-like neck scales and the southern subspecies (*Varanus indicus kalabeck*), from New Guinea and its environs, exhibits widely separated, weakly keeled neck scales.

SCHMIDT'S MONITOR
(Varanus karlschmidti)

Very similar to the mangrove monitor (*Varanus indicus*), and possibly attributable to the same species, is the poorly known and seemingly rare Schmidt's monitor (*Varanus karlschmidti*) (Fig. 6.7). Only a few specimens of this rainforest form have ever been collected, from the Sepik River in New Guinea and from Jobi Island, just off the northern New Guinea coast. It was named in honour of Karl Schmidt of the Chicago Natural History Museum, who undertook extensive exploration in New Guinea in the 1920s and 1930s. Just over 1m (3¼ft) in length, *Varanus karlschmidti* is claimed to differ from *Varanus indicus* in being smaller, more elongate and exhibiting a tendency to yellow coloration on the head and neck.

MERTENS' WATER MONITOR
(Varanus mertensi)

Two rather small, water-adapted monitors occur in the humid northern regions of Australia.

▲ **Fig. 6.7 Schmidt's monitor *(Varanus karlschmidti).***

Mertens' water monitor (*Varanus mertensi*), grows to about 1.25m (4¼ft) in length and occurs in the Kimberley district of Western Australia (south to the May and Mary Rivers), in the far north of Northern Territory and on Cape York Peninsula (Fig. 6.8).

The species is clearly specialized for aquatic life, having a strongly laterally compressed tail bearing a double-keeled crest, but also possesses long legs and feet (kept pressed against the body when swimming), with toes that end in slender black claws, well adapted for climbing trees, which this monitor does with alacrity if alarmed at any substantial distance from a suitable pool or river refuge. It is never found very far from water, however, although it seems to avoid the coastal mangrove swamps favoured by *Varanus indicus*. Usually, it prefers to remain among the roots of trees growing along the banks of lakes or streams, sometimes basking on overhanging branches or on partly submerged rocks and logs. The prey is predominantly aquatic, as might be anticipated, and includes fish, frogs and crabs, along with beetles, water nymphs, shrimps, amphipods and dragonflies, but such terrestrial victims as spiders, ants, snakes, birds and small mammals are also taken, along with reptile eggs.

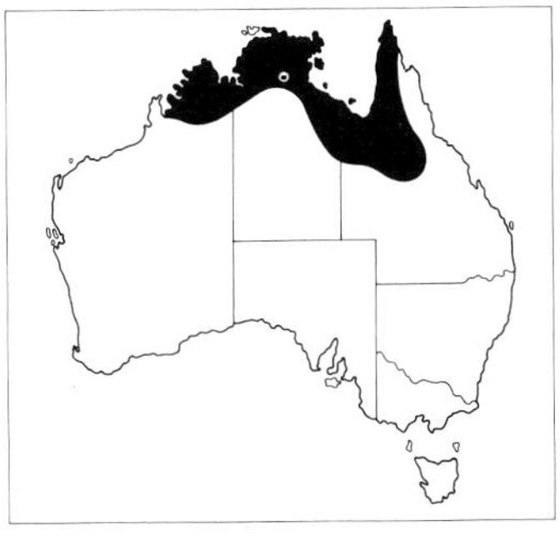

◀ **Fig. 6.8 Distribution of *Varanus mertensi.***

The head of Mertens' water monitor is over half as broad as long, with a slender snout, depressed at the tip. The oval nostrils are latero-dorsal in position, nearly twice as far from the eye

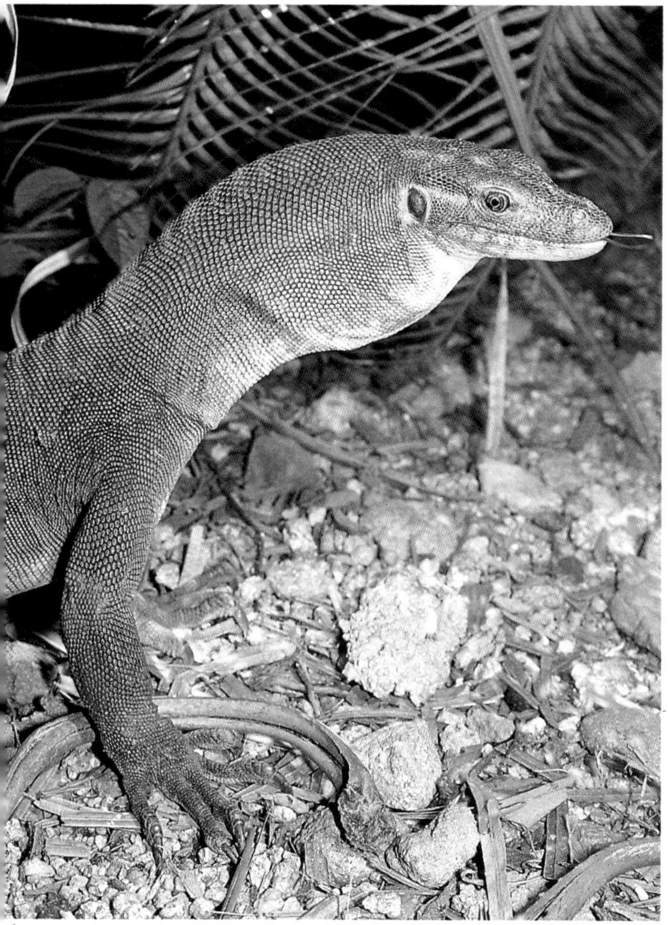

▲ **Mertens' water monitor *(Varanus mertensi)* has a broad head with a slender snout depressed at its tip.**

as from the tip of the snout, and provided with a valve that is closed when the animal is under water. The cranial scales are flat, smooth and of substantial size, with irregular outlines, the supraoculars being large and well differentiated.

Coloration is dark olive-grey or brown above, with white blotches on the head and small, sparse, black-edged, greyish white or yellowish white spots on the body; these become rings around the proximal part of the tail and on the outer aspects of the limbs. A whitish yellow ring around the ear aperture is joined at the top to a whitish streak from the eye, while the upper and lower lips are barred with dark grey and brownish white. The lower surfaces and the inside of the limbs are cream or white, with irregular dark spots, bars or reticulation.

Mertens' water monitor is most active in the wet season, but breeds during the dry months, the sexes being of about equal size. Females construct their nests in a burrow, using decaying vegetation, leaf mould, etc. After laying clutches of 10–14 eggs, each measuring 6 × 3.5cm (2½ × 1½in), the monitor seals the opening. Emergent hatchlings are about 12cm (5in) long.

The populations of Mertens' water monitor in lakes and rivers have been observed to migrate in about December (just before the wet season), away from the main body of water. They mostly head upstream to smaller or temporary waterholes, near which their eggs are laid. The diet consists mainly of small fish, which swim upstream in floods and are left stranded in pools, and frogs and crabs emerging from the sand as water floods in. Sometimes this monitor will move sideways through shallow pools, concentrating fish and crustaceans within the arc formed by its body and tail, leaving the water briefly to position large fish, i.e. those over about 8cm (3in) in length, for swallowing. Mertens' water monitor has become semi-tame near some human habitations and will enthusiastically eat sausages in camping areas, often becoming a permanent resident at such sites, actively soliciting food.

▲ **Fig. 6.9 Threatening behaviour exhibited by *Varanus mertensi*, which includes turning its back on a prospective antagonist and everting its head.**

▲ **Fig. 6.10 Mitchell's monitor *(Varanus mitchelli)***

A captive specimen of this species, placed in an enclosure containing several large iguanas and a Gould's monitor at Dallas Zoo, exhibited various types of threatening behaviour. This included: bounding bipedal flight; a bipedal stance with the anterior trunk expanded and the posterior trunk dorso-ventrally compressed, presenting the flattened dorsum to the adversary while arching the neck and looking over the shoulder; undulating lateral flexures; hyper-extension or adpression of the forelimbs and pivoting upon the hind limbs; tilting the trunk towards the adversary; commencing an exaggerated jerky gait with limbs hyper-extended; and, on one occasion, striking a congener with the tilted dorsum by jumping sideways (Fig. 6.9). However, the animal was not seen to open its mouth aggressively, hiss or flick its tongue. The tail may be used for slapping.

MITCHELL'S MONITOR *(Varanus mitchelli)*

The other small water monitor from northern Australia, Mitchell's monitor (*Varanus mitchelli*) (Fig. 6.10), named in honour of Francis J. Mitchell of the South Australian Museum in Adelaide, has similar habits to Mertens' water monitor but grows to about only 70cm (28in) in length. Occurring in the Kimberley district south to the King Leopold Range and Lake Argyle, and thence through the northern part of Northern Territory to extreme northwestern Queensland (Fig. 6.11), this diminutive reptile is found along the banks of lagoons or water courses and in swamps, often sheltering in *Pandanus* vegetation. It frequently enters the water to hunt frogs, tadpoles or fish (especially during the wet season) but is quite capable of climbing trees, sometimes hiding itself away in hollow limbs or beneath loose bark. Other prey, providing food in the dry season, includes spiders, crabs, beetles, orthopterans, roaches, caterpillars, ants, centipedes, small reptiles (skinks), mice, cicadas, hemipterans and reptile eggs.

The tail of Mitchell's monitor, which has a dorsal double keel, is less laterally compressed than that of Merten's water monitor and there are not so many mid-body scale rows (fewer than 130, compared with over 140 in Mertens' monitor). The nasal openings are about half way between the eyes and the tip of the snout and the supraocular scales are relatively undifferentiated from the proportionately large, smooth cranial scalation; on the tail, the dorsal and lateral scales are rather small, with low keels.

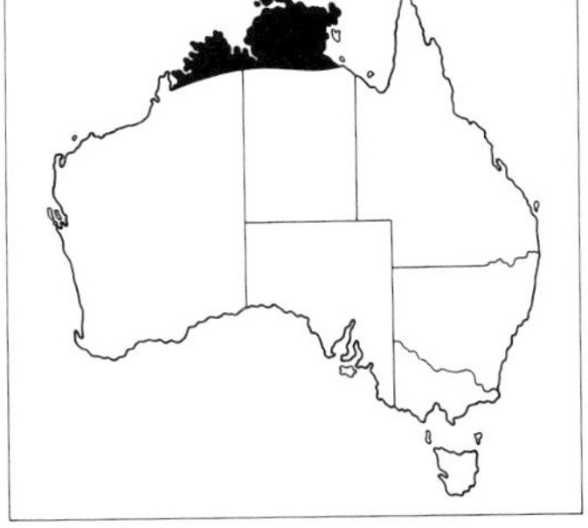

◀ **Fig. 6.11 Distribution of *Varanus mitchelli*.**

Ground coloration is dark grey, blackish grey or dark olive-grey dorsally, variably marked with black and white. In the Kimberley population, small dark spots occur on the foreback and sides of the neck, with white dots on limbs, hindback and often neck and foreback. In animals from Northern Territory, there are indistinct, pale, black-centred ocelli alternating transversely with irregular black bands, and white spots on the legs. Ventral surfaces are whitish with narrow grey cross-bands, the lower part of the tail being mostly dark greyish brown in colour and the tail tip unpatterned.

Mitchell's monitor is most active in the wet season but breeds during the dry months. Males and females are of nearly equal size. Up to about 12 eggs, measuring approximately 2.5 × 1.3cm (1 × ½in), are laid in each clutch. Hatchlings attain a length of some 8cm (3in) at emergence.

LACE LIZARD *(Varanus varius)*

A powerful monitor, up to 2m (6½ft) in length, ranges lowlands and coastal forests throughout the whole of eastern Australia, from the southeastern Cape York Peninsula to southeastern Victoria, extending westwards to about Broken Hill and into southeastern South Australia (Fig. 6.12). The lace lizard (*Varanus varius*) is Australia's second biggest living lizard, surpassed in size only by the gigantic lace lizard (*Varanus giganteus*), and, in the southeastern portion of its range, the only larger native predator present is the dingo.

Essentially terrestrial foragers, systematically investigating every nook and cranny that could conceal possible prey, lace lizards will race for safety up trees if approached, climbing the trunk on the side furthest from the perceived threat to reach the topmost branches that will bear their weight; they are therefore also commonly known as tree goannas. It is claimed that a thoroughly panicked lace monitor will, like the gigantic lace lizard, try to climb any convenient upright object, even an unsuspecting man or horse.

Lace lizards usually live in holes in trees and can often be seen sunning themselves on the sides of a trunk, especially on cool spring and autumn days. One specimen, a large male weighing 4.2kg

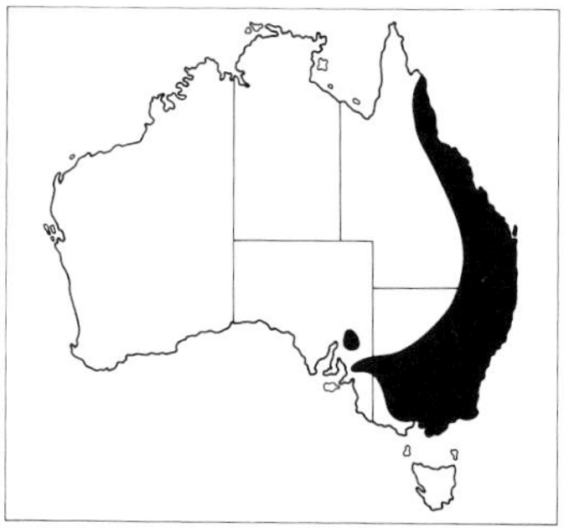

◀ **Fig. 6.12 Distribution of *Varanus varius.***

(9¼lb), had a temperature-signalling radio-transmitter implanted in its abdominal cavity and was then released where it was captured (Cruikshank Station, 40km/25 miles north of Griffith, in New South Wales). This animal was observed at ranges of 55–90m (60–100yd) for a period of 5 days, during which it travelled over 18km (11 miles). At night, it took refuge in various hollow trees, all of which appeared to be familiar to it. Morning re-emergence took about half an hour; the monitor would initially bask with its body upright against the tree trunk, the top of its head and its back to the sun, eventually flicking out its tongue several times and turning its head from side to side (presumably to ensure there was no danger in the vicinity) before climbing down. It would often bask again briefly on reaching the ground and, warming at a rate of 0.14°C (0.25°F)/minute, took less than 1 hour to reach its normal temperature.

Before taking refuge for the night, it would bask at the base of its 'home' tree, upright against the bole, which raised its temperature by 1 or 2°C (1.8 or 3.6°F) before it retired for the night. During the hours of darkness, the body temperature fell at the rate of 0.02°C (0.04°F)/minute. The mean body temperature for the average 11-hour active period varied by only 1.2°C (2.5°F) from day to day and averaged 35.5°C (95.9°F) in a range of 35–36.2°C (95–97°F).

The adult diet includes fox cubs, rats, mice, young rabbits, other lizards (e.g. blue-tongued lizards), birds' eggs and nestlings, snakes, frogs, spiders, turtle eggs, insects, beetles, grasshoppers and any form of carrion, including dead kangaroos. At Lake Cowal, New South Wales, *Varanus varius* is known to eat the eggs and chicks of the little black cormorant *(Phalacrocorax sulcirostris)*, little pied cormorant *(Phalacrocorax melanoleucos)*, royal spoonbill *(Platalea regia)*, silver gull *(Larus novaehollandiae)*, rainbow bee-eater *(Merops ornatus)* and white-winged chough *(Corcorax melanorhamphus)*.

The lace lizard has a depressed snout, with anteriorly located, suboval nostrils. The toes are long and the elongate, slender tail is laterally compressed towards its end, although it is of rounded cross-section at its base.

There appear to be two distinct colour forms of *Varanus varius*. Throughout its range, there is a common variant with a prominent juvenile skin patterning comprising a pale bluish grey ground colour spotted with yellow, black banding across the neck and back, black and yellow banded forelimbs, black and yellow spotted hind limbs, black and yellow banded tail, and yellow ventral surfaces banded with black. In adults, these markings gradually merge into overall dark grey or dull bluish black, with just a faint trace of banding or pale spots, although some bright yellow and black chin markings are usually retained. In subhumid areas from northern New South Wales to mid-eastern Queensland, there is a distinct banded variety, with a yellowish brown to bright yellow ground colour, that has broad irregular, dark transverse bands from shoulders to tail tip, an overall fine black mottling, and black and yellow banding on limbs and lower surfaces.

The lace lizard is regarded as a pest by many poultry farmers because of its proclivity for egg stealing and is shot on sight. Lace lizards have been observed attempting to steal kitchen scraps from Australian bush turkeys *(Alectura lathami)* in backyards, but the bird turns its back on the monitor and uses its strong legs to kick back a barrage of stones, sand and litter that puts the reptile to flight. Even large monitors up to 1.5m (5ft) in length are deterred by this strategem. Their departure from the scene is speeded by the bird delivering sideways kicks to project further debris, a procedure which it repeats six or seven times from alternate flanks, producing about half-a-dozen kicks on each occasion during some 5 minutes. The goanna eventually takes flight with its tail held in a tight curl, a pursuing turkey on one occasion being seen to deliver a severe peck at the reptile's tail. It is probable that lace lizards enter the incubation mounds of bush turkeys to take eggs or chicks.

Fully mature lace lizards are large enough to lose their fear of predation, even regarding people (other than poultry farmers) with relative equanimity. Camping sites often have a resident lace monitor that scavenges for scraps and openly solicits for titbits. They can bite viciously, however, and once they have sunk their teeth into a victim it is very difficult to force the jaws open again. If cornered on the ground, a lace lizard will raise itself high on its legs, inflate its body with air and stand at bay, with mouth agape and tail lashing, emitting a prolonged, loud, hissing noise. The tail of a large specimen is heavy enough to throw a man off balance and can inflict a painful blow on an unprotected leg.

Intraspecific ritualized fighting has been observed, lasting 20–30 minutes and involving bipedal combat (apparently quite vicious), after which the contestants lie locked in an embrace for perhaps five minutes. They then fight violently again in standing and supine positions. When overthrown, the loser lies prone while it is straddled by the victor.

Breeding takes place in early summer in New South Wales and in mid-summer in southern

▶ **Fig. 6.13 Lace lizards (*Varanus varius*) mating.**

▲ With this fiercely gaping maw, it is not surprising that lace lizards *(Varanus varius)* are accomplished egg stealers, with domestic poultry notoriously frequent victims of their raids.

◀ The lace lizard *(Varanus varius)* reaches 2m (6½ft) or more in length and is surpassed in size among living Australian monitors only by the gigantic lace lizard. This powerful terrestrial forager is an able tree-climber and usually rests in holes in tree trunks at night.

Victoria, with numerous males aggregating around a receptive female and frequently engaging in ritualized combat. A successful male approaches a prospective mate from behind with all four legs stiffened, the body off the ground, the neck nearly vertical and the head high and jerking from side to side. He seizes her with claws and jaws, biting at her neck. Often the female will run off, carrying the male, for about 3m (10ft); she then usually stops and the male begins to rub her neck with his snout, exploring her back and sides with his forked tongue. His hind leg scratches the side of the female's tail; she responds by recurving her back and lifting her tail (Fig. 6.13). The females are not aggressive and copulation lasts for up to four minutes, the pair then separating; 20–30 pelvic thrusts were observed in about 60 seconds. Pairs mate frequently, the male using his hemipenes alternately.

Although lace lizards sometimes nest in the humus of an old tree stump, the favourite egg-laying site is a termite nest. After depositing her clutch, the female escapes through the hole which she has excavated in the side of this structure, leaving the eggs secure inside to hatch in the warmth of the nest, where the heat generated by decaying wood helps to maintain a relatively high temperature. Clutches comprise 6–12 eggs, each about 7 × 4cm (3 × 1½in) and weighing 6.5g (about ¼oz); they are roughly similar to a hen's egg but narrower, with a flexible leathery shell, and are laid in mid-summer (December to early January). The female returns 9 months later to dig out the newly hatched juveniles but leaves them to fend for themselves once they have made an exit from the termite nest. It sometimes takes her several weeks and the digging of a number of holes to locate her brood.

Hatchlings measure about 30cm (12in) in length and weigh about 23g (1oz). They are exceedingly aggressive as soon as they emerge, blowing out the throat pouch in a threatening manner and lashing the tail if approached. Juveniles are brightly coloured (black ground tone, with yellow and green markings and broad muzzle and tail bands), display a high level of activity (moving exceedingly quickly on the ground), and corkscrew quickly up trees if alarmed. They are preyed on by the kookaburra, raven, butcher bird, currawung *(Strepera)* and snakes. The bright colours become duller and darker after 2 years.

Lace lizards, which have survived in captivity for over 20 years, possess unusually complex lungs, incorporating far more diverticula than seem necessary for a reptile of their size, even an unusually active one. The suggestion has been made that the extant *Varanus varius* population may therefore be descended from very much larger ancestral stock that presumably roamed eastern Australia during the Pleistocene, when the enormous marsupials were to be found there, along with the huge *Megalania*.

PLAINS GOANNA *(Varanus spenceri)*

Across arid regions of northern Australia, from central-eastern Northern Territory to the western interior of Queensland (Fig. 6.14), the flat 'black soil' (generally putty-coloured in reality) areas and Mitchell grass downs are the home of the plains goanna (*Varanus spenceri*).

Up to about 1m (3¼ft) in length, this robustly proportioned monitor has a long neck and an unusually shaped head that has been likened to the distinctive profile of an Arab horse. The tail is rather short, thick and rounded at its base, becoming compressed laterally further back along its length, with a dorsal keel. The coloration is grey to greyish brown or dull red-brown, with pale bands and dark interspaces (four in number and V-shaped on the neck, with 20–50 from the shoulders to the tail tip). The pale-hued lips have dark grey or black bars and the light grey ventral surfaces, with 115–120 transverse scale rows, are spotted with dark grey or brown.

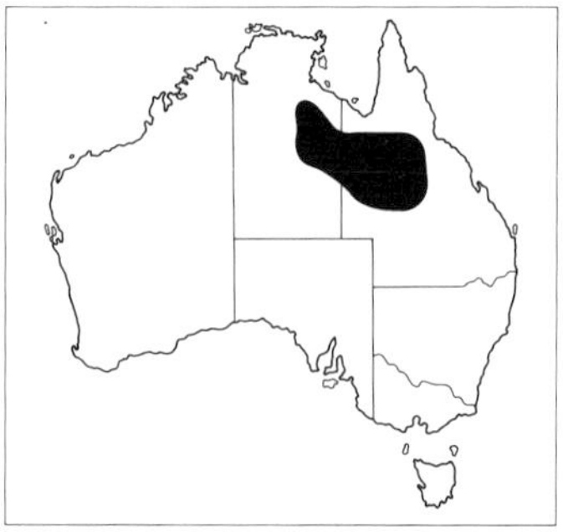

◀ Fig. 6.14 Distribution of *Varanus spenceri*.

Plains goannas habitually shelter in cavities below rocks, or in deep soil cracks, emerging on hot, still days to forage for small vertebrates, arthropods and carrion, adopting a bipedal stance occasionally to survey the vicinity for possible danger. Sometimes they dig burrows or move into the burrows of other animals; they tend to remain in hiding when strong winds blow across the dessicated plains.

The plains goanna seems to be a notably amiable species and one specimen, which was being filmed as it walked along, took to following the photographer, ultimately halting in his shadow.

Clutches of about 10–30 eggs, each measuring about 3 × 5cm (1¼ × 2in), are laid in spring. Emergent juveniles are 22cm (9in) long and are brightly coloured, with two or three broad V-shaped markings on the neck. The back is velvet brown, with eight or nine yellow bands, and the tail is ringed by four to six bands, which break up towards the tip into irregular spots and stripes; the belly is a uniform white. By 9 months of age, the youngsters have attained a length of about 34cm (13in) but the prominent, sharp-edged juvenile markings become diffuse and fade with approaching adulthood.

SALVADOR'S MONITOR or PAPUAN MONITOR *(Varanus salvadori)*

One very large monitor inhabits the northern part of the Australasian region and is usually regarded as a distinct subgenus, *Papusaurus,* as its home is the island of New Guinea. Up to 2m (6½ft) in length, Salvador's monitor (*Varanus salvadori*) (Fig. 6.15) is an arboreal species with a long, flattened head and a convex nasal profile. The oval, elongate nasal opening is situated towards the tip of the snout and the cranial scales are small, with irregular-shaped supraocular scales. Dorsal scalation is elongate and keeled and the ventral scales, arranged in about 80–105 transverse rows, display especially prominent keels. There is a notably long tail (about two and a half times as long as the combined head and body measurement), exhibiting a rounded cross-section near its base, but becoming weakly compressed laterally further back, with a dorsal double keel.

Coloration is black above, with bands of yellow spots running across the back, the tail exhibiting irregular yellow transverse bands; ventral surfaces are yellow but bear black marking and banding. The dentition is long and pointed, with weakly recurved tips, there being eight to nine

▼ Fig. 6.15 Salvador's monitor or Papuan monitor (*Varanus salvadori*).

▲ **Most at home in the trees, where it preys on birds and their eggs, Salvador's monitor *(Varanus salvadori)* can reach 2m (6½ft) in length.**

premaxillary teeth, 10 pairs of teeth in the maxillae, and 12 pairs in the lower jaw.

A powerful carnivore that, because of its adaptations for life in the trees is a regular predator of birds and their eggs, Salvador's monitor has (like the lace monitor, *Varanus varius*) unusually complex lung diverticula, suggesting derivation from an earlier giant form.

GREEN LACE LIZARD or EMERALD MONITOR *(Varanus prasinus)*

Several tree monitors from the New Guinea area and the fringes of northern Australia seem to be possible descendants of the mangrove monitor (*Varanus indicus*) or the big, wide-ranging water monitor (*Varanus salvator*). They have taken to life in the trees, acquiring a green skin pigmentation (sharing this feature with *Varanus indicus* and the butaan, *Varanus olivaceus*) that may be so dark as to appear nearly black.

The beautiful little green lace lizard or emerald monitor (*Varanus prasinus*) (see opposite) measures just under 1m (3¼ft) in length and occurs in New Guinea and adjacent islands, on the islands of the Torres Strait, and on the eastern part of the Cape York Peninsula (Fig. 6.16).

Slender and long-limbed, with a prehensile, more or less rounded tail, about twice the length of the combined head and body measurement and lacking any distinct keel, this purely arboreal monitor has short toes terminating in elongate, curved claws. The snout is depressed anteriorly, with the rounded or oval nostrils located nearer to the tip of the nose than to the eye, their orientation being more or less outwards and upwards. The cranial scales are large, smooth and flat, those between the orbits being the largest, while the supraocular series comprises three or four transversely broadened elements. Scalation in the posterior dorsal region, on the ventral surface and along the tail is keeled; the scales of the back are long and oval, the abdominal series is arranged in 70–90 transverse rows, and the tail is regularly ringed with scales.

As its common name implies, the green lace lizard generally has a bright green back, sometimes with a black network forming transverse or small ocellate markings (especially in the shoulder region), while the lower surfaces are yellowish and spotted. However, almost black melanistic populations occur on some small islands and on the Australian mainland, these forms possessing a pale bluish green muzzle, sometimes with a short yellowish bar extending from behind the eye back to the area above the ear opening.

The habitat of the green lace lizard seems to range from monsoon-rain and palm forests to mangrove swamps, the handful of specimens collected in Australia having been caught in vine forests or eucalyptus forest. Completely at home in the foliage of the upper forest canopy, where soft, black sticky tissue on the soles of its feet gives it a firm grip on tree trunks and branches,

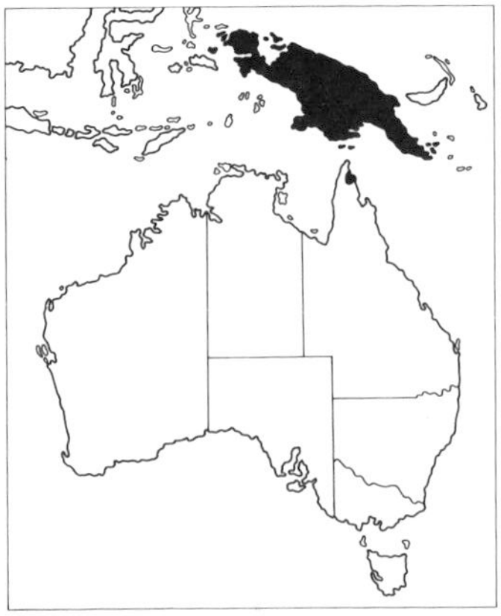

◀ **Fig. 6.16 Distribution of *Varanus prasinus*.**

this elegant little varanid lives mostly on orthopterans and beetles, as well as taking roaches, stick insects, centipedes, spiders, rodents and possibly frogs and geckos. It shares with the butaan the distinction among monitor lizards of being a partial vegetarian and, in captivity, readily eats fruit.

Varanus prasinus prasinus
The principal subspecies, *Varanus prasinus prasinus*, occurs widely in the lowland forests of New Guinea but is absent from mountainous areas. It is also present on Salawatti and Misool (at the western end of New Guinea), on Goodenough Island in the d'Entrecasteaux archipelago (off eastern New Guinea), on islands in the Torres Strait (Murray, Dauan) and in the McIlwraith Range of the Cape York Peninsula.

Varanus prasinus bogerti, Varanus prasinus beccari* and *Varanus prasinus kordensis
Varanus prasinus bogerti is a melanistic form occurring in the d'Entrecasteaux group of islands, *Varanus prasinus beccari* is from the Aru Islands

▲ **One of the most beautiful of all monitors, the green lace lizard *(Varanus prasinus)* is an eye-catching emerald colour.**

(with a possible occurrence in West Irian at Fakfak) and *Varanus prasinus kordensis* is a dark-coloured subspecies from Wiak (Kordo) Island off western New Guinea that may ultimately prove to have been merely based on a solitary dark specimen of *Varanus prasinus prasinus*.

Varanus telenesetes* and *Varanus teriae
Still rather poorly known, and indeed only first described in 1991, *Varanus telenesetes*, from Roussell Island (Papua New Guinea), closely resembles *Varanus prasinus* but has pale-coloured palmar surfaces, with mottled patterning on the ventral surface of the body and smooth belly scales. *Varanus teriae* is a robustly proportioned, melanistic tree goanna from Australia's Cape York Peninsula, with yellow dorsal spots forming thin, paired chevrons and caudal rings, a pronounced temporal streak, and pale yellowish lower surfaces.

CHAPTER 7

Australasian Dwarfs

Not only has Australia been the home of the largest known monitor lizards from the past, and remains the domicile of some of today's biggest varanids, but this area of the world is also where the smallest living members of the group are to be found, some 15 or so diminutive species collected together as the subgenus *Odatria.*

None of these tiny monitors exceeds 1m (3¼ft) in length and some barely reach 20cm (8in). They have relatively deep heads with a straight skull profile and a small supratemporal opening in the cranial roof for jaw muscle insertion. The nostrils tend to be closer to the end of the snout than to the eye and incorporate a short, convex septomaxillary bone with a more or less smooth surface. There are seven to nine premaxillary teeth, with seven to ten teeth in the maxilla and in the dentary. The dentition lacks serrations but the crowns are pointed and laterally compressed.

The neck of odatrias is protected by enlarged nuchal plates and the scalation of the often rather short and generally uncompressed tail is arranged in rings. With short, stout limbs and rather stubby toes, odatrias are mostly denizens of dry areas in the Australian tropics and subtropics, the tail probably being used as a food store to see the animal through unfavourable seasons. In most species, the tail is of little use as an aid to swimming and, consequently, these midget monitors are usually disinclined to enter the water, except as a last resort.

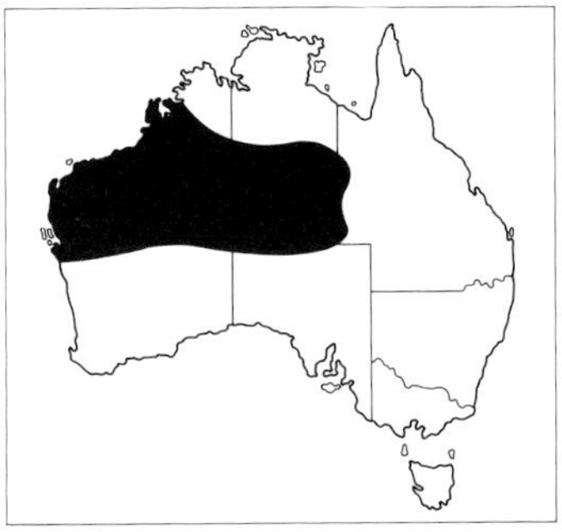

◀ **Fig. 7.1 Distribution of *Varanus brevicauda*.**

SHORT-TAILED ODATRIA

(Varanus brevicauda)

The smallest of all the odatrias, and hence the most diminutive living monitor, is *Varanus brevicauda* (Fig. 7.2), a tiny reptile, only about 20cm (8in) long when fully grown, that occurs in the arid northwest of Australia, from the Great Sandy Desert of Western Australia (as far south as Carnarvon and Wiluna Districts) to the Tanami and Simpson Deserts of Northern Territory (Fig. 7.1).

A reddish brown or yellowish brown species with cream underparts and faint dark flecks or reticulum on the body and limbs, the short-tailed odatria is extremely shy, living in shallow burrows beneath hummock grasses or occupying the existing burrows of other small lizards. There is usually a dark streak running from the snout back above the eye, which has a distinctive orange- or red-coloured iris. The dorsal and lateral scales are strongly keeled and there are about 75–80 transverse rows of ventral scales. No other monitor has such a proportionately short tail, usually less than the length of the creature's head and body; it is covered in spiny scales and has a depressed base, but becomes circular in cross-section further back and, in seasons of plenty, accommodates substantial fat deposits.

The short-tailed odatria is a terrestrial species, foraging for arthropods, caterpillars, insects, beetles, roaches, isopods, grasshoppers, small lizards and reptile eggs over its preferred habitats of acacia-eucalyptus-spinifex dunes and sand plains. The testes of males are at their largest during August, which is presumably the breeding season. Clutches do not usually include more than half-a-dozen eggs.

EYED ODATRIA or SPINY-TAILED GOANNA *(Varanus acanthurus)*

Widely distributed across hard soils and rocky areas of the subhumid or arid northwestern two-thirds of Australia, the eyed odatria *(Varanus acanthurus)* is a robustly proportioned species that grows to about 75cm (30in) in length. This small monitor is also known as the spiny-tailed goanna because of the prominent spiny scutes that ring the top and sides of the rounded, unkeeled tail. Once this creature has taken refuge in a hole or cavity, the backwardly projecting scales around the tail make it almost impossible to pull it out and the spiny tail is, in fact, very often deliberately held in front of the body to afford protection. Dismembered tails are sometimes found lying about on the surface, having apparently been discarded by a predator which found the spiky caudal appendage of the eyed odatria to be an unappetizing morsel. The snout of the eyed odatria is short and depressed towards the tip, with rounded nostrils. Cranial scales are very small and equal in size, the supraoculars being diminutive and granular. Dorsal trunk scalation is small, elongate and tectiform, with 56–115 rows of scales around the middle of the body.

The eyed odatria is blackish, dark brown or reddish brown in colour, with numerous rows of cream, yellow or pale reddish ocelli around the body and sometimes across the top of the neck (hence the common name). The head is brownish in colour, embellished with yellow or cream spots, which sometimes become longitudinal stripes down the neck, while a dark brown stripe runs along the snout and through the eye, to continue as a broad temporal band extending down to the forelimb, bordered by light yellow spots or stripes; a yellow stripe also traces back from the lower jaw. The tail is dark brown with narrow cream, yellow or white rings (sometimes rather indistinct) and a dark-hued tip, and the limbs are spotted with white, cream or pale reddish brown. Lower surfaces are pale brown or yellow, spotted with brown down the throat, along the belly, under the hind limbs and below the depressed base of the tail.

In Western Australia, *Varanus acanthurus* extends through the tropical region south to beyond North West Cape, reaching the Hammersley range, Lake Disappointment and the Gibson Desert. The Northern Territory population extends as far south as the Kintore and Macdonnell Ranges, while in Queensland this species is restricted to the northwestern part of the state (Fig. 7.3). It also occurs on a number of

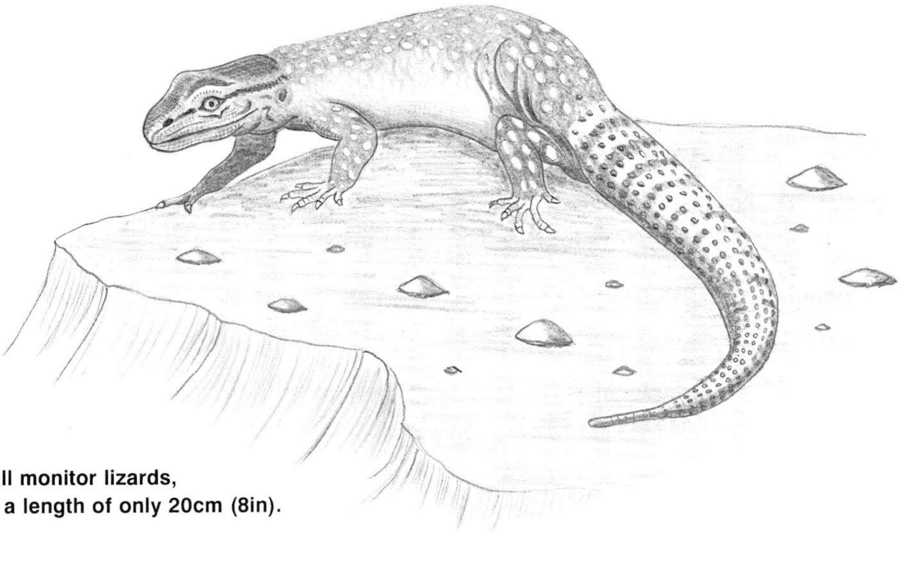

▲ **Fig. 7.2 The smallest of all monitor lizards, *Varanus brevicauda*, attains a length of only 20cm (8in).**

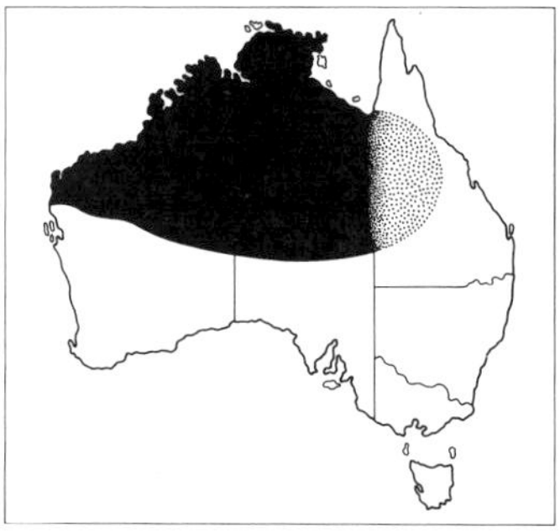

◀ **Fig. 7.3 Distribution of *Varanus acanthurus*.**

The eastern population, stippled, has an acrocentric chromosome 5 and is chromosomally monomorphic, whereas throughout the rest of its range the species is polymorphic.

offshore islands along the western Australian coast, from Sir Graham Moore Island southwest to South Muiron Island, the populations on some of these islands having become rather distinctive (e.g. those on Barrow and South Muiron Islands).

From the northern to the southern limits of its range, *Varanus acanthurus* becomes paler and redder in colour but the distribution and variation is too continuous to justify division into northern and southern subspecies. However, chromosomal analysis has disclosed two karyotypes. The Queensland population is chromosomally monomorphic but, in Northern Territory and Western Australia, *Varanus acanthurus* exhibits a pericentric inversion polymorphism of chromosome pair 6, which is present in three different forms, one corresponding to the monomorphic type (submetacentric), the other two being aberrant (metacentric/acrocentric heterozygous, acrocentric monozygous). The species also exhibits a secondary constriction of the short arm of chromosome pair 1 and has a ZZ/ZW sex chromosome system; the eastern population has an acrocentric chromosome pair 5. While the western, central and eastern populations are separated by deserts (Tanami, Gibson and Great Sandy) and by the Barkly Tableland (a vast grassland prone to extensive flooding and dissected by many rivers), these obstacles are probably not effective barriers to gene flow. It is not known whether chromosomal polymorphism arose during an east–west colonizing radiation or became established in an already extant distribution.

Typical habitats of the eyed odatria are rocky outcrops (providing hiding places beneath boulders or in deep crevices), tufts of spinifex *(Triodia)* grass, hollow logs and abandoned termitaria. It is not particularly agile and can often be encountered basking on rocky ledges. Food consists mainly of insects, mice and very small lizards, but the species is an acknowledged cannibal. A consignment of several individuals sent to the Australian Museum in a single container was reduced to just one specimen (the largest of the original group) when the box was opened at its destination.

The ovaries and ova of females in northern Australia begin to increase in size during April/May, remaining well developed until October, with 2–11 oviducal eggs (depending on body size) present from August to November. Females apparently usually breed every year but only lay one clutch each season, while males exhibit spermatozoa from April to November, with a July–October peak. Incubation takes 3–4 months, the nest being a small chamber at the base of a laterally curved S-shaped tunnel that is usually situated some 40cm (16in) below the surface, with the entrance often concealed by a small rock. Hatching occurs in December/January, the newly emergent young having a head and body length of 6–7cm (2½–3in). Sexual maturity is reached after 190–270 days, so some individuals become sexually mature during their first year of life.

Spiny-tailed goanna
(Varanus acanthurus acanthurus)

The subspecies from northwestern Australia, the spiny-tailed goanna *(Varanus acanthurus acanthurus)*, occurs north of Broom. This form attains a length of 60cm (24in) and has smooth ventral scales arranged in 65–75 transverse rows.

Ridge-tailed goanna
(Varanus acanthurus brachyurus)

Slightly smaller than *Varanus acanthurus acanthurus* (up to 38cm/15in long), the ridge-tailed goanna *(Varanus acanthurus brachyurus)* is present right across northern Australia, extending south of Broom and westwards to the Monte Bello

Islands, but absent from the Great Sandy Desert and northern Queensland. Where the ranges of this subspecies and the spiny-tailed goanna overlap, the ridge-tailed goanna is a frequent prey of its larger congener.

Occurring in flatter country more often than *Varanus acanthurus acanthurus*, the ridge-tailed goanna, which has 56–71 transverse rows of ventral scales, prefers slight slopes or the flats between hills, where it will take to the trees if threatened; in winter, it is often found in hollow limbs of snappy gum and grey box. It also tunnels under rocks and crevices, often constructing multiple entrances to a maze of interconnecting galleries that occupy an area of perhaps 45 × 90cm (18 × 36in) but are no deeper than 25cm (10in). Adjacent shallow retreats are also often maintained and the subspecies frequently takes refuge under builders' scrap, such as galvanized iron.

Varanus acanthurus insulanicus

On islands in the Gulf of Carpentaria (Groote, Marchinbar), there is a large, long-tailed melanistic subspecies, *Varanus acanthurus insulanicus,* that has strongly developed dark markings in the form of broad cross-bands on the back, constituting a large-meshed network, with black and yellow longitudinal head and neck stripes.

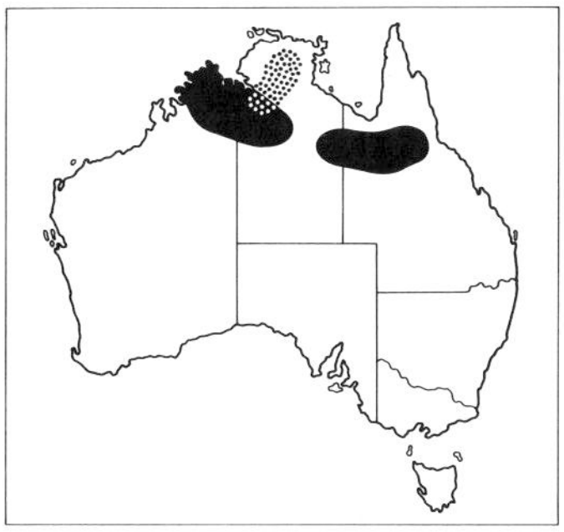

◀ **Fig. 7.4 Distribution of *Varanus storri* and (stippled) *Varanus primordius*.**

PYGMY RIDGE-TAILED GOANNA or DWARF MONITOR (*Varanus storri*)

Very similar to *Varanus acanthurus*, but only about half the size, with fewer mid-body scale rows (up to about 91), fewer transverse rows of ventrals (no more than 58) and a much weaker colour pattern, the pygmy ridge-tailed goanna or dwarf monitor *(Varanus storri)* (Fig. 7.5) is a small, spiny-tailed odatria occurring in two separate populations (representing different subspecies): one is found in the Charters Towers area of Queensland and the other around the Kimberley region of Western Australia and in the adjacent Northern Territory (Fig. 7.4).

▼ **Fig. 7.5 The pygmy ridge-tailed goanna (*Varanus storri*).**

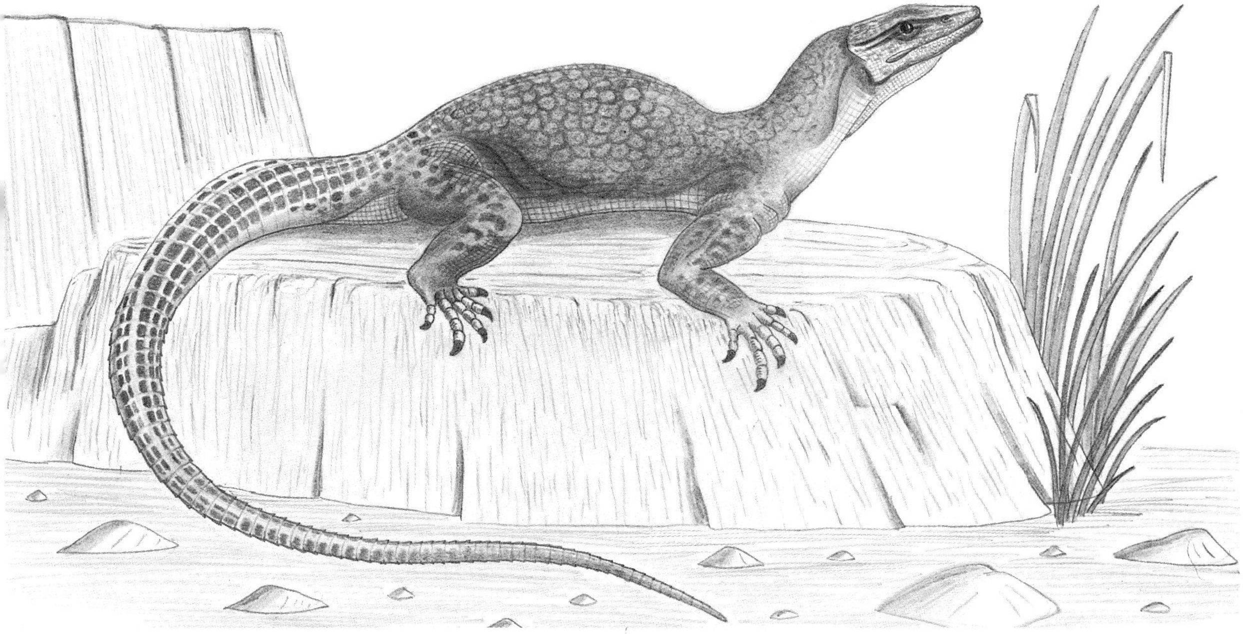

The tail of this diminutive varanid is rather short, with strongly spined scales along the top and sides, forming perfect whorls with the ventral caudal scalation; slightly depressed at its base, the tail then becomes rounded in cross-section and bears a two-keeled crest. The nostrils are dorso-laterally located on a swollen bony ridge (canthus rostralis) and the head scales are small and smooth, the supraorbitals being the most diminutive although not sharply demarcated.

Dorsal coloration is reddish brown, the head usually being flecked with blackish brown (the dark pigment is confined to the tubercles). The dorsal and upper lateral surfaces of the body and the upper surfaces of the limbs have a blackish brown reticulum, the enclosed spots sometimes being paler than the ground colour. The sides of the head, body and limbs are usually spotted with blackish brown and there are spots on the lips and temples which tend to form irregular vertical bars; a dark streak (sometimes pale edged) runs from the eye to the ear opening. Ventral surfaces are pale brown to whitish.

The pygmy ridge-tailed goanna is locally quite abundant in some areas of its range. A terrestrial monitor, favouring rocky hillsides, it lives in tunnels under small slabs of rock and in holes among spinifex grass on rocky hillsides, but is also found under piles of builders' scrap (galvanized iron, etc.). One colony of about 50 individuals that was studied near Charters Towers lived in burrows below rocks among Queensland spear grass *(Heteropogon contortus)*. In early spring (late September), some two-thirds of the population were males, several of the females were gravid, one or two not quite fully grown individuals were present, but no juveniles from the previous year's broods were detected. Animals lived individually in U-shaped burrows, which were to be found under rocks at least 16cm (6in) high. This was presumably to ensure adequate insulation, the interior of the burrows being 5–8°C (9–14.4°F) cooler than the outside temperature (25–27°C/77–80.6°F). Smaller, flat rocks are used only as temporary hiding places if the goanna is pursued by a predator.

Between 09.00 and 11.30 hours, the burrows were empty because their occupants were out foraging for grasshoppers, orthopterans, beetles, roaches, ants, caterpillars, centipedes, spiders and geckos (e.g. *Heteronotia binoei*). The pygmy ridge-tailed goannas retreated to their burrows during the heat of the day but, if the rocks above their excavations were lifted, they scattered with great agility into the long grass. Predators included foxes, snakes and birds of prey. To protect themselves from attack, these little varanids blocked the entrance to their burrows with the formidable spiky tail, effectively deterring all but the most persistent of antagonists.

About five to seven eggs, each measuring 3 × 2cm (1¼ × ¾in), are laid in a clutch and require 70–112 days to hatch. The juveniles measure about 12cm (5in) in length after 12 months' of growth.

Varanus storri storri

The subspecies from Northern Territory and northern Queensland is *Varanus storri storri* (named in honour of G.A. Storr, a scientist at the Western Australian Museum)

Varanus storri ocreatus

From the Kimberley district of Western Australia (east of 126°E) and adjacent Northern Territory, *Varanus storri ocreatus* is distinguished by the presence of enlarged scales beneath the distal part of the hind leg, a proportionately longer tail and limbs, and fewer mid-body scale rows and transverse rows of ventral scales.

VARANUS PRIMORDIUS

Among the rocky ranges and outcrops of northwestern Northern Territory, there is a small monitor distinguished from *Varanus storri* only by its more greyish ground colour and less spiny tail. Described in 1942 by the famous German herpetologist, Robert Mertens, as *Varanus primordius*, this form was unfortunately based on only a single indifferent specimen and is of doubtful taxonomic validity. Furthermore, a range of morphologically intermediate individuals occurs between the *Varanus storri* communities and the *Varanus primordius* population, which suggests that these two forms may in reality be just a single species exhibiting regional variation.

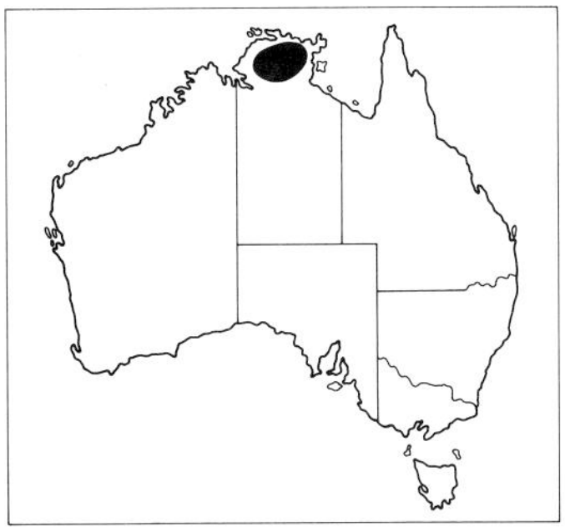

◀ **Fig. 7.6 Distribution of *Varanus baritji*.**

VARANUS BARITJI

Another small, spiny-tailed odatria, rather more elongate than *Varanus storri*, is to be found only in Arnhem Land, north of 15°S (Fig. 7.6). *Varanus baritji*, measuring slightly over 50cm (20in) in length, was named in honour of Dr Neville White, who brought the holotype to the Northern Territory Museum of Arts and Science in Darwin. Dr White had worked for a number of years with aboriginal people in northern Arnhem Land, in whose language *baritji* means 'white'.

In this species, the mid-body scales number 80–112 around the abdomen and there are 57 ventral scale rows. The tail is surmounted by a double crest, with a strongly spinose keel present on the dorsal and lateral scales; a cluster of 12 enlarged ventral caudal spines occurs in rows behind the cloaca.

Coloration above is ochre with black spotting but no ocelli, the top of the head being mottled mid-brown, relieved by a few black spots and distinct lateral facial stripes. Ventrally, the head and chin are light coloured, the gular region of the throat is lemon yellow and the undersurfaces are buff coloured.

Varanus baritji was first described only in 1987 and its biology is largely unknown.

DWARF MONITOR (*Varanus caudolineatus*)

The dwarf monitor (*Varanus caudolineatus*) (Fig. 7.7) is a tiny odatria from the coast and interior of central Western Australia, mainly but not exclusively arboreal, that attains a length of only about 30cm (12in) – scarcely larger than the diminutive *Varanus brevicauda*.

The snout of the dwarf monitor is very short, depressed anteriorly, and exhibits only an indistinct canthus rostralis. The rounded nostril is situated mid-way along the muzzle and the tail is proportionately rather short (not greatly exceeding the head and body in length), with a rounded cross-section, although it is depressed at its base. There is no dorsal caudal keel but the upper and lateral scales of the tail bear small spines. Head scales, including the supraoculars, are small and subequal, while the dorsal scales are small, round and simply convex, with 80–110 scale rows around the middle of the body. The ventral scales are smoothly sculptured and arranged in 62–74 transverse rows.

Coloration is yellowish grey above, with round dark brown spots, a dark brown temporal streak and four longitudinal dark brown stripes along the tail. The lower surfaces are pale yellow, lightly flecked with dark brown, and the throat is brown spotted.

The range of the dwarf monitor encompasses the western half of arid and semi-arid Western Australia south to the northern wheatbelt and the eastern goldfields (Fig. 7.8). North of the Ashburton River, the species tends to be larger, with more numerous mid-body scale rows and a tendency for dark spots on the base of the tail to align transversely. Specimens of the dwarf monitor have apparently been accidentally transported to the Esperance coastal plain in consignments of

▲ **Fig. 7.7 The dwarf monitor (*Varanus caudolineatus*).**

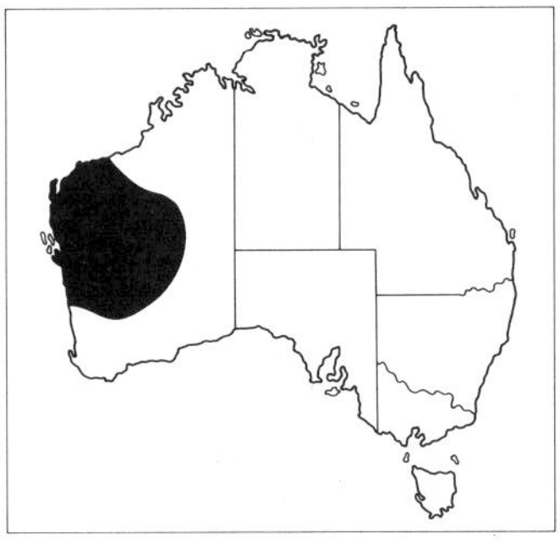

◀ **Fig. 7.8 Distribution of *Varanus caudolineatus.***

mulga wood *(Acacia aneura)* but there is no evidence that colonization of southern Western Australia has taken place through this route.

The normal habitat of dwarf monitors seems to be healthy mulga woodland and shrubland, on hard, stony soils, where they take refuge under the loose bark and in the hollows of mulga trees; they also occur in eucalypt hollows and the rock crevices of exfoliating granitic outcrops (tree-dwelling lizards often occur among rocks, since loose bark and the cavities and cracks of exfoliating rock are comparable). The dwarf monitor does not occur in spinifex habitats or on sand plains, however.

The prey includes to a large extent the widespread arboreal gecko, *Gehyra variegata*, which spends the day under loose bark, in tree hollows and in rock crevices. Ground-living geckos *(Heteronotia binoei, Rhynchoedura ornata)* are also taken, together with grasshoppers, spiders, centipedes, cicadas, beetles and moths.

The breeding season is apparently July–August, with four or five eggs, each measuring about 12 × 20mm (½ × ¾in) and weighing 3g (1/10oz), being laid in November–December. The dwarf monitor is most active in the summer months, generally near the middle of the day. Body temperature ranges from 34 to 40°C (93.2–104°F), with an average of about 38°C (100.4°F), which is 5°C (9°F) or so above ambient temperatures.

GILLEN'S PYGMY MONITOR
(Varanus gilleni)

Rather similar in its habits to *Varanus caudolineatus*, Gillen's pygmy monitor *(Varanus gilleni)* is slightly larger – up to 40cm (16in) long – but also favours mulga woodland and shrublands, and likewise hides out beneath loose bark or in the hollows of dead trees, either standing or fallen. The range, however, does not apparently overlap that of *Varanus caudolineatus*, Gillen's pygmy monitor occurring in Western Australia, through the northern and eastern arid zones, from southern Kimberley south across the Great Sandy, Gibson and Great Victoria Deserts to the vicinity of Neale Junction, extending southeastwards through the southern deserts of Northern Territory into South Australia (almost as far south as Port Augusta) (Fig. 7.9). The boundary between sandy deserts and the harder soils of the Pilbara–Hamersley region may constitute a dividing line between the ranges of *Varanus gilleni*, which occurs in spinifex habitats and sand plains, and *Varanus caudolineatus*, which does not. The preferred habitat of Gillen's pygmy monitor is loams and sand plains supporting mulga stands, together with inter-dunes bearing desert oak *(Casuarina decaisneana).*

Varanus gilleni can be distinguished from *Varanus caudolineatus* by the streaked head markings and the presence of bands rather than spots across the body. The nostril is dorso-lateral in position and slightly nearer to the eye than to the end of the nose. The ventral scales occur in 82–87 transverse rows and there are 90–125 scales around the middle of the body; the rather short tail is of rounded cross-section, with no trace of a dorsal keel.

The dorsal coloration is reddish brown, greyish brown with a slight reddish tinge, or (rarely) yellowish brown, with blackish brown or dark reddish brown streaks on the head and foreneck (transverse on the snout, reticulate on the crown, longitudinal on the neck), narrow cross-bands on

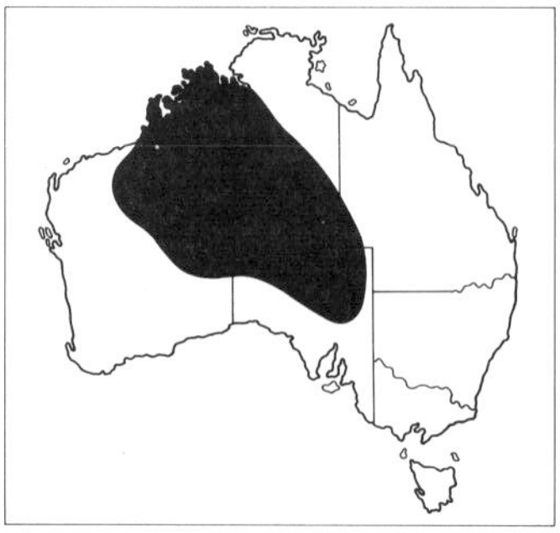

◀ **Fig. 7.9 Distribution of *Varanus gilleni.***

the body and anterior region of the tail, and longitudinal lines on the distal caudal region. Small dark spots occur between the dorsal bands, usually in single transverse rows, and the legs may be spotted or finely banded with dark reddish brown. Undersurfaces are whitish, freckled with reddish brown on the throat venter. There is a temporal streak running from the eye to above the ear aperture. Northern animals have proportionately longer legs and tails than those from the south, while counts of mid-body scale rows and subdigital lamellae decrease slightly from north to south.

A small, docile, inoffensive lizard, *Varanus gilleni* is poorly known, despite having been first described as long ago as 1895, when it was named in honour of F.J. Gillen, the chief officer of the Alice Springs telegraph office. It seems (like *Varanus caudolineatus*) to feed largely on the widespread arboreal gecko, *Gehyra variegata*, juvenile Gillen's pygmy monitors often being found to contain autotomized tails of this gecko in their stomachs. Other prey includes ground-dwelling geckos, large grasshoppers, scorpions, orthopterans, beetles and termites, together with birds' eggs.

Breeding apparently takes place in September–October, up to about seven eggs being laid in a clutch; these hatch in December. Emergent hatchlings are approximately 13.5cm (5¼in) in total length and require about 24 hours to struggle out of the egg. Once the head appears, it is constantly turned from side to side, with the tongue flicking, but it is withdrawn quickly at the slightest hint of danger. Although apparently exhausted by the effort of escaping from the egg, juveniles quickly recover and, within 18 hours, will take grasshoppers and young skinks.

When threatened, Gillen's pygmy monitor expands its gular area, compresses the trunk laterally, lashes its tail and makes short rushes with the mouth open. Ritualized combat between rival males has been witnessed, initiated by individuals flattening the trunk dorso-ventrally. One male then approaches the other from behind and straddles its opponent, seeking to secure a hold with the hind legs in the pelvic region. The subordinate animal may twist laterally to achieve mutual

▲ Mulga woodlands and shrublands or interdunes bearing desert oaks are the favoured habitats of Gillen's pygmy monitor *(Varanus gilleni)*.

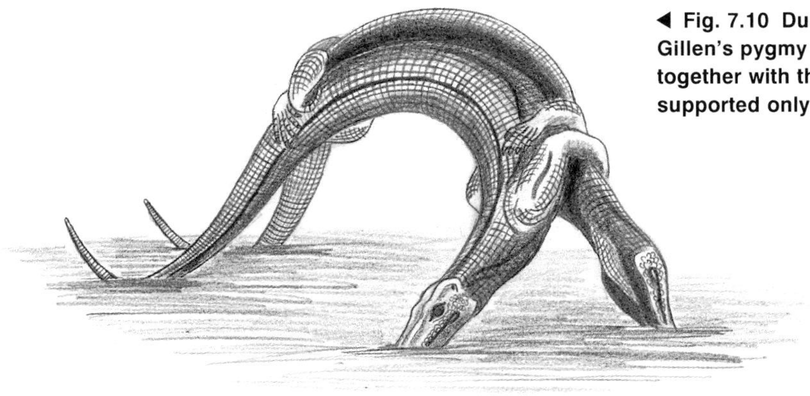

◀ **Fig. 7.10 During ritualistic combat, males of Gillen's pygmy monitor (*Varanus gilleni*) wrestle together with their bodies locked in an embrace, supported only on their snouts and tails.**

belly contact while the two adversaries seek to embrace one another with their fore- and hind limbs. Lateral bending of the bodies serves to form a rising arch, supported only by the snouts and tails of the contenders, the arch structure swaying, rising, falling and ultimately collapsing as the adversaries push against each other and change their grips to secure an advantage. Most bouts last 5 seconds or less before the arch collapses, the victor being apparently the positionally superior male at this juncture (Fig. 7.10). He may then, for the first time, bite at the vanquished (up until this point their mouths will have been kept closed). After the collapse of an arch the bout may be recommenced, sometimes after the subordinate has reversed its position by flipping its adversary over. Occasionally, there is an aggressive face-off, the lizards walking slowly forwards on stiffened legs, with the head flexed downwards from the slightly raised neck, at times reaching out with a foreleg as if to grasp at the opponent. The combatants seem oblivious to their surroundings during their struggles and watching females will sometimes crawl over them without eliciting any reaction.

DESERT PYGMY MONITOR *(Varanus eremius)*

A beautiful little red odatria, the desert pygmy monitor *(Varanus eremius)* occurs in arid and semi-arid areas of Western Australia from Pilbara and the Great Sandy and Tanami Deserts south to the far north of the wheatbelt and to the Great Victoria Desert, thence through southern Northern Territories into South Australia and southwestern Queensland (Fig. 7.11).

In this species (Fig. 7.12), which is only about 45cm (18in) long, the very large nostrils are located rather nearer to the tip of the snout than to the eye, and the face has a concave 'hollow-cheeked' appearance. Head scales are small and obtusely keeled, with conspicuous interorbitals and somewhat smaller supraorbitals. The tail tends to a triangular cross-section, with a dorsal crest towards the tip and keeled (but not spiny) scales. Ventral scales are arranged in 67–77 transverse rows, with 85–110 scales around the middle of the body.

Coloration is reddish or greyish brown above, rarely yellowish brown. The neck, back, limbs and base of the tail are usually covered with small blackish brown spots and frequently also with pale brown spots (usually dark edged) or pale flecks. There is a dark streak running through the top of the orbit to above the ear aperture and a whitish line extends from the lips to the foreleg, bordered above by a dark streak. The tail has four blackish brown longitudinal stripes. Ventro-lateral surfaces of the body are grey, occasionally bisected by a whitish strip, the belly being whitish and the lower part of the tail pinkish. On the chin and

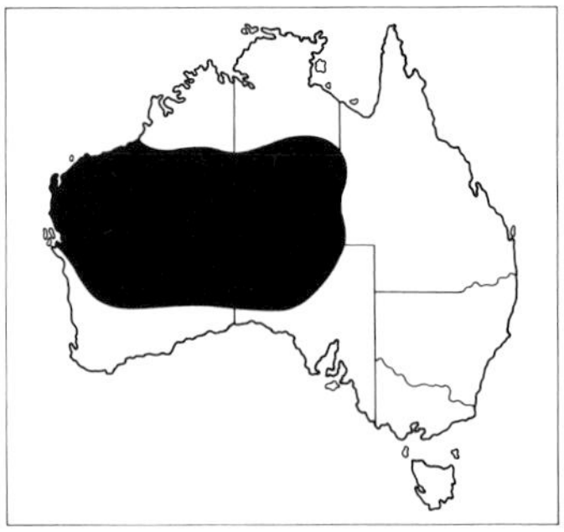

◀ **Fig. 7.11 Distribution of *Varanus eremius*.**

down the throat, there are a median and usually two lateral grey streaks, confluent at the chin to form an arrowhead-like pattern.

The keeled head scales and the dark streaks on the throat distinguish *Varanus eremius* from *Varanus caudolineatus* and *Varanus gilleni,* and its habits seem to be almost exclusively terrestrial rather than favouring a woodland or shrub environment. It lives in burrows among sand dunes and spinifex grass and, unlike most larger goannas, which usually become inactive in winter, does not hibernate and may even be more active in winter than in summer. On hot days, it is abroad by 08.00 hours but spends the hours of greatest heat underground, while on cold days it emerges later but forages through the mid-day period, maintaining a body temperature of about 37°C (98.6°F), even when the ambient figure is as much as 9°C (16.2°F) lower. The frequency with which its unique and conspicuous tracks are seen in sandy deserts suggests that it is quite common and covers large distances (up to a kilometre a day) but it is wary and seldom seen. Gillen's pygmy monitor is quickly attracted to fresh holes or excavations and often visits fresh man-made diggings.

Prey is normally caught above ground rather than being sought by digging, although the burrows of other lizards (notably the complex diggings of the nocturnal skink, *Egernia striata*) are often explored, whether for food, refuge or thermoregulation is uncertain. The diet consists mostly of other small lizards and large insects (especially grasshoppers), with occasional roaches, centipedes, scorpions and caterpillars. The number of grasshoppers eaten approximately equals the number of lizards but, in terms of volume and energy yield, reptile prey is considerably more important than invertebrate food. The lizards known to be regular victims of Gillen's pygmy monitor include species of *Ctenotus, Delma, Physignathus* and *Lerista.*

Male desert pygmy monitors have their testes much enlarged in September, October and November, although specimens have been collected most frequently in August and September, is presumably the mating season these lizards are particularly active. Eggs of relatively large size (ovarian eggs already measure 5–6mm/¼in in diameter in November) are laid in clutches of three to six during January and February. Hatchlings, with a head and body length of about 6.5cm (2¾in), appear from March until June and, within a year, have attained a length of about 8cm (3in).

▼ Fig. 7.12 The desert pygmy monitor (*Varanus eremius*).

LONG-TAILED ROCK MONITOR
(Varanus kingorum)

Extremely wary, rarely venturing far from shelter and occupying a very small geographical range in the eastern Kimberley region and adjacent Northern Territory (Fig. 7.13), the long-tailed rock monitor *(Varanus kingorum)* is a poorly known species with a total length of only some 40cm (16in), two-thirds consisting of the long slender tail.

This dull greyish brown to rich reddish brown odatria has small blackish spots, often coalescing over the head, body, limbs and most of the tail to form a fine reticulum that sometimes develops into an obscure striped pattern on the distal portion of the tail. The yellowish brown ventral surfaces are dotted with blackish brown on the throat and belly. The head scales are small and smooth and there are 97–108 rows of scales around the middle of the body. At its base, the tail is somewhat depressed, becoming subtriangular in cross-section at mid-length and finally acquiring an elliptical section; there is no evidence of a dorsal crest, and the upper and lateral caudal scalation is large, with low, moderately sharp keels. The nostrils are located about half way between the eyes and the tip of the snout.

Compared to *Varanus caudolineatus* and *Varanus eremius*, the long-tailed rock monitor has a much longer tail, lacking longitudinal stripes, and is additionally distinguishable from *Varanus eremius* by its smooth head scales and shorter, thicker and more strongly curved claws. Compared to *Varanus storri*, it has a much longer and smoother tail. Presumably insectivorous, *Varanus kingorum* is a terrestrial form, living in rocky areas, where it shelters beneath sandstone slabs or in vertical crevices on low outcrops.

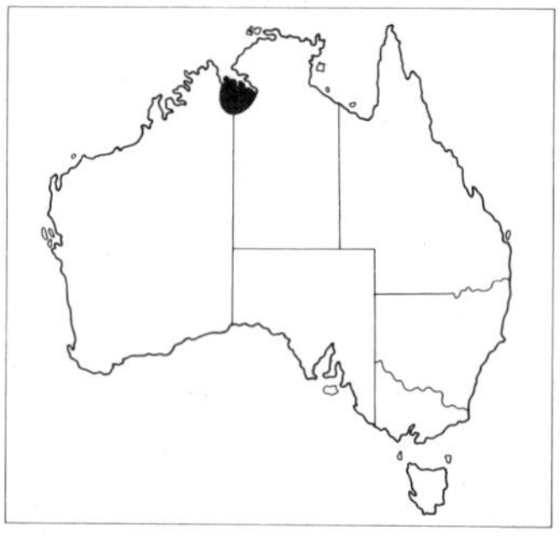

◀ **Fig. 7.13 Distribution of *Varanus kingorum*.**

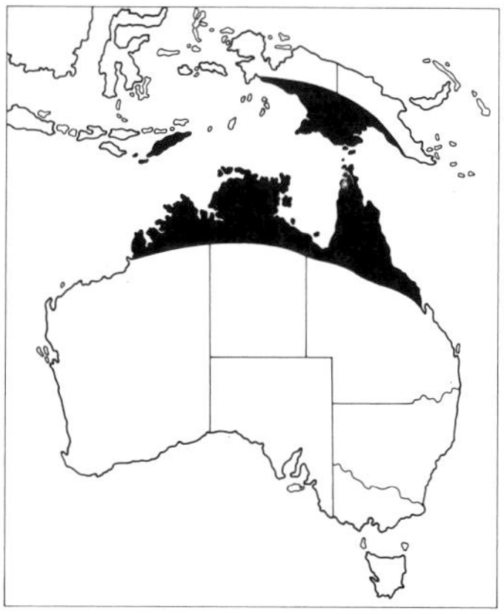

◀ **Fig. 7.14 Distribution of *Varanus timorensis*.**

***Varanus timorensis* occurs in southern New Guinea and the Timor archipelago; *Varanus timorensis scalaris* is the Australian form and may represent a species in its own right.**

SPOTTED TREE MONITOR
(Varanus timorensis)

Only one species of the subgenus *Odatria* occurs outside Australia and that is the spotted tree monitor *(Varanus timorensis)*, a rather variable, non-aggressive species, about 80cm (32in) long, that favours an arboreal habitat and is found in the Timor archipelago (Timor, Samao, Roti and Sawu, but not Sumba) and southern New Guinea (Fig. 7.14).

The spotted tree monitors of the islands to the north of Australia have a rather deep head with a short nose and nostrils located about mid-way along the snout. The cranial scales are small and smooth, with diminutive, poorly differentiated supraorbitals, and the tail is circular in cross-section at its base, subsequently becoming rounded, then triangular and finally elliptical. The dorsal and lateral caudal scales are mucronate, with a low keel, and the ventral scale rows number 70–85. The limbs are proportionately short, with toes ending in thick, strongly curved claws.

Dorsal coloration is brownish grey to black, with transverse rows of well-separated, greyish white, black-centred spots on the back. The first

▶ **The only species of the subgenus *Odatria* to occur outside Australia, the spotted tree monitor *(Varanus timorensis)* is found in the Timor archipelago and southern New Guinea.**

half of the tail is ringed with brownish or greyish white, and the undersides are whitish.

Food includes snakes, skinks and scorpions, as well as smaller items, such as orthopterans and insects. These monitors spend a good deal of time hiding out in tree stumps but, on the Timor archipelago, may sometimes be seen basking on the coral limestone walls of native settlements, taking refuge in crevices between the stonework if they are alarmed.

Mating is initiated when a male approaches a female and straddles her. He then uses a hind leg to lift the female's tail, his claws often making abrasions and causing the tail to bleed. The male then embraces the female with his forelegs just behind her forelegs, often rubbing his snout along the side of her snout and face. To achieve intromission, the male twists his cloacal region below the female's while she remains passive. Coupling may last for up to 45 minutes, with pelvic thrusting at intervals of 5–22 seconds.

Australian spotted tree monitor (*Varanus timorensis scalaris*)

A very similar tree monitor, which ranges across northern Australia, may either be a subspecies (*Varanus timorensis scalaris*) or a separate but closely related species in its own right. Substantial diffferences in the morphology of the hemipenes suggest that it is indeed a separate species rather than a subspecies of the New Guinea and Timor archipelago form. In addition, *Varanus timorensis scalaris* (or *Varanus scalaris*) exhibits spinose post-anal scales in males, has a spotted colour pattern on the head and neck, and is only about 60cm (24in) long. Its range extends from the Kimberley division of Western Australia south to northern Dampier Land, Fitzroy Crossing and Lake Argyle, then across northern Northern Territory to northern Queensland, with populations also present on some of the islands of the Torres Strait (Wales Island, Thursday Island, Murray Island) and the Gulf of Carpentaria (Groote Island).

Varanus timorensis scalaris favours a woodland habitat, occurring even in rainforest in Queensland, sheltering in hollow trunks or limbs and occasionally beneath loose bark. The colour pattern is very variable but usually includes prominent transverse white, yellow or pale grey ocelli with dark centres or spots along the upper flanks. A dark streak, demarcated by a lighter-coloured edge, runs from the eye, above the ear opening, onto the neck, and pale pigmentation spots the limbs, while irregular pale bands ring most of the tail. Rarely seen on the ground, this form, like the spotted tree monitors of Timor and New Guinea, lives mostly on a diet of skinks, scorpions, insects and orthopterans.

GLAUERT'S MONITOR (*Varanus glauerti*)

Distinguished with difficulty from *Varanus timorensis*, Glauert's monitor (*Varanus glauerti*) (Fig. 7.15) was in fact initially described as a subspecies of the Timor monitor, named in honour of Ludwig Glauert, the English-born former director of the Western Australian Museum in Perth.

A smooth, slender, flat-headed, dorsally depressed species, measuring up to about 80cm (32in), with a very long, slightly compressed tail, Glauert's monitor has nostrils situated slightly nearer to the tip of the snout than to the eyes. The head scales are small and smooth, the interorbitals being the largest and the supraorbitals the smallest. There are 120–160 scale rings around the body and the dorsal and lateral caudal scales are smooth proximally but then develop very small keels distally; males have two or three vertical rows of raised, enlarged scales ventrolaterally at the base of the tail, separated from the cloaca by small scales. The feet have short, thick, markedly curved claws and one to three (usually two) blackish brown, round, flat tubercles beneath the toes, with similar tubercles on the soles of the feet (increasing in size towards the heel).

Scales on the top of the head are greyish white, with a black centre, while the neck, foreback (usually) and upper surfaces of the forelegs are dark or bluish grey. The remainder of the back, the upper surface of the hind legs and the slightly depressed base of the tail bear a broken black or dark greyish brown reticulum enclosing smoky blue-grey or greyish white ocelli, each with a central dark spot or cluster of dots, tending to become narrow vertical stripes on the body sides.

▲ **Fig. 7.15 Glauert's monitor (*Varanus glauerti*).**

The tail is proximally speckled with black and white, becoming banded black and white distally. Lower surfaces are whitish, sometimes indistinctly banded with grey or brown, and a blackish temporal streak with pale edging runs through the eye to the temple.

Wary and shy, living mostly in rocky gorges or on escarpments, Glauert's monitor rarely ventures far from sanctuary and, if discovered skulking in one of the deep, narrow crevices in which it habitually takes refuge, is almost impossible to pull out of its hiding place. Its range is limited, extending from northern Kimberley south to Yampi Sound and the Kununurra District, as well as offshore islands from Sir Graham Moore Island southwest to Byam Martin Island, while an apparently isolated population is located in the Arnhem Land Escarpment of Northern Territory (Fig. 7.16).

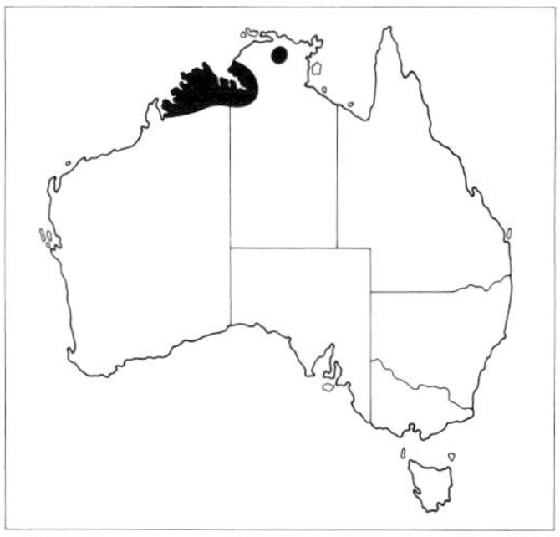

◀ **Fig. 7.16 Distribution of *Varanus glauerti*.**

Food includes the usual mix of orthopterans, spiders, roaches, caterpillars, small lizards and reptile eggs that the *Odatria* group of monitors typically subsist on, but the life habits of Glauert's monitor are poorly known.

SHINY-FOOTED GOANNA
(Varanus glebopalma)

The least known and hardest to find of all the Australian goannas, *Varanus glebopalma* (Fig. 7.17) is distinguishable from the very similar *Varanus glauerti* principally by having the last two-fifths of the tail whitish and unbanded (rather than having most of the tail boldly banded in black and white).

Up to about 1m (3¼ft) in length, the shiny-footed goanna has highly polished black pads on the soles of its feet, from which the scientific name derives; the largest of these are located at the base of the toes (Fig. 7.18). It lives in crevices in the rocky outcrops, pegmatites and granite boulders of the sandstone hills, plateaux and islands of Western Australia's Kimberley region from Kalumburu southwest to Yampi Sound (including Koolan Island), through the northern part of Northern Territory to extreme north-western Queensland (Mount Isa) (Fig. 7.19). Once it has gone to ground in a deep crevice, it is very

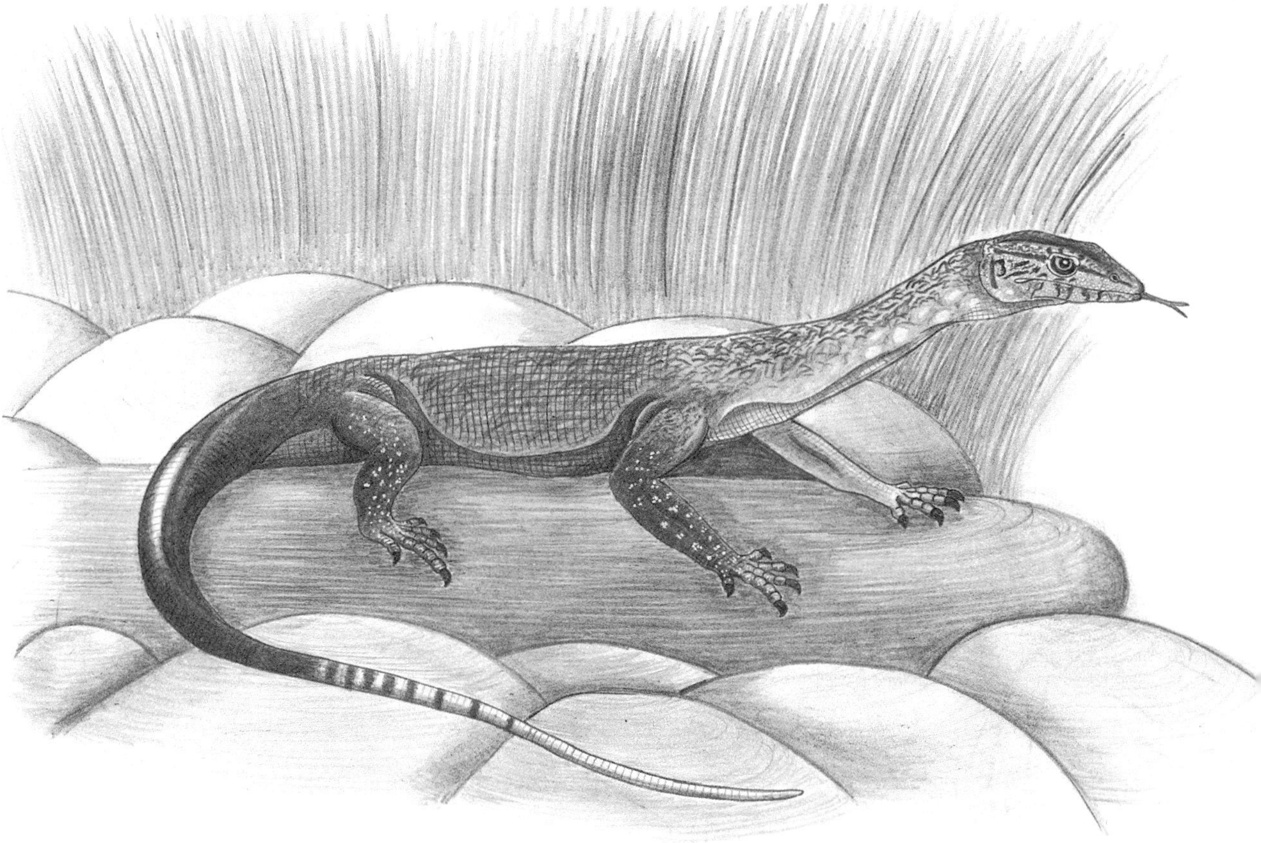

▲ **Fig. 7.17 Shiny-footed goanna (*Varanus glebopalma*).**

▼ **Fig. 7.18 Hind foot of *Varanus glebopalma*, showing the sole with its shiny black tactile pads.**

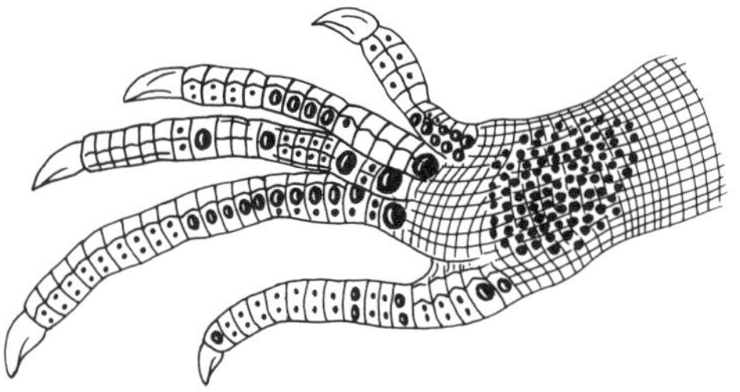

difficult to extricate and can usually only be caught while sunning itself, foraging, or hiding in a relatively shallow crack.

The nostrils are oval and located nearer to the tip of the snout than to the eye. Upper head scales are slightly larger than the temporal scales but smaller than the interorbitals. The triangular ear opening is slightly oblique and body scales number 130–170 around the middle of the trunk, with about 126 transverse rows of smooth abdominal scales. There is a slight depression at the base of the unusually long tail (which is up to twice the head and body length) but the tail then becomes laterally compressed and covered with uniform, obtusely keeled scales that do not rise to a spine. Some slightly prominent scales occur each side of the vent in male individuals, a site where species of *Odatria* frequently have spinous squamation.

Generally the ground colour is pale or dark grey to reddish brown. Narrow transverse dark lines usually become joined to form a reticulum on the body, side of the head, chest, throat and base of the tail. The top of the head is flecked blackish brown and the sides of the head and neck are pale coloured. Yellow or white spotting occurs on the blackish limbs and the ventral surfaces are brownish white, transversely barred with light purplish fawn. On the anterior half of the tail, black scales are dominant but, towards

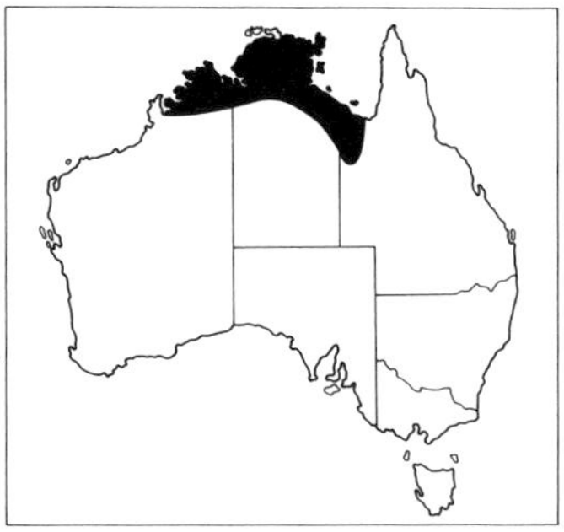

◀ Fig. 7.19 Distribution of *Varanus glebopalma.*

the tip, the basal coloration lightens to pale brown, yellow and finally white, although juveniles exhibit narrow dark bands right to the tail tip.

The first specimen of *Varanus glebopalma* to be scientifically described (a male) was shot in 1948 near the southern end of Lake Hubert, in Arnhem Land, in the crevice of a sandstone boulder. Two further examples were reported in 1957 and, within a couple of decades, some 20 more specimens had been obtained.

The shiny-footed goanna is very agile and alert and has been observed making spectacular leaps from boulder to boulder and climbing with facility up sheer rock faces. In hot weather, it tends to be active mostly at twilight and has been seen still hunting in caves after darkness has fallen. Food includes small lizards (skinks, pygopodids and lesser species of goanna), frogs and toads, spiders, orthopterans and centipedes.

PILBARA ROCK MONITOR

(Varanus pilbarensis)

The Pilbara region of northwestern Western Australia (Fig. 7.20) has its own exclusive species of rock monitor. *Varanus pilbarensis* (Fig. 7.21) is a

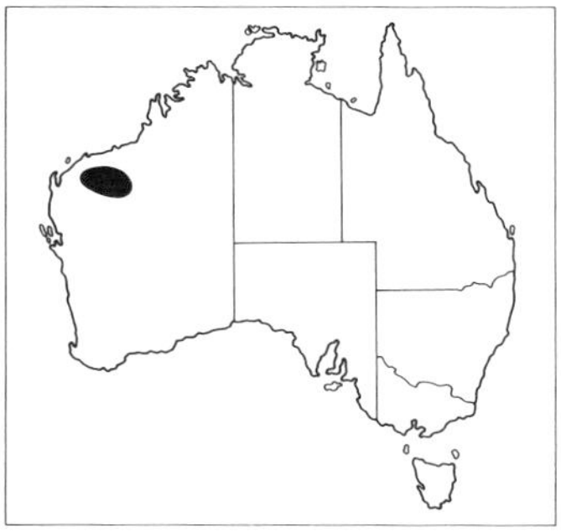

◀ Fig. 7.20 Distribution of *Varanus pilbarensis.*

▼ Fig. 7.21 The Pilbara rock monitor *(Varanus pilbarensis).*

small reddish-coloured form, no more than 50cm (20in) long, that lives on rocky hills, on cliff faces and in gorges, sheltering in crevices or cavities and displaying a high level of co-ordinated agility as it leaps from boulder to boulder.

The Pilbara rock monitor has small, smooth head scales, the supraorbitals being much inferior in size to the interorbitals but not sharply differentiated from them. The nostrils face upwards and outward and are located about half way between the tip of the snout and the eye. There is a slight proximal depression of the tail, which then becomes circular in cross-section and finally elliptical towards its tip. The dorsal and lateral caudal scales bear low keels and, just behind the cloaca, on each side, there are four to six curving rows of long, narrow, pointed scales, which increase in size, elevation and spininess outwards and are usually white (sometimes reddish brown) in colour. The claws are very short, thick and strongly curved, and there are 110–135 scales around the middle of the trunk.

Dorsal coloration is pale (occasionally moderately dark) reddish brown, tinged with olive on the neck and back but palest on the snout and tail. Dark reddish brown dots or flecks occur on the head and neck, sometimes coalescing into narrow, wavy cross-bands. The back and the base of the tail bear small, blackish brown or very dark reddish brown spots, aligned in short, variable transverse bars, between which are barely discernible greyish spots, transversely confluent and aligned in short, variable cross-bars. Dark rings around the tail become grouped in couplets distally and, towards the tip, the members of each couplet usually merge to form wide, dark reddish brown bands. The limbs have irregular, pale grey or whitish spots, sometimes dark edged or dark centred. The side of the head is a pale reddish brown, marked with reddish brown vertical bars on the lips, oblique bars on the temples and, occasionally, a narrow streak from the front of the eye backwards and upwards to above the temples. Throat and venter are greyish white, irregularly and indistinctly cross-banded or clouded with grey, and the undersides of the limbs are greyish white with an indistinct grey reticulum on the hind legs (occasionally also on the forelegs).

RUSTY MONITOR *(Varanus semiremex)*

The rusty monitor *(Varanus semiremex)* (Fig. 7.23), attaining a little over 50cm (20in) in length, is unusual for an odatria in being aquatically adapted. Its principal home is among the mangrove trees of coastal and estuarine swamps along the subhumid eastern shoreline of Queensland (Fig. 7.22). It frequently shelters in hollow trunks or branches, sometimes taking refuge beneath loose bark, and is also found in the vegetation dominated by the paperbark tree *(Melaleuca)* around the margins of creeks, lakes and rivers. The rusty monitor preys mostly on arthropods, crustaceans (notably crabs) and small vertebrates (e.g. fish, geckos, the more diminutive mammals). It often enters the water during the course of its foraging expeditions and swims efficiently, with the assistance of its proportionately rather short tail.

The tail is rounded in cross-section near the base but becomes laterally compressed further back and constitutes an efficiently adapted swimming organ, although it lacks a median keel. The head scales are small, smooth and glossy, but irregular in shape, and the nostrils are slightly nearer to the tip of the snout than to the eyes. There are 85–105 scales around the middle of the body and 74–92 transverse rows of ventral scales.

Two distinct colour forms of the rusty monitor occur. The eastern variant (present from Yeppoon northwards into the southern Cape York Peninsula) possesses a greyish brown ground colour with blackish flecks that often form a reticulum over the neck and body. The limbs bear variegated blackish brown markings, spotted with cream, and the dark grey-brown tail has a barely discernible patterning. Ventral surfaces are white

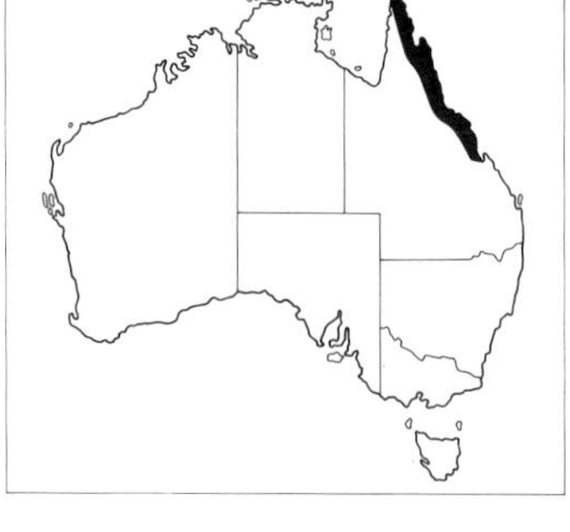

◀ **Fig. 7.22 Distribution of *Varanus semiremex.***

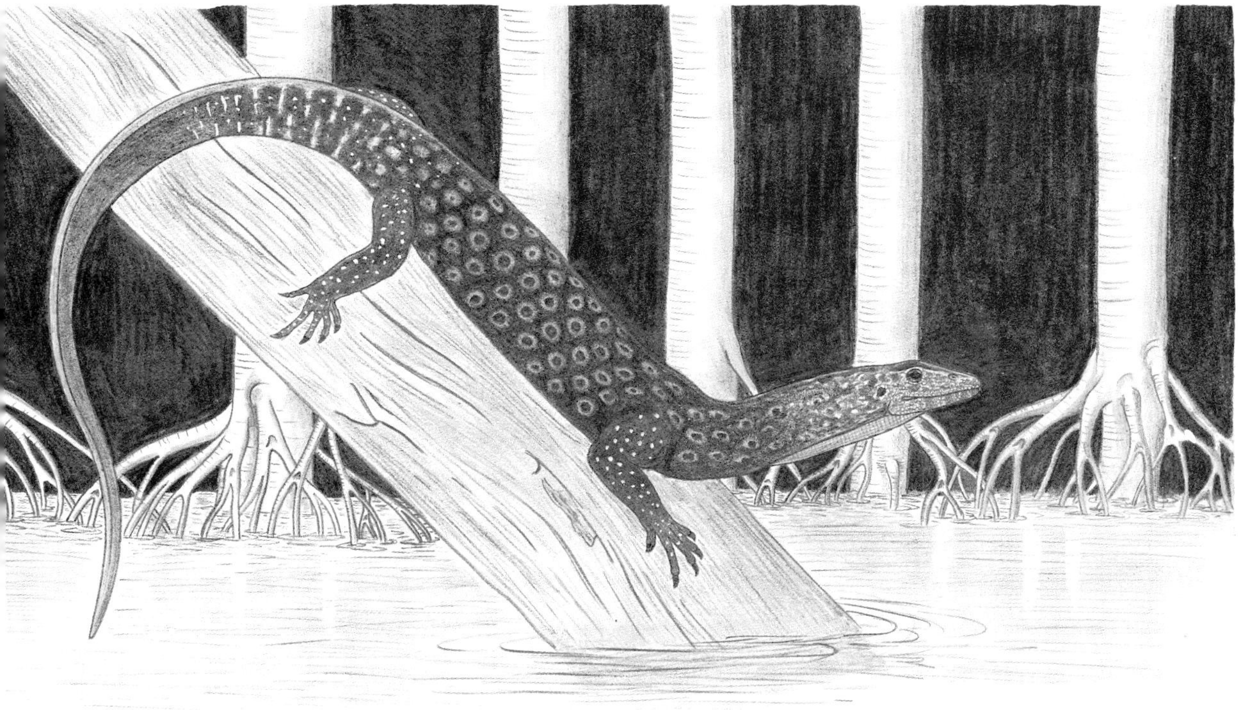

▲ **Fig. 7.23 The rusty monitor (*Varanus semiremex*, northern race).**

or pale yellow, with irregular brown bands, and the head is dark above but paler on the sides, the lips bearing dark brown bars. A northern form, present towards the tip of Cape York Peninsula, has a darker ground colour and stronger patterning, with white ocelli transversely aligned on the neck and body.

There have been reports of the rusty monitor along the Ord River in northwestern Australia, so it is possible that this species has a wider range than the generally accepted distribution down eastern Queensland. Some authorities have suggested that *Varanus semiremex* is only a variant of *Varanus timorensis.*

The rusty monitor may not in fact be the only odatria that is at home in the water. Mitchell's monitor *(Varanus mitchelli)* is not usually regarded as an odatria (see page 91), largely because it is an aquatic monitor, but researchers have determined that this small form has the same chromosome karyotype and exactly the same lactate dehydrogenase isozyme as typical odatrias, and should therefore perhaps be included in the same subgenus.

VARANUS TRISTIS

Occurring throughout most of Australia's subhumid or arid woodlands, *Varanus tristis* is essentially an arboreal odatria but will also make its home on rocky outcrops and ranges if necessary. Such adaptability has allowed this medium-sized, long-tailed goanna to colonize more than three-quarters of the continent. It is absent only from extreme southerly Western Australia (south of Peak Charles), the southern portion of South Australia, Victoria, south and eastern New South Wales, and the southeastern corner of Queensland (Fig. 7.24).

◀ **Fig. 7.24 Distribution of *Varanus tristis*.**

▲ **Throughout most of Australia's subhumid or arid woodlands there is to be found *Varanus tristis*, populations in the western and eastern portions of the continent being distinguishable by variations in their coloration.**

Growing to about 80cm (32in) in length, *Varanus tristis* has a rather short, strongly depressed and relatively sharp-snouted head, with hollow cheeks and laterally oriented nostrils, located if anything slightly closer to the nose than to the eye. The head scales are small and smooth, a sharp differentiation existing between the large interorbitals and the small supraorbitals. The tail is depressed proximally but then becomes round in cross-section, and the ventral scales are arranged in 77–85 transverse rows, with 105–155 scales around the middle of the trunk. Dorsal and lateral caudal scales are moderately large, with a low sharp keel ending in a sharp spine, and there is a circular or squarish cluster of large, black or black and white scales on each ventro-lateral surface at the base of the tail (smaller and less spiny in females and immature males). The limbs are relatively long, with toes terminating in rather short, thick, strongly curved claws.

In the northern part of Australia, *Varanus tristis* is active throughout the year, foraging up to 2km (1¼ miles) a day in search of small lizards (e.g. *Moloch, Ctenotus, Lerista* and the diminutive *Varanus caudolineatus*), nestling birds, eggs (both avian and reptilian), spiders, ants, abundant grasshoppers, roaches, beetles, cicadas and caterpillars. The voracity of this particular monitor is demonstrated by the discovery, in a specimen itself weighing only 126g (4½oz), of a 35g (1¼oz) agamid.

In more southerly parts of Australia, *Varanus tristis* becomes inactive during the winter months, building up fat reserves in autumn to see it through the inclement season. In its preferred arboreal habitat, it is very hard to spot, its coloration merging with the rough bark of coolibahs, box or bauhinias; when at rest on a branch it achieves further camouflage by curving its body to conform to the shape of the tree limb against which it is flattening itself. It prefers to take refuge in the deeper hollows of tree trunks (as opposed to pipes within the branches) and is sometimes discovered beneath the loose bark of a ring-barked tree, possibly searching for geckos, spiders, etc. Its tracks habitually run from tree to tree, so it presumably ascends each in turn in search of prey. In arid areas, it shelters in rock crevices and under slabs, or occasionally uses the mud nests of swallows and martins.

Oviducal eggs are present in *Varanus tristis* by November, so breeding probably takes place in about September, with clutches of 5–17 proportionately rather small eggs, laid in late spring. At an incubation temperature of around 27°C (80.6°F), hatching takes place in 116–140 days. The newly emergent juveniles are 20cm (8in) long and weigh 4–6g (⅛–¼oz).

Two colour phases of *Varanus tristis*, sometimes distinguished as separate subspecies, occur respectively in western and central Australia (*Varanus tristis tristis*, the black-headed monitor) and eastern Australia (*Varanus tristis orientalis*, the freckled monitor), but intergradation does occur between these two different types and it is doubtful whether they are much more than geographical races.

Freckled monitor (*Varanus tristis orientalis*)

The eastern Australian freckled monitor (*Varanus tristis orientalis*) has a brown ground colour (ranging from a pale hue to almost black), with prominent greyish white ocelli transversely aligned across the neck and back, and pale grey, yellow or reddish spots and ocellations on the limbs. The anterior portion of the tail bears banded or variegated pale markings, which give way posteriorly to largely unpatterned dark brown or black. The top of the head is flecked greyish brown and there is a pale-edged dark streak extending from the eye to above the ear, while the lips are pale with brown bars or mottling. Undersurfaces are whitish, with dark spots or bars.

The range of the freckled monitor extends westwards to central Australia and northern Northern Territory, the rest of this species' range being occupied by the black-headed monitor.

Black-headed monitor (*Varanus tristis tristis*)

In western and central Australia, *Varanus tristis* is represented by the black-headed monitor (*Varanus tristis tristis*), in which the ocelli tend to be smaller and integrated into a fine dark reticulation, while the head, neck, body and tail are dark brown or black. Individuals from the extreme southwest of Western Australia are almost totally lacking in any pattern at all and there is a tendency throughout the range of *Varanus tristis* for old animals to acquire a darker ground colour and lose their patterning.

An attempt to delineate a central Australian subspecies (*Varanus tristis centralis*), with intermediate coloration, has not met with a great deal of scientific support.

* * *

In all probability, the subgenus *Odatria* evolved within the Australian continent from a larger ancestor whose descendants became progressively dwarfed, conceivably as an adaptation to increasing aridity in the area during the Pleistocene. Odatrias have clearly been very successful and resourceful in eking out an existence among the deserts and sand dunes, even taking advantage of the escape strategy habitually practised by the tiny geckos on which many odatrias feed (or try to). If caught by the tail, geckos can shed this appendage (subsequently growing a replacement) and it seems that at least some odatrias deliberately seek out discarded gecko tails, which are in fact a quite valuable source of protein in their diet.

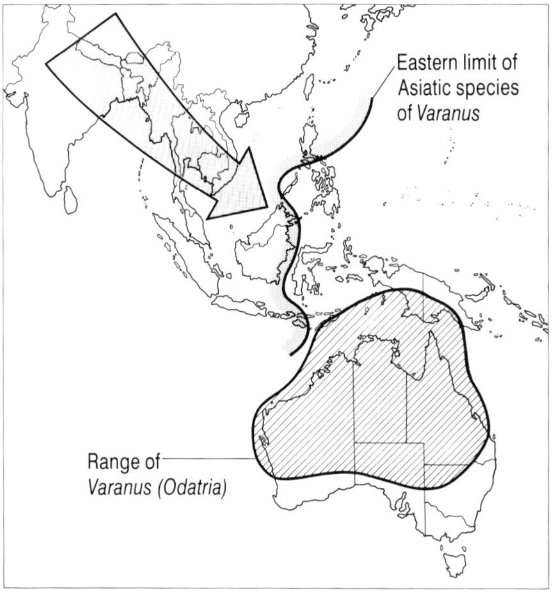

▲ **Fig. 7.25 The monitor kingdom of Australasia, showing the eastern limit of Asiatic varanids migrating from the west (arrow) and the range of the subgenus *Odatria*.**

The precise ancestor of *Odatria* has not yet been pinpointed. One suggestion is that there was a progression from the huge *Megalania* down to *Varanus gouldi* and finally to *Odatria*, the argument being that most monitors are large and a steady down-scaling in size is a more probable scenario than the alternative hypothesis that proposes a large ancestral form giving rise to tiny odatrias, which then again generated a series of large species, such as *Varanus gouldi*. One difficulty with postulating the descent of *Odatria* from a large progenitor is that all the odatrias seem to have smooth, slender lungs, but large monitors need to have complexly folded lungs to supply their substantial energy requirements and might have been expected to hand down such a bronchial structure even to dwarf descendants.

Given the predominantly Australian distribution of *Odatria*, it seems more likely that occurrences of the subgenus in outlying areas, e.g. New Guinea, Timor, are the result of emigration rather than an indication of an extra-Australian centre of evolution and subsequent immigration via the Timor Sea or the Torres Strait. It is noticeable that *Odatria* is not present across the extreme south of Australia, whether because the climate there is not warm enough in winter or because there has been insufficient time for it to diffuse south from a northerly point of origin is not known.

Australia's monitors, both the large species and the odatrias, have a clearly defined distribution (Fig. 7.25) that excludes Tasmania and New Zealand in the south and is limited towards the northwest by a line of demarcation running up through Flores in the Lesser Sunda islands, through the Makassar Strait between Borneo and Celebes, west of Palawan, and across the Philippines south of Luzon – a boundary that also marks the most easterly occurrence of Asiatic species of *Varanus*. (This line of demarcation is not dissimilar to Wallace's Line, which supposedly marks the boundary between Oriental and Australasian faunas and passes through the Selat Lombok between Bali and Lombok, then up through the Makassar Strait and finally across to the south of Mindanao. This was drawn in the nineteenth century by the British naturalist, Alfred Russel Wallace).

Clearly the Antipodes latterly became a major centre of varanid evolution, geographical isolation providing an environment in which the group flourished and evolved both giant species and very small dwarf forms.

CHAPTER 8

Venomous American Dragons

The southwestern USA, western Mexico and Guatemala are home to the Gila monster (named after the Gila region of Arizona) and its close relative, the Mexican beaded lizard. Plumply proportioned reptiles, usually brightly coloured with black and yellow markings, but in some parts of their range almost black, these lizards are collectively known scientifically as *Heloderma.* They enjoy a less than savoury reputation because their bite is poisonous – a unique feature among lizards.

A large *Heloderma* can be up to 90cm (36in) long and the venom of such a sizeable reptile, injected into the victim through channels in the lower teeth, may cause very unpleasant symptoms in a human being and is likely to prove fatal to a small mammal or a bird. A number of human deaths from *Heloderma* venom have, in fact, been recorded but, invariably, the reptile evidently struck in self-defence. The venomous capability of *Heloderma* is not, it seems, employed as an offensive ploy to secure prey.

Such a heavily built, sluggish lizard seems an unlikely relative for the sleek and active monitors of the Old World but two significant features of its anatomy strongly suggest such an affinity. The lower jaw of one *Heloderma* species has a varanoid type of joint half way along its length and all the members of the genus possess elongate, slit-like nasal openings in the skull. In addition, both helodermatids and varanids have a sutured latero-ventral process of the frontal bone below the brain's olfactory lobe, maxillary bones that are excluded from the intra-orbital cavity, rings of granules around the scales on the back, osteoderms underlying scales in general, four vertebrae supporting sternal ribs, and a count of two, three, four, five and three phalanges respectively in the five front and back toes. The evidence may be only rather limited but it nonetheless seems to lead to the valid conclusion that *Heloderma* is a varanoid, despite the fact that there are also significant differences: the skull of monitors has an incomplete post-orbital arch (although a temporal arch is retained), coalesced nasal bones and a parietal opening, while the scales of monitors bear pits (not present in *Heloderma*) and their slender tongues lack a villose basal portion, such as that found in the Gila monster group.

Heloderma has a short, broad and relatively low skull (Fig. 8.1), which, in typical lacertilian fashion, lacks temporal arches, but the jaws are powerful and stoutly constructed, and capable of crushing proportionately quite large prey. Well-developed osteoderms protect the head and body (fused to the skull in the cranial region) and the feet have five short toes adapted for digging. The rather short or stumpy tail is a unique fat store, which can be drawn upon to sustain the animal through adverse climatic conditions that engender hibernation – or at any rate to allow withdrawal to a subterranean lair – when dry or cold seasons supervene.

MEXICAN BEADED LIZARD
(Heloderma horridum)

There are two species of *Heloderma*, of which the more southerly, *Heloderma horridum,* is the most conservative. Popularly known as the Mexican beaded lizard, this form attains a length of about 1m (3¼ft) and occurs from southern Sonora in the north to southeastern Guatemala in the south. It is absent from the USA and, even in Mexico, is restricted to the Pacific drainage of the country's western region (Fig. 8.2).

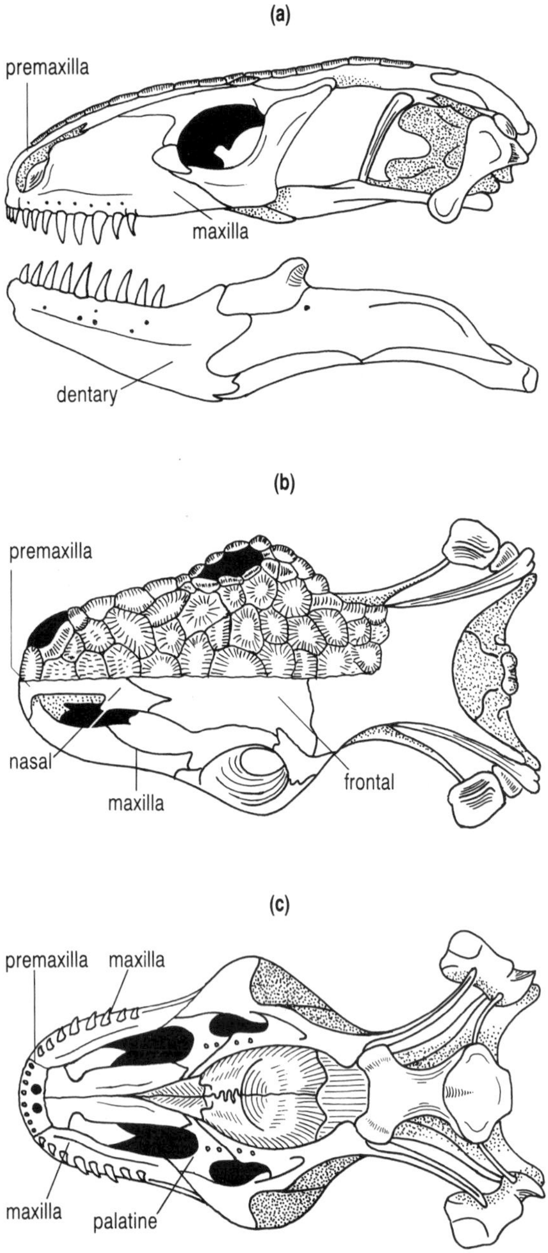

▲ **Fig. 8.1 Skull of *Heloderma horridum*: (a) lateral aspect, with osteoderms removed; (b) dorsal view, with osteoderms partially removed; (c) palatal surface.**

▶ **Fig. 8.2 Distribution of *Heloderma* in the southwestern USA and Mexico.**

Heloderma horridum was the first member of the family to be described by the early European colonists of the New World. In 1615, one Hernandez referred to the *acaltetepon* that occurred in the fields of Cuernavaca, Nova Hispania (now in the Mexican state of Morelos). Proper scientific publication had to wait until 1829, when this reptile was formally described as *Trachyderma horridum,* subsequently amended to *Heloderma horridum* when it was discovered that the designation *Trachyderma* had already been used for a totally different reptile.

The tail of *Heloderma horridum* is rather short by the standards of lizards in general but still represents at least 65 per cent of the measurement from the tip of the snout to the vent. It has 40 caudal vertebrae (there are less than 30 in the northern species) and 73–87 rows of scales beneath it (the maximum number in *Heloderma suspectum* is 62). The Mexican beaded lizard also has only six or seven maxillary teeth and retains teeth on the palatine bone in the roof of the mouth. Its claws, furthermore, are proportionately long. The upper surface of the head is virtually all black and juveniles possess six or seven black bands round the tail.

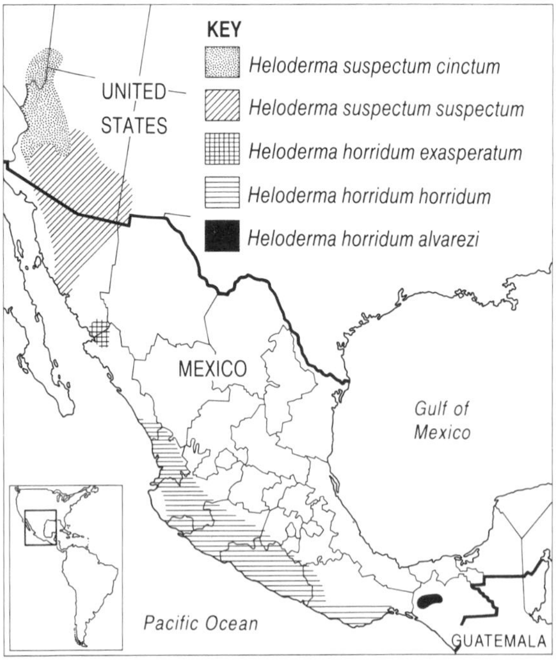

Rio Fuerte beaded lizard
(Heloderma horridum exasperatum)
There are four subspecies of *Heloderma horridum*, of which the most northerly is *Heloderma horridum exasperatum*, from southern Sonora and northern Sinaloa, where it occurs in the drainage basin of the Rio Fuerte, an area of deep canyons *(barrancas)* where the rivers have eaten back into Mexico's central plateau. Consequently, it is known as as the Rio Fuerte beaded lizard.

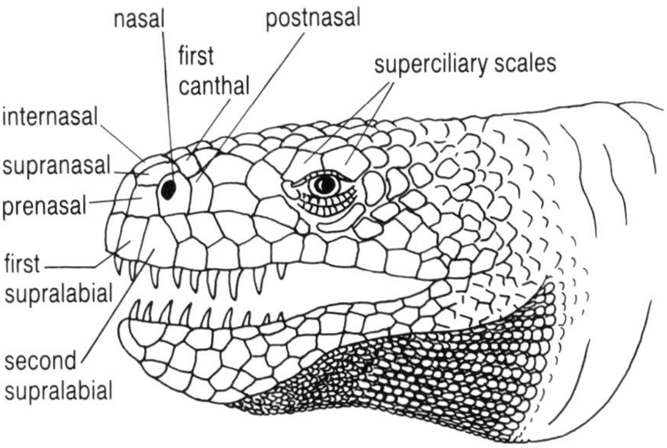

▲ **Fig. 8.3 Facial scalation of *Heloderma horridum*.**

The light, yellowish or pinkish ground colour of its skin equals or exceeds in area the black or dark brown regions. It is further distinguished by details of the scalation around the nostrils: the supranasal scale is usually in contact with the postnasal scale (not separated from it by the first canthal), there are up to eight scales across the head between the superciliaries, and the second supralabial is always in contact with the nasal or prenasal plates (Fig. 8.3). Up to about 60cm (24in) in total length, this rather small subspecies principally inhabits deciduous forest at altitudes of 300–1070m (1000–3500ft) above sea level, where there is about 700mm (28in) of rain a year, with a summer rainy season through July and August and a dry, almost rainless spell from March through May.

Heloderma horridum horridum
Further south in Sinaloa, *Heloderma horridum exasperatum* probably intergrades with *Heloderma horridum horridum*, the largest subspecies of the genus, which has an extensive range along Mexico's Pacific drainage from southern Sinaloa through Nayarit, Jalisco, Michoacan and Guerrero to the eastern boundary of Oaxaca, with occurrences further inland in Mexico and Morelos.

Popularly known as the *escorpion* in Mexico, this form – the true Mexican beaded lizard – is identifiable by scalation details of the head, notably the separation of the supranasal from the postnasal by the first canthal, the presence normally of less than eight scales across the top of the head, and 11 or fewer scales along the mid-line of the head between the internasals and the occiput.

Although juveniles of *Heloderma horridum horridum* from throughout the extensive geographical range of this subspecies all have a rather similar colour pattern of light and dark markings, adults show considerable variation, depending on where they come from. Generally speaking, however, the black or brown markings tend to cover a greater area than in the Rio Fuerte subspecies, while the yellow areas comprise dots, bars or irregular spots that are more or less bilaterally symmetrical.

The preferred habitat of *Heloderma horridum horridum* seems to be tropical deciduous forest or thorn forest, occasionally savannah or pine/oak forest, where winters are dry but the overall climate is humid or subhumid. The heavy rains that affect northwestern Jalisco and western Nayarit seem to deter the reptile, since it does not occur in these areas. This subspecies is present from sea level (the coastal plain in the middle area of its range) up to altitudes of at least 1500m (nearly 5000ft) inland, with some populations occurring as much as 275km (over 170 miles) from the coast.

Black beaded lizard or Chiapan beaded lizard
(Heloderma horridum alvarezi)
In the west-central region of Chiapas there is a race of *Heloderma* that loses virtually all its juvenile skin patterning as it matures and, as an adult, is almost black, retaining only the faintest vestiges of light-coloured markings. *Heloderma horridum alvarezi* is consequently known as the black beaded lizard, *escorpion negro*, or (a reference to its home territory) the Chiapan beaded lizard.

A rather small race, with an overall length of about 50cm (20in), the black beaded lizard exhibits faint yellow markings only on the belly and the lower surface of the tail, where indistinct cross-bars are all that remains of the juvenile coloration; the rest of the skin is slaty-black or dark brown. Occurring on the headwaters of the Rio de Chiapa, which drains into the Atlantic, the black beaded lizard is apparently a denizen of the tropical deciduous forest that occurs in the central depression of Chiapas; it may also frequent the gallery forest along streams and perhaps the lower reaches of pine/oak forest on the hills of the area.

Heloderma horridum charlesbogerti

A fourth subspecies of *Heloderma horridum* was described in 1988 from the Motagua Valley of southeastern Guatemala, an arid area with less than 50mm (2in) of rain a year, falling mostly in June, July and August, the months of January through May being almost totally without precipitation. *Heloderma horridum charlesbogerti* occurs in the tropical deciduous forest of the valley floor. This forest comprises acacia, mimosa, thorn scrub, spiny grasses, cacti and, on the higher slopes, oaks – a flora similar to that preferred by *Heloderma* throughout its range. This race of Mexican beaded lizard is quite widely separated from other populations of the species, possibly due to the formation of a high volcanic cordillera in southern Guatemala during the Pleistocene, which cut off this group of helodermatids from the other subspecies of *Heloderma horridum.*

The head and neck of *Heloderma horridum charlesbogerti* are uniformly black, while the upper surface of the body has a dark ground colour with pale yellow spots and blotches across the hinder region. Forwards of the vent, there are no complete bands, rings or rosettes. Females of this subspecies exhibit considerably enlarged pre–anal scales – a feature more generally found in the northern species, *Heloderma suspectum.*

GILA MONSTER *(Heloderma suspectum)*

Commonly known as the Gila monster, and ranging from southern Nevada and Utah, south through Arizona, to southwestern New Mexico and the Mexican state of Sonora, *Heloderma suspectum* is readily distinguished from *Heloderma horridum* by its smaller size (maximum length less than 60cm/24in) and much shorter, stumpier tail, which represents less than 55 per cent of the snout to vent measurement; it has only 25–28 caudal vertebrae and fewer than 62 rows of subcaudal scales. Additionally, the splenial bone on the inside of the lower jaw overlaps the coronoid bone above it, the maxillary teeth number eight or nine (with no palatine dentition), and there is a pair of enlarged pre-anal scales just in front of the vent. The upper surface of the head is mottled with pink, except for the snout, and juveniles of the species have only four or five black rings around the tail.

There are two subspecies of the Gila monster and, throughout their ranges, they seem to favour environments of rocky, semi-arid regions, usually found in the foothills of mountain ranges, such as the Santa Catalinas near Tucson, Arizona or the Santa Rita Mountains. They occur in areas where cactus plants, creosote bushes, mesquite, yucca, cholla and paloverde trees grow prolifically, as well as ranging up into oak forests at higher elevations, with specimens reported from altitudes that can be as great as 1525m (5000ft) in Arizona.

Banded Gila monster *(Heloderma suspectum cinctum)*

The most northerly population of *Heloderma suspectum* comprises the subspecies *Heloderma suspectum cinctum* (the banded Gila monster), which occurs in the drainage of the Colorado River, from extreme southwestern Utah, through the most southeasterly corner of Nevada, to the northwestern region of Arizona, with occasional reports from the Mojave Desert of California (San Bernardino County and Inyo County).

It is distinguished by its rather pale coloration and the retention of juvenile markings in the adult. On the upper surface of the body, there are four black 'saddles' (irregular, double cross-bands) containing lighter spots, together with four or five black or dark brown bands around the tail (including the tip), which are either much broader than the intervening black-mottled light bands or else heavily mottled with pink or yellow. In some areas, unusually dark-coloured individuals apparently occur, exhibiting predominantly black markings combined with salmon-coloured (rather than flesh-toned) light areas. A black basaltic lava flow in Washington County, Utah, has yielded a specimen of this particular type, suggesting that selection for skin patterning is influenced by the habitat, this factor over-riding the normal trend for paler-coloured northern Gila monsters.

Heloderma suspectum suspectum

The southerly race of Gila monster, *Heloderma suspectum suspectum*, occurs from Guaymas on the Sonoran coast, northwards into most of southern Arizona (probably intergrading with *Heloderma suspectum cinctum* in the western region of this state) and extending into extreme southwestern New Mexico. In this form, the juvenile skin pattern is lost by adulthood, the coloration becoming mottled or blotched with black and pink and the dark tones tending to be dominant along the back. On the tail, the lighter bands are mottled, streaked or blotched with black, while the four or five dark rings (including the terminal tip) are either broadened by encroachment on the lighter bands or else irregularly interrupted by rows of light scales.

* * *

Helodermas are not true desert animals and avoid really barren arid regions, especially if the soil is hard and affords little facility for digging or finding burrows. They need water and an annual rainfall of at least 50mm (2in) during the warm season seems essential for them. It is noteworthy that their extension westwards is apparently limited by the lack of summer rainfall west of the Colorado River, where on average less than 50mm (2in) of precipitation occurs during April–September, most rain falling in the winter, when it is too cold for Gila monsters to venture forth. These lizards are only active within an ambient air temperature range of about 25–35°C (77–95°F) and maintain their body temperature at about 30°C (86°F); temperatures above 45°C (113°F) or much below 5°C (41°F) are likely to be fatal.

When the cold season supervenes, they hibernate in subterranean shelters, often burrows taken over from other animals but occasionally possibly dug by the helodermas themselves. There they remain throughout the dry, low-temperature months, living off the fat stored in their bodies and stumpy tails, until the next moist warm season. They also go into hiding during the heat of the day in summer and, unlike monitor lizards, are frequently to be seen during the cool hours of the night. The inference must be that helodermas are relict forms, basically needing access to water and now squeezed into a small, contracting area of a formerly much wider range by increasingly arid climatic conditions.

Certainly fossil helodermas are much more widely distributed, with a species (*Heloderma texana*) present in Texas during the Early Miocene, 20 million years ago. There is also evidence of *Heloderma* in Florida at about the same time, while a closely related genus, *Lowesaurus*, with triangular frontal bones (as opposed to the trapezoidal frontals in *Heloderma* itself) and 11 pairs of maxillary teeth occurred in northeastern Colorado and Nebraska in Oligocene times (about 30 million years ago), possibly surviving into the Early Miocene of Nebraska.

Further back still, at the end of the Eocene or beginning of the Oligocene, there was a member of the family in Europe, *Eurheloderma*, represented by skull and jaw bones and vertebrae from the Quercy phosphorites of France – famous since the middle of the nineteenth century for fossil animal remains. The evolutionary history of the family traces back ultimately to *Paraderma*, known from skull and jaw fragments discovered in the Late Cretaceous of Wyoming, and *Gobiderma*, whose 5cm (2in) long skull was found in the Late Cretaceous of the Gobi Desert, demonstrating that helodermatids existed before the end of the Age of Dinosaurs, over 60 million years ago. In 1995, fossil helodermatid bones were reported to occur in the Lower Cretaceous rocks of Utah, which indicates the presence of this family over 100 million years ago.

Helodermas seem to have two principal sources of food: the eggs of lizards or ground-laying birds, and juvenile mammals of such small species as ground squirrels, cottontails or jack rabbits. When helodermas emerge from their winter hibernation, to a greater or lesser extent emaciated from a period of several months' starvation, it is spring and breeding time for precisely those species whose eggs and young the helodermas so greatly relish. Vision does not seem to be of significant importance in the location of prospective food but great reliance is placed on the forked tongue, which constantly flicks in and out, supplying particles to Jacobson's organ for assessment; normal olfaction also doubtless plays an important role. Helodermas have been seen to seek out eggs hidden as deep as 13cm (5in) below the surface of the ground with unerring accuracy. Once the eggs are located and excavated, the reptiles explore the shells with their tongues before taking an egg in their jaws. They then either swallow the egg, if it is small enough, or else crack the shell (a procedure usually assisted by pressing the egg against a firm support, often simply the ground) and then lap up the contents. In experiments with captive Gila monsters, it was found that a trail made by moving an egg along the ground was carefully followed, although an egg left in plain view on the surface was not noticed, even when the animal passed within 15cm (6in) of it.

Vision is evidently a markedly subordinate sensory attribute among helodermas, although it does play a part in the final seizure of small juvenile mammals. Confronted with live prey, helodermas react surprisingly quickly for such notoriously sluggish creatures, usually seizing the victim by the head with the first bite; if this is not achieved, the prospective meal is then quickly repositioned for swallowing head first. Inertial feeding is practised, the reptile slackening its grip momentarily while throwing the prey further back in the jaws until it is finally engulfed, a process that may take about 2 minutes; the heloderma's head is finally bent downwards to assist the throat musculature in forcing the meal back down the oesophagus.

In the wild, helodermas presumably raid the burrows of rodents and rabbits to secure young victims, or the nests of ground-dwelling birds for eggs, doubtless locating them by olfaction and the use of Jacobson's organ. The rapidity with which a captive Gila monster was seen to flee from the vicinity of a simulated nest area, clutching a juvenile hamster in its jaws, suggests that escape from enraged parents is an urgent prerequisite. Nestling birds seem to be rarely if ever taken but small reptiles, such as lizards, may be eaten. Birds that build their nests above the ground seem to be relatively safe from egg predation by helodermas, since these reptiles have a limited climbing ability. They have, however, been seen to ascend trees, such as desert willows or cholla cactus plants, while foraging, sometimes to a height of 2.5m (8ft). Their climbing movements are cautious and the descent is accomplished head first by inching downwards on the forelimbs and using the hind legs to provide a steadying anchorage.

The strength of a heloderma's jaw musculature is substantial – sufficient to break an egg or to kill a small mammal by crushing its body. Its venom is too slow acting to be of any help in predation and must therefore be regarded as having a purely defensive function. The poison glands are large, modified salivary glands that lie along the outside of the lower jaw bone, immediately beneath the skin. Each gland is invested with a capsule of fibrous tissue and comprises three or four lobes, increasing in size from front to back and more or less club-shaped, with a swollen, rounded, glandular secretory region at the bottom and a narrow, upper, excretory portion. From this excretory portion, venom is discharged near the bases of the lower teeth, where it fills a shallow longitudinal channel, subdivided by obliquely transverse folds of tissue that probably form temporary reservoirs for the poison.

The teeth of helodermas are elongate and conical, and the largest (the fourth to the seventh) occur in the middle of each tooth row. These fangs have grooves running up their anterior and (usually) posterior faces, flanked by a sharp flange that forms a cutting edge. When the reptile sinks its teeth into a victim, venom is drawn up the grooves in the lower teeth (Fig. 8.4) and enters the puncture wounds inflicted by the bite. The upper fangs, slightly smaller than the lower ones, may also carry poison, in this case drawn from the venom reservoirs of the lower jaw when the mouth is closed and the tips of the upper teeth

▲ Conspicuously coloured when caught in the open, but well camouflaged in its usual environment of rocks and vegetable debris, the Gila monster *(Heloderma suspectum)* is unaggressive, but if molested will inflict a highly poisonous bite.

▶ This example of the Gila monster *(Heloderma suspectum)* from the Sonoran desert of Mexico, is a representative of the northern population of the genus.

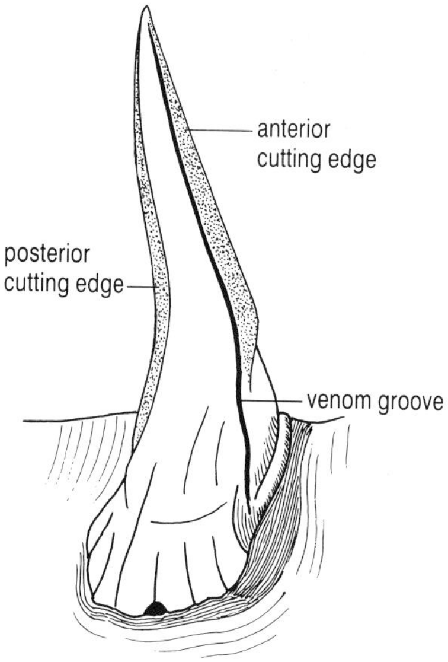

▲ **Fig. 8.4 Lower jaw tooth of *Heloderma*, viewed from the inner (lingual) aspect, showing the venom groove and prominent cutting edges.**

protrude down into the pockets along the venom channel. The front and back teeth are considerably smaller and are either only feebly grooved or lack grooves altogether.

Heloderma venom seems to have a toxicity comparable with that of cobra venom, although it is of different composition, since antivenins prepared for use against the bites of cobras and vipers seem to have no effect against it. Dried *Heloderma* venom injected at a dosage of about 10mg/kg of body weight will kill a dog, mouse or rabbit, although mice are slightly more resistant (minimum lethal dose about 40mg/kg of body weight). Death is apparently caused largely by interference with respiratory function. Experiments have shown that, in warm-blooded animals injected with lethal doses of *Heloderma* venom, the heart sometimes continues to beat for up to half an hour after breathing ceases (for several hours in the case of frogs), suggesting that the poison does not primarily affect the heart. Post-mortem examination disclosed congestion and oedema of the lungs, together with dilation of the intestines by fluid and gas, and haemorrhagic lesions in the digestive tract, liver and also the kidneys.

The venom of helodermas has been found to consist for the most part of macromolecular proteins that can be precipitated with trichloracetic acid and ammonium sulphate. It contains a very active hyaluronidase, a phospholipase A (present in many animal venoms), a kinin-releasing enzyme, an acidic protein which acts as a neurotoxin (gilatoxin), and an apparently hypothermic toxin (helothermine), which, in experimental mice, causes lethargy, partial paralysis of the hind limbs and lowering of the body temperature. The toxic factor is heat-stable, remaining unaffected by heating to 100°C (212°F) for 15 minutes.

There have been a number of human fatalities following bites by helodermas and, when European settlers reached Mexico and the American southwest, they found that the native Indians were fully acquainted with the venomous capability of these reptiles. One early record of a European who succumbed to a Gila monster's bite concerns a miner, Johnny Bostick, who died in an Arizona mining camp in 1878 or 1880, 3 months after receiving a bite from a Gila monster that left him paralysed down one side. In 1884, a Colonel Yeager (also referred to as Yearger or Yager in various accounts) died an hour after being bitten by a Gila monster that he was teasing for the benefit of a crowd. In the 1890s, Arthur James, a tourist, who was encamped in an Arizona cave with a companion, was awakened at dawn by something crawling over him, attempted to brush it off, and was severely bitten on his wrist by a Gila monster. His arm quickly became greatly enlarged and discoloured and, delirious and half crazed with pain, he eventually ran howling to a nearby stream, where he died with his head in the water and his teeth fixed in the engorged arm.

The venomous capabilities of helodermas were thus soon demonstrated to settlers from the east who found their way into the Gila monster heartland of Arizona. A careful account by a French scientist, Marie Phisalix, who was bitten on her right index finger by a specimen she was handling at a menagerie in France, stated that the wound bled freely and violent pain spread up the median nerve pathway to the armpit, accompanied by purple-coloured swelling of the hand and wrist. After 5 minutes, she experienced profuse generalized perspiration, paleness with mottling of the face, faintness and sudden temporary loss of consciousness. After 3 hours, she began to recover from the most severe effects of the venom but her arm remained painful for a week and fainting spells, profuse sweating and weakness consequent upon the least exertion persisted for about 5 months.

If a heloderma sinks its teeth deeply enough into a victim, and its jaws cannot quickly be prised free (the bite is immensely strong, so this is not an easy task), sufficient venom may be injected into the punctures to cause severe symptoms, or even death, in a human being. Individuals who are elderly or under the influence of alcohol (e.g. the unfortunate Yeager, according to eye witnesses) would be especially vulnerable. Some bites from helodermas prove to be relatively innocuous, perhaps because only the front teeth (which are likely to carry little or no venom) enter the victim's flesh, or because the reptile is in poor physical condition or has recently used up its store of venom.

First aid for victims of heloderma bites consists mainly of supportive measures to ease the pain and counter shock. A tourniquet may be applied above the bite (not too tight, and loosened for a few seconds every 15 minutes or so) and suction should be applied to the punctures in an attempt to withdraw at least some of the venom. The application of antiseptic will counter the pathogenic organisms introduced along with the venom from the lizard's mouth (some of the bacteria cultured from the mouths of Gila monsters are highly virulent and could by themselves generate serious symptoms). The patient should avoid exertion and be taken to a doctor or hospital as quickly as possible. It should be remembered, however, that helodermas employ their venom purely as a means of defence and, if they are left alone, they will not be aggressive.

They have few enemies, save humans, and the majority of potentially predatory animals seem aware of these lizards' venomous capabilities. Most subspecies of *Heloderma* appear very conspicuous when observed in a cage or crossing an asphalt road but, in fact, they do not exhibit 'warning coloration'. When observed in a desert environment, against their natural background of rocks and vegetable debris, their coloration is essentially a camouflage device; at night especially, the sharply contrasting light and dark markings break up the creature's outline in a most effective manner.

If they feel threatened, the first reaction of helodermas is to remove themselves from the scene of danger. They are not fast movers and can run no faster than about 20m / minute (22yd / minute) for brief distances of about 10m (11yd), which enables them to find refuge in a burrow or hole, or beneath a rock or vegetation. Helodermas can swim adequately in emergencies although they are by no means agile in the water.

These reptiles can probably survive for more than a year without food, living off the fat reserves in the tail (two deposits run along above the level of the vertebrae and two larger ones below the vertebrae, separated by muscle). When they emerge from winter hibernation, they are thin, often to the point of emaciation, but quickly attain healthy breeding condition on a diet of bird or reptile eggs and small baby mammals.

Rival males have been seen to engage in a ritualized form of combat, pushing against each other with their heads and seeking to secure an opportunity for asserting superiority by straddling the opponent.

Mating seemingly occurs during early or midsummer, although captive specimens in Seattle Zoo apparently mated in December or January, the male mounting the female after first rubbing his chin along her head, neck and back, with copulation usually taking about 3 minutes (Fig. 8.5). Up to 12 oval, rough-shelled white eggs measuring some 7.5 × 3.5cm (3½ × 1½in) and weighing about 40g (1½oz) are laid during July or August in the wild, although a female in Seattle Zoo laid in May and, in Mexico, egg deposition may be delayed until as late as November (the end of the wet season). Nests are excavated in warm but slightly moist sand, in sites exposed daily to warm sunshine. Incubation requires 30–130 days (probably depending on temperature) and the hatchlings are about 10–20cm (4–8in) long on emergence from the egg.

◀ **Fig. 8.5** ***Heloderma suspectum*** **mating.**

Helodermas may legitimately be regarded as endangered but are by no means rare. Because they hide themselves away below ground during the winter, and even in summer tend to avoid the heat of day by emerging only at night or early in the morning, they have never been conspicuously abundant. Probably 95 per cent of a heloderma's life is spent underground. They have negligible commercial value, the skin being of little use for leather because it contains abundant osteoderms, and although the venom has been exploited as a homeopathic remedy, its efficacy is uncertain.

Indian supersitition has endowed helodermas with supernatural powers, including influence over the weather and the menstrual cycle of women. These reptiles are often regarded as unlucky omens and, because they are difficult to kill, they were reputed to be potentially immortal. It was therefore customary to hang up a (presumed) dead heloderma on a bush until it was so decomposed that there could be no doubt about its demise. In Mexico, the meat from the loins was eaten as an aphrodisiac, although elsewhere the flesh of helodermas is regarded as poisonous.

Various myths were also propagated by European settlers, including the suggestion that these reptiles were so sluggish that they needed little food and consequently had no anus, simply voiding waste matter occasionally through the mouth, leading to a further fiction which attributed venomous qualities to the foetid breath. Helodermas do not spit venom, as sometimes alleged, although an angry specimen will often hiss and, in so doing, possibly accidentally expel a few drops of venom from the mouth; nor do they possess the jumping powers occasionally attributed to them. Helodermas do not need to throw themselves on their backs before biting to ensure that venom runs down into the wound, they are not vulnerable to their own poison, and their teeth (adapted for grasping) cannot readily snip out a section of flesh.

CHAPTER 9

The Earless Dragon

The shyest, least offensive and most poorly known of all varanoids lives less than 1600km (1000 miles) away from the mighty Komodo dragon on the Indonesian island of Borneo.

About 45cm (18in) in length, the so-called 'earless' monitor *(Lanthanotus borneensis)* (Fig. 9.1) apparently spends most of its time underground, emerging only at night. It is able to remain dormant for long periods of time, breathing so slowly and shallowly that it is difficult to be sure it is still alive.

With its weak, diminutive legs, *Lanthanotus* looks and moves more like a snake than a lizard. The neck and forward part of the trunk seem to be quite strongly muscled, however, probably to aid in burrowing through loose soil or enlarging pre-existing subterranean cavities, which it does by employing the flattened, blunt-pointed head. The eyes are small, with movable lids, the lower one incorporating a window for vision when the eyes are closed, as they usually are in daylight. This suggests that sight is not a particularly significant sense to *Lanthanotus* and is very much subordinate to smell, although the upward-facing external nostrils, located near the tip of the snout at the summit of two raised projections, are also of insignificant proportions. Probably the forked tongue is an important sensory receptor, as it is in monitors generally, *Lanthanotus* tending to leave this organ protruded for a few seconds at a time rather than flicking it rapidly in and out. The common name of 'earless monitor' refers to the absence of an external auditory opening and *Lanthanotus* certainly seems to be unresponsive to sounds, despite the occurrence of a fully developed ear structure below the skin.

The tail is nearly as long as the animal's body, cannot be shed if the creature is seized, and may serve primarily as a fat store, with the subsidiary function of aiding balance, locomotion or swimming. Some prehensile capability is evident, so the tail may help *Lanthanotus* to keep its footing on slippery or irregular surfaces, further aided by the quite long, sharp, curved claws of its five-toed feet, or to anchor it in fast-flowing streams.

The brownish-coloured skin is covered in small granular scales, with longitudinal series of large, keeled, tubercular scales, arranged in six to ten rows along the body (where they rest on a bony layer of osteodermata) but becoming fewer down the tail. This nodular epidermis usually acquires a covering of adherent earth particles that make this reclusive little reptile totally inconspicuous even when it does venture out.

And venturing out is not something that *Lanthanotus* does very often. It seems to be exclusively nocturnal, spending the daylight hours underground and only emerging for at most a few hours during darkness. What it feeds on in the wild remains problematical: the teeth are long, widely spaced, taper to points and curve slightly backwards, while the structure of the palate suggests that its food must be soft or easily swallowed. *Lanthanotus* is usually found in the vicinity of water and, when in captivity, will spend long periods of time lying in water. It also possesses a number of aquatic specializations, notably the nostrils at the tip of the snout, which face slightly backwards, and the clear scale on the lower eyelid, and it is an accomplished swimmer, searching downwards with its head while the body twists gracefully in serpentine fashion.

The first scientific description of *Lanthanotus* was published by the Vienna-based zoologist, Franz Steindachner, in 1878. This specimen was about 43cm (17in) long and had been obtained from Borneo, the Indonesian island which eventually proved to be the earless monitor's only home. Initially, Steindachner thought his discovery was related to the *Heloderma* group because the teeth were erroneously believed to possess venom grooves comparable to those of the Gila monster. Consequently, the newly identified *Lanthanotus* (which means 'hidden ear') was assigned to the Helodermatidae but, in fact, it is not venomous.

It resembles *Varanus* itself in such specialized features as the presence of nine cervical vertebrae (one more than in lizards generally), the occurrence of small peduncles beneath the cervical and caudal centra to support (respectively) the hypapophyses (ventral projections of the neck vertebrae to which the hypaxial muscles are attached) and the chevron bones, the existence of a posterior fenestra in the coracoid bone of the shoulder girdle, reduction of the sternal ribs to less than four, and fusion of the astragalus and calcaneum (two important bones of the ankle joint), but it is now generally regarded as an intermediate form between the relatively conservative helodermatids and the quite progressive varanids. For instance, ventral peduncles on the cervical and caudal vertebrae are absent in *Heloderma*, small in *Lanthanotus*, and large in *Varanus*.

Specialized skeletal features of the earless monitor include lack of an overlap between the clavicles and the rod-like interclavicle in the shoulder girdle, loss of a bone (a phalanx) from the fourth toe of the forefeet and the hind feet, and the presence of a tubercle near the outer end of the fifth metatarsal. A juvenile specimen of *Lanthanotus* was found to have a ninth (and last) cervical vertebra that still retained rudimentary sternal ribs, indicating a final stage in the 'cervicalization' of what was once the first thoracic vertebra.

The flattened skull of *Lanthanotus* (Fig. 9.2) has lost its temporal arch and, when viewed from below, it can be seen that the ventral processes of the frontal bones fail to meet below the brain. There are eight anterior upper jaw teeth in the premaxillary bones and, like one species of *Heloderma*, this enigmatic little lizard has retained palatal teeth on the pterygoid bones – the extinct mosasaurs also had palatal teeth, but modern monitors have lost them.

For nearly a century after Steindachner's original discovery, the earless monitor remained largely a mystery. Only half-a-dozen more specimens came to light, all from Borneo, and it was widely assumed to be extremely rare and perhaps verging on extinction. In the 1950s, however, Tom Harrisson, the curator of Sarawak Museum in Kuching, launched a programme to survey the reptile fauna of Borneo. A major objective was to secure specimens of the elusive *Lanthanotus* but, in this respect, the scheme was initially disappointing. Plenty of other reptiles were found by professional and amateur native collectors but

▲ **Fig. 9.1 The earless monitor (*Lanthanotus*).**

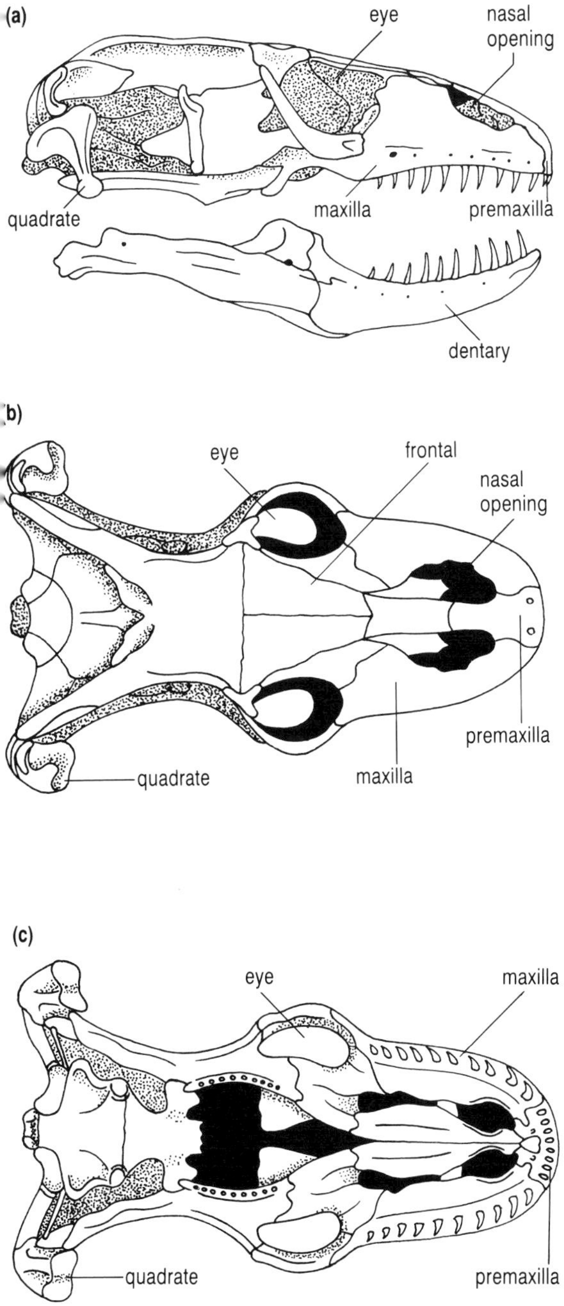

▲ **Fig. 9.2 Skull of *Lanthanotus*: (a) lateral elevation; (b) dorsal aspect; (c) palatal view.**

not a single specimen of the earless monitor materialized. Until January 1961, that is, when one of the museum's full-time collectors, Jommel bin Bogol, was working on an archaeological site at the Niah Caves. Reports reached him of an unusual lizard that had been found in a hole 25cm (10in) deep by a Dyak while hoeing the heavy loam of his pepper garden. Hurrying to the spot, Bogol found himself in possession of a live earless monitor.

The precious specimen, some 32cm (13in) long, was taken back to Kuching in a tin of earth. Tom Harrisson and his wife Barbara installed it in a plastic cage in their air-conditioned bedroom, with a deep, dark box to provide a refuge. As a pet or a subject of scientific study it proved to be singularly disappointing, remaining so torpid as to appear dead for hours or even days at a time. It was amenable to being handled, never trying to bite, although it clearly preferred Mrs Harrisson's attentions to those of her husband, and would swim gracefully when given the chance of a regular dip in the washbasin. It would emerge from its box voluntarily during the night but periods of activity rarely lasted for more than about 5 minutes; excursions by day were a rare occurrence and the animal was evidently predominantly nocturnal. It would also lie in water for 24-hour periods, sometimes remaining totally submerged for over 30 minutes.

Initially it refused any sort of food but eventually began to accept the raw yolks of marine green turtle eggs. It was found that, without regular bathing, the earless monitor's skin became too dry, while, if it was allowed to become too damp, a fungal infection attacked the eyes and nostrils. The little reptile required constant attention to keep it alive and, when the Harrisson's had themselves to visit the Niah Caves, where the Sarawak Museum had a permanent research station, they felt obliged to take it with them. By this time, it had been persuaded to take fresh raw hens' eggs (fortunately, since turtle's eggs could not be obtained at Niah) but, in April, some 2½ months after its initial capture, it suddenly died. Its health had been declining steadily and its faeces, which were originally white, hard and gritty, had acquired a liquid consistency, so its demise was not perhaps too unexpected. Nonetheless, it took some time to confirm that the creature was actually dead, so lethargic had it always been.

Having found one of these cryptic creatures, it now proved much easier to locate further specimens, especially when the local Dyaks were offered a bonus for bringing in specimens of the earless monitor. Most were discovered in the coastal plain area of Borneo, but some also emanated from the vicinity of the narrow, steeply banked streams with gravelly beds that run through the primary forest of the hills.

Attempts to keep these lizards alive on a diet of egg yolk proved only partially successful and it was eventually discovered that earless monitors will readily take fish: fresh or frozen mackerel, plaice or whitebait are eaten with relish. They seem to prefer a temperature of about 22–25°C (71.6–77°F), which is perhaps on the low side for a reptile whose home is at the equator. Observation of numerous captive specimens has confirmed that *Lanthanotus* is a supremely indolent creature, movement being rare by day and of only a few minutes duration at night, the lizard collapsing into a moribund, flattened heap immediately after these efforts, having seemingly exhausted its strength. When attempting to break up sizeable pieces of fish, the lizard will thrash about relatively energetically, using the half-coiled tail and splayed out hind limbs to provide a secure purchase for its efforts. The bite is quite strong and, if the piece of fish it is feeding on is picked up, the creature can be lifted up along with its meal.

The question of how *Lanthanotus* lives in the wild is still unanswered. While captive specimens have demonstrated an evident enthusiasm for frozen fillet of plaice, as purchased from supermarket freezers, this is clearly not its natural diet. Perhaps in the wild *Lanthanotus* takes tadpoles, small fish or worms (captive specimens have been persuaded to eat earthworms); a disinterest in stale fish suggests that carrion is not to its liking but caged specimens will eat pig or chicken liver.

Usually the earless monitor occurs in rice paddies or other wet places, but it is sometimes found in holes that are some distance from the nearest water. Whether it actively burrows is doubtful, since the forelimbs are so weak and really serve only to steer the creature when walking, locomotory thrust being generated by the hindquarters, assisted by undulatory, snake-like movements of the spine. When at rest, the forelimbs are often left in a passive, trailing position. Perhaps it can thrust its snout below fallen vegetation, rocks or logs to wriggle out of the daytime heat and sunlight.

The apparent lethargy may be to some extent an artefact of captivity, since specimens kept in conditions approximating their natural environment tend to be more lively than the less fortunate early captives. While the original live specimens responded hardly at all to being touched or prodded, lying torpid for hours or days on end, it was subsequently found that earless monitors could become quite excitable, aggressively waving the end of the tail, and even biting, although the tiny teeth do little harm to a human finger and there is no evidence of a reaction to venom.

One specimen was observed to shed its skin during the second half of the year (July–December) and this animal was found with 6 eggs measuring about 2.9 × 1.7cm (1¼ × ½in), with a parchment-like skin. It is not known if they were *Lanthanotus* eggs or a prospective meal.

There is just one known possible fossil ancestor of the earless monitor: *Cherminotus*, with a head measuring 3cm (1¼in) and a long slender snout, is represented by fossil skulls from the 75 million-year-old Late Cretaceous of the Gobi Desert. Today, *Lanthanotus* occurs only in Borneo and whether it formerly enjoyed a wider range in the recent past is problematical. The earless monitor is not itself the 'missing link' between lizards and snakes, although snakes in all likelihood did evolve from lizard stock of probably subterranean habits in which the body became progressively more elongate, limbs and eyes regressed, and the number of vertebrae increased. *Lanthanotus* seems to have diverged from the central varanoid stem after the helodermatids branched off, and this obscure little Bornean reptile must have independently pursued its lonely, but seemingly successful, evolutionary path for many millions of years. Contrary to the early impressions of its extreme rarity, the evidence suggests that *Lanthanotus* may in fact be quite numerous in Borneo but its shy and retiring life style makes it so inconspicuous that it largely escapes notice.

CHAPTER 10

Extinct Sea Dragons

The extinct mosasaurs, the great sea dragons of the Cretaceous, were probably more reminiscent of sea serpents than anything else. Up to 15m (50ft) in length, these monstrous aquatic lizards had not become as fully adapted to their new home in the oceans as other groups of reptiles (such as the ichthyosaurs) or, in later times, some of the mammals (such as dolphins).

Mosasaurs still had relatively sinuous bodies (with up to 50 pre-sacral vertebrae) and long tails inherited from land-living forebears whereas fully adapted, aquatic, air-breathing vertebrates became fish-like in form, with abbreviated necks, shortened, deeply proportioned bodies and tails converted into powerful swimming organs (vertically oriented in ichthyosaurs, as in fish, but horizontal in dolphins). In most genera, however, there was probably little or no connection between the mosasaur spine and the pelvic bones, indicating that aquatic specialization was advancing rapidly, this loss of articulation being a feature of wholesale adaptation to life in the water. Some mosasaurs had tails modified for swimming with a laterally compressed configuration towards the tip.

The heads of mosasaurs were still almost entirely monitor-like, affording unequivocal evidence of varanid relationship, although the skull bones do offer some identifying distinctions; for example, the premaxillae are extended to reach the frontal elements (which are fused), while the nasal bones (already small in monitors) are reduced to mere splints. The snout was very long, with the slit-like external nostrils situated on the dorsal surface, as befitted air-breathing animals whose lives were spent in the sea.

The eyes were large and incorporated a ring of sclerotic plates (about 14 in each socket) to maintain the configuration of the cornea and support the sclera, visual orientation being predominantly lateral rather than forwards, with a slight upward-anterior direction.

Mosasaur skulls, like those of monitor lizards, were constructed of five subunits, between which a greater or lesser degree of movement (cranial kinesis) was possible (Fig. 10.1). A parietal unit on top of the head and a flat basal unit in the floor of the skull were transversely hinged to the muzzle unit. The quadrate unit (incorporating the ear drum and jaw hinge) articulated dorsally with the suspensorial process of the occiput but swung more or less freely ventrally in a backwards and forwards direction, constrained only by a ligament which presumably replaced the lost lower temporal bar. The occipital unit comprised a central cranial component to which the parietal, basal and quadrate units were articulated. These constituent sections would have been bound together by ligaments.

Each half of the lower jaw was divided into two components by a joint near the lower edge on either side. The function of this kinetic skull and jaw structure was probably to facilitate the biting action of the jaws. When the mouth was widely opened to strike, the effective size of the gape was increased by raising the muzzle relative to the posterior part of the skull and by lowering the front portion of the jaws; strong muscles attached to the skull and mandible provided the motive power. The various joints also no doubt served to absorb some of the shock generated by the strike, the lower jaw hinge being particularly effective in this role.

Once the prey had been seized, the jaws would close and their vice-like grip could be augmented by downward movement of the muzzle to meet

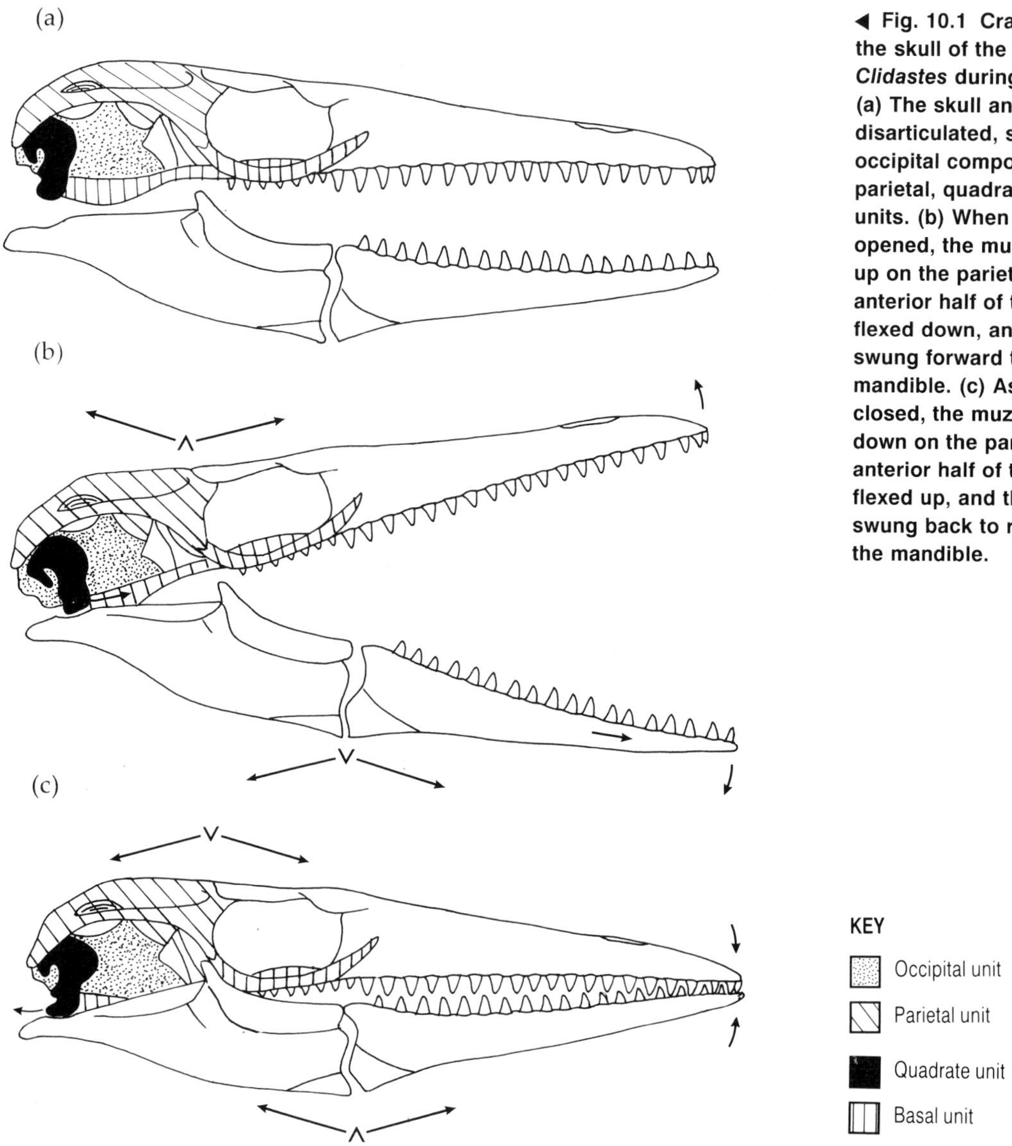

◀ **Fig. 10.1 Cranial kinesis in the skull of the mosasaur *Clidastes* during biting. (a) The skull and lower jaw, disarticulated, showing the occipital component and parietal, quadrate and basal units. (b) When the jaws opened, the muzzle unit flexed up on the parietal unit, the anterior half of the lower jaw flexed down, and the quadrate swung forward to protract the mandible. (c) As the jaws closed, the muzzle unit flexed down on the parietal unit, the anterior half of the lower jaw flexed up, and the quadrate swung back to retract the mandible.**

an upwardly hinging front section of the lower jaw. As a result, the jaws would be closed most tightly at the front and a struggling prey probably sought to escape by wriggling towards the back of the gape. This, however, was towards the yawning cavern of the mosasaur's throat, and also brought the wretched victim within range of the recurved teeth located along the pterygoid bones – palatal elements, forming part of the basal unit, which were thrust forwards as the jaws opened by the action of muscles on the jointed skull. As the mouth closed, the pterygoids, with their teeth impaling the prey, were drawn back by muscle contraction and hastened the engulfment of the victim. In addition, the quadrate bones, because they had lost their contact with the lower temporal arcade, were free to move more or less independently, so that the lower jaw could be displaced horizontally backwards and forwards relative to the upper jaw. An ammonite shell, which had been repeatedly bitten by a mosasaur, displays grooves cut into the conch that bear eloquent testimony to the fierceness with which the lower jaw could be retracted. Living monitors swallow their prey by gravitational inertia: with the victim in the jaws, the head is drawn up and back, then thrust forwards as the grip is momentarily released, thus throwing the prey back into the throat.

The kinetic skull structure present in the earlier mosasaurs remained very varanid-like, although the upper temporal arcade was quite firmly attached to the muzzle unit by extensive suturing of the postorbitofrontal bones to the ventral surface of the frontal element (as the muzzle unit was rotated up, the upper temporal arcades were depressed, and vice versa), while the supratemporal bone was firmly attached to the braincase where it received the upper end of the quadrate. There seems little evidence that the lower jaw joint ever permitted any lateral flexion to facilitate the swallowing of large prey and active rotation around the occipital unit was lost in later forms. The density of the water, inhibiting rapid closure of the jaws, may have been a factor in the loss of kinesis.

Streptostylic (i.e. freely swinging) quadrates nonetheless remained a feature of mosasaurs throughout their existence and presumably assisted them to force prey down their throats without the aid of claws, gravity, or any point of leverage. It is noteworthy that, in an ammonite which had been bitten by a mosasaur, and savaged at least 16 times before the living chamber was crushed, the upper and lower teeth marks are not always aligned, due presumably to the independently movable quadrates. The teeth, which were the weaponry operated to such deadly effect by this specialized jaw apparatus, were impressive indeed, most species possessing conical, slightly recurved fangs, with somewhat swollen bases, that were firmly located in shallow pits. A few mosasaurs, however, evolved blunt, crushing teeth, presumably for breaking open the hard shells of invertebrate prey. The pterygoid teeth of mosasaurs are characteristic of the family but must be regarded as a rather conservative feature, occurring in many early reptiles but lost in modern varanids.

A calcified tympanic membrane was present, which may have facilitated underwater hearing and also possibly prevented damage to the ear drum by water pressure when these reptiles dived deeply. Hearing above the water surface was probably impaired, however, in order to secure greater auditory acuity when submerged.

Compared to most lizards, the chest region of mosasaurs was concentrated unusually far forward; the rib cage was expanded and the first five thoracic ribs were attached to the sternum, as in primitive terrestrial lizards. The posterior ribs of the trunk had also been reduced, so the flanks were probably slender and merged smoothly into the fleshy base of the tail, which must have formed quite an efficient sculling organ. The fore and hind limbs were of approximately equal size but had been converted into paddles, initially with slender digits enclosed in a loosely knit, turtle-like paddle. Later, the major bones became shorter and broader, with flattened carpal and tarsal (wrist and ankle) bones, and clawless fingers and toes (usually incorporating additional phalangeal bones) enclosed in a more efficient fleshy paddle.

Presumably these paddles served mainly to orient the body when swimming. The forepaddles would be held at a low angle to the trunk, and abduction and adduction, accompanied by minor inversionary or eversionary flipper movements, would enable them to function in the manner of an aircraft's elevators, the axis of rotation extending along the leading edge. The joints at elbow and wrist, and at knee and ankle, had lost their original special mobility, so that the paddle structure now became uniformly resilient, with the replacement of bone by fibro-cartilage producing a particularly flexible flipper. The investing membrane had a concave margin between the fourth and fifth digits, before extending inwards to make a broad connection with the flanks of the body.

Mosasaurs apparently swam primarily by lateral undulations of the tail and posterior region of the body. Although their body shape is not so well suited to fast swimming as the more hydrodynamically efficient silhouettes of many bony fishes, sharks and porpoises, a long, slender configuration might deliver propulsive energy more effectively at slower speeds. The large size of mosasaurs may, in any case, have enabled them to generate sufficient power to overtake smaller, more streamlined prey.

The diet of mosasaurs included fish, other marine reptiles and ammonites, and the larger mosasurs were capable of swallowing a 364kg (800lb) bulldog tarpon; an expandable throat pouch may have provided temporary food storage. Flattened, spheroidal objects, 50cm (20in) long, presumed to be mosasaur coprolites, contain fragmentary fish remains, and fossil stomach contents have revealed that their prey included sharks, primitive flightless sea birds *(Hesperornis)* and other mosasaurs.

The sea dragons were probably the only Late Cretaceous marine reptiles with the massive jaw structure necessary to prey on ammonites, and they singled out pelagic forms with either smooth, discoid shells (incorporating narrow umbilici and sharp or narrow venters, such as the rapid-swimming *Placenticeras* and *Sphenodiscus),* or elongate, nearly straight shells (baculitids, which were probably floating plankton feeders). A fossil specimen of *Placenticeras,* 42cm (17in) in diameter, from the Bearpaw shale of Alberta, bears five teeth marks apparently inflicted by a huge mosasaur. Attacking from behind and below the floating prey, the mosasaur seems to have first punctured the shell, destroying the ammonite's hydrostatic system with two savage bites, then seized the living chamber with the front teeth and shaken the creature out of the shell. Evidence of ammonite predation by mosasaurs is especially abundant in the Campanian, when mosasaurs were at their most varied, but becomes less common in the subsequent Maastrichtian division of the Cretaceous period, when mosasaur variety was declining as extinction began to approach.

Mosasaurs probably executed slow turning movements by simple lateral bending of the long, muscular neck and the anterior portion of the trunk, but the tail and most of the body were almost totally inflexible in the dorso-ventral direction, so for abrupt, high-speed turns a more complex procedure was required. It has been suggested that the body was first turned on its side by using the forepaddles, after which the neck was arched in the direction of the required turn while the forepaddles were abducted so that their flexor surfaces faced into the current. Meanwhile the hind paddles rotated to force the hind part of the body in the opposite direction to that in which the front of the animal was moving, thus pivoting the mosasaur about its centre of inertia. For diving, the head and neck were presumably flexed downwards, while adduction of the forepaddles depressed the front of the body and abduction of the hind paddles raised the back of the body. The atlas/axis joint and the occipital articulation evidently permitted a very full range of movement, including rotation in a transverse plane, which must have materially assisted in the seizure of agile prey at close range (Fig. 10.2).

The body was probably completely covered in rhomboid scales, of moderate size (i.e. about 5 × 3mm / ¼ × ⅛ in) on the flanks and belly in a 5m (15ft) mosasaur, slightly larger on the back (perhaps 8 × 7mm / ⅜ × ¼in), and quite big (10 × 8mm / ½ × ⅜ in) on the limbs. Since fish living on the continental shelves are commonly reddish grey or silver-grey, mosasaurs (which occupied a similar habitat) probably had a comparable coloration. Shallow-water forms or young individuals living inshore might have been more variably coloured.

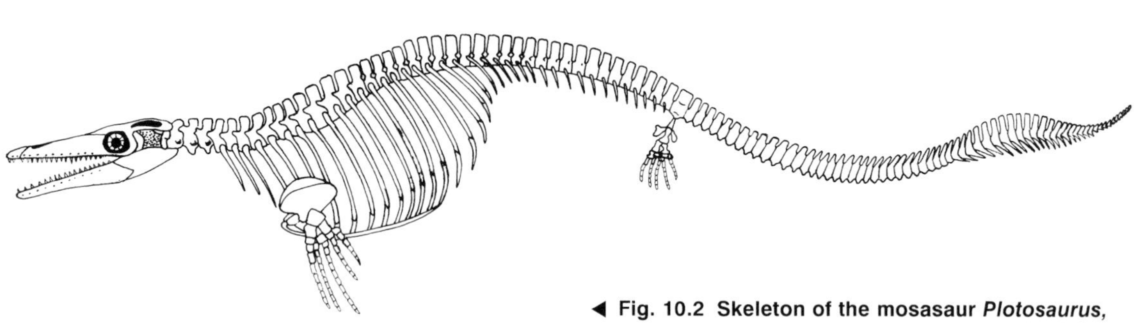

◀ **Fig. 10.2 Skeleton of the mosasaur *Plotosaurus*, about 10m (30ft) in length.**

A few juvenile mosasaur fossils have been found in shallow-water deposits but they are conspicuously absent from rocks laid down under deep water, such as the famous Niobrara chalk. No adults with embryos preserved within the body cavity are known, as they are in the case of ichthyosaurs. This evidence that ichthyosaurs brought forth their young alive solves the problem of how such reptiles contrived to breed, for the conversion of their limbs to paddles, allied to the presence of a fish-like tail, would have made it impossible for ichthyosaurs to come ashore for egg laying.

How, then, did mosasaurs breed? There is no positive evidence with which to answer this question but, since modern marine turtles, with otherwise totally aquatic habits, contrive to haul themselves ashore in order to lay their eggs, it must be presumed that mosasaurs were also able to drag themselves onto a suitable beach and deposit eggs. Modern varanids do not display any sort of parental care for their young and it is unlikely that mosasaurs did either. Clutches would simply have been left to take their chance of surviving predators and the vicissitudes of climate and weather, with hatchlings making their own hazardous way to the sea after emergence, possibly using the brighter light from the direction of the sea as a guide, after the manner of marine turtles.

The specimens of very young mosasaurs that have come to light, however, include one specimen, only 107cm (3½ft) long, found in Alabama, that may be a juvenile of *Clidastes* – a common genus in that area. Subsequent examination of a fossil pelvis belonging to a specimen of *Clidastes* has disclosed a very interesting feature. It seems that the upper pelvic bones (the ilia) articulate with the spine through a special joint comprising an elliptically shaped condyle on each ilium that fits into an oval socket on either side of the sacral vertebra. Previously, it had been supposed that, in mosasaurs, the connection between the spine and the pelvis had either been lost altogether or was tenuously retained through the intermediary of the sacral ribs. The special joint found in the *Clidastes* specimen is of more appropriate strength and suggested, firstly, a capacity for either streamlining the pelvic region (with the ilia rotated inwards) or providing maximum hydrodynamic deployment of the hind paddles (with the ilia swung out laterally) and, secondly, the further possibility that outward rotation of the ilia would provide a wide enough birth canal for the passage of embryo mosasaurs which had undergone their early development within the mother. Reproduction would then have been of the ovoviviparous type, the eggs being retained in the maternal birth canal until the young were sufficiently well formed to be born alive.

The reign of the mosasaurs was relatively brief in geological terms. They first appeared about 80 million years ago, in the Turonian stage of the Cretaceous period, and vanished suddenly 65 million years ago, at the end of the Mesozoic era, in company with the dinosaurs and several other major groups of animals, all victims of mass extinction. The world in which they lived bore little relationship to that of today. Even the continents occupied different positions, with the Atlantic Ocean only just beginning to open up, so that the eastern and western hemispheres were separated by a relatively narrow interval of sea, while the dispersal of a previously conjoined southern supercontinent, Gondwanaland, had barely begun. South America and Africa were being split apart by the future Atlantic, connections between Antarctica, Australia and southern Africa had been only recently severed, and peninsular India was drifting northwards, destined for a future collision with southern Asia.

A mild, equable climate extended even to high latitudes, and snowy polar caps were either absent altogether or had only undergone incipient development. The old mountain ranges of the Palaeozoic era had been largely eroded away, new ones were yet to rise and large areas of the low-lying continents had been invaded by warm shallow seas, with oceanic waters dividing North America in two from the future Gulf of Mexico to the Beaufort Sea.

Such conditions offered matchless opportunities for marine life to proliferate. There was an abundance of bony fish, sharks, rays, marine turtles and all kinds of invertebrates (especially ammonites and belemnites). Amid this cornucopia of life, the mosasaurs prospered. They seem to have preferred the inshore environment where the water was less than 180m (600ft) deep, and there are indications that they were still only imperfectly adapted to deep diving. Mosasaur vertebrae display evidence of avascular necrosis – destruction of bone tissue that occurs in human deep-sea divers and, in severe cases, can lead to collapse of the vertebral structure. In mosasaurs, the condition did not apparently progress to this crippling stage but some genera (e.g. *Platecarpus, Tylosaurus)* exhibit vertebral necrosis in up to one-third of their backbone. Presumably, these creatures would normally have adjusted their behaviour patterns to avoid the pathological consequences of abrupt deep diving but, when evading a predator or injudiciously pursuing prey, their natural limits might occasionally have been overstepped. In the course of a single individual's lifetime, these rare excesses would not have led to crippling or life-threatening damage. Other mosasaurs, such as *Clidastes,* seem not to have suffered any incidence of vertebral necrosis and presumably avoided deep diving.

There were apparently two or three separate lines of mosasaur evolution and the slender *Clidastes,* 6m (20ft) long, with a disinclination to venture into deep water, seems to represent the rather generalized Mosasaurinae. In this central group, the teeth along the edges of the jaws are very numerous and the tenth, eleventh and twelfth cranial nerves emerge from the skull through two openings. Also, the tail is relatively short, supporting a prominent fin-like structure, the body is by comparison rather long (with over 30 pre-caudal vertebrae), and the articulations of the limb bones exhibit a minimal covering of cartilage. In contrast, the other lines of mosasaurian evolution, comprising the subfamilies Plioplatecarpinae and Tylosaurinae, had rather sparsely disposed teeth along the jaws, only a single skull opening for the tenth, eleventh and twelfth cranial nerves, a long tail, quite a short body (usually less than 30 pre-caudal vertebrae) and a thick covering of cartilage on the articular surfaces of the limb bones. The plioplatecarpines were specifically distinguished by a divergent fifth digit in the forefeet, while tylosaurs had reduced shoulder girdle elements and carpal bones,

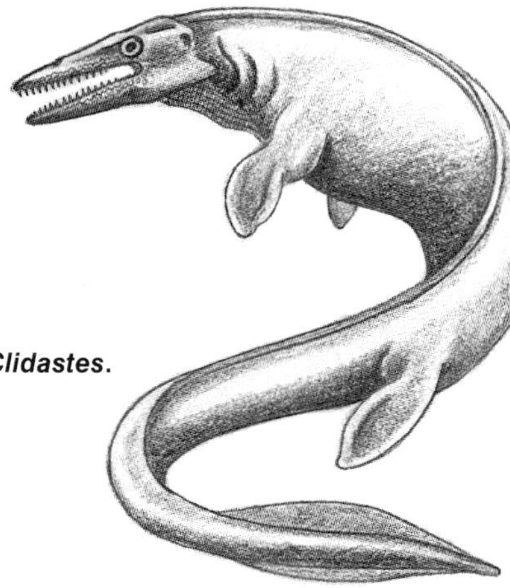

▶ **Fig. 10.3** ***Clidastes.***

although otherwise displaying affinities with the Mosasaurinae that hint at direct derivation from mosasaurine stock.

The skull of *Clidastes* had a shortened temporal region but relatively long jaws, armed with about 18 pairs of trenchant teeth. The body was elongate and the paddles rather small, which perhaps indicates somewhat limited aquatic agility (Fig. 10.3). However, the vertebrae towards the end of the tail had dorsal and ventral processes that must have supported a fin-like structure possibly capable of generating considerable speed through the water.

The dentition suggests a capability for rapid biting and, since the jaws of mosasaurs could be moved horizontally because of the streptostylic quadrate bones, *Clidastes* was probably able quickly to saw up its prey into small, swallowable pieces. In all likelihood, this mosasaur fed on fast-moving fishes with only a limited capacity for evasion, and tended to remain close inshore – certainly, its fossil bones occur principally in shallow-water deposits.

Clidastes was quite a common form along the Cretaceous interior sea-way that bisected North America from the Arctic to the Caribbean. Its remains occur abundantly in the Niobrara chalk of Kansas, a deposit laid down some 80 million years ago under warm temperate conditions, with waters of above average salinity and an organic-rich black or chalky shale sea floor, where inoceramid bivalves lived in such profusion that their huge, flat shells formed vast shell 'islands'.

Another mosasaur of the '*Clidastes* group' also occurred in the Niobrara Sea, the rather rare *Halisaurus,* with a comparatively short, stout skull but quite slim limb bones, not greatly different in general proportions to those of a terrestrial lizard.

Clidastes remained a conspicuous feature of the North American inland sea-way during the episodes of deposition that immediately succeeded the Niobrara stage, in company with a new incursion of more advanced mosasaurines. These included *Mosasaurus* itself, about 9m (28ft) long, with an advanced skull structure lacking cranial kinesis, large firmly rooted teeth, and paddles of a more truly flipper-like construction. *Mosasaurus* probably hunted mostly in the surface waters, seeking giant marine turtles. The contrasting *Globidens* had massive jaws, furnished with blunt spherical teeth, evidently developed for crushing thick-shelled invertebrates.

Mosasaurs were also enjoying substantial success in the Late Cretaceous waters of the proto-Atlantic. Remains of *Halisaurus* and *Mosasaurus* occur on the North American eastern seaboard and in northwestern Africa; a unique but poorly known genus, *Amphekepubis,* has turned up in Mexico and the waters that submerged California at that time harboured *Plotosaurus,* a large-eyed, slender-jawed form (Fig. 10.2). Like *Mosasaurus, Plotosaurus* had lost the kinetic skull structure of early mosasaurs and possessed a somewhat ichthyosaur-like appearance that suggests it was probably a hunter of small fish. It had narrower paddles than the related *Clidastes* and a more highly developed tail fin, so it may have been an even faster swimmer.

Across the broadening Atlantic Ocean, Europe was largely submerged beneath an incursive shallow sea, from which areas of higher land projected as islands. Here, too, conditions favoured mosasaurs and the mosasaurine family was represented by: *Liodon,* with strongly compressed, very smoothly enamelled posterior teeth; *Mosasaurus* itself, a common form in the Late Cretaceous of Belgium and the Netherlands, but also possibly present in the USA, Sweden, Bulgaria, western Africa, Poland, Japan and New Zealand; and *Carinodens,* a derivative of the blunt-toothed *Globidens,* with slightly less robustly constructed teeth and a more slender lower jaw, that seems to have been widespread, occurring in Morocco and Brazil as well as Europe. Elsewhere in the world, the Mosasaurinae have been reported from such widely disparate Late Cretaceous localities as Nigeria, Israel and the former USSR, while in New Zealand this group was represented not only by *Mosasaurus* but also by *Moanasaurus* and *Rikisaurus,* together with the more distantly related *Taniwhasaurus.*

The short-tailed Plioplatecarpinae evolved in parallel to the Mosasaurinae and occupied the same habitats in the same geographical areas. Presumably the life styles of the two groups did not overlap or, if they did, then, somehow or other, there was a measure of accommodation between the subfamilies that managed to avoid competition.

Platecarpus seems to have represented the central stem of the plioplatecarpines. This mosasaur, up to 7.5m (23ft) in length, possessed a short, high, exceedingly kinetic skull, a deep body of reduced relative length, proportionately large paddles and negligible development of a tail fin (Fig. 10.4). The scales were of typical rhomboid

▼ **Fig. 10.4** ***Platecarpus.***

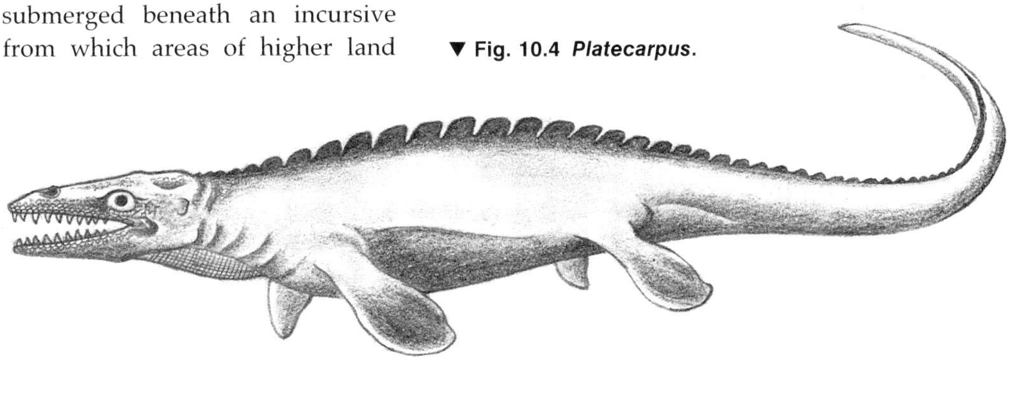

mosasaurian pattern but lacked the longitudinal ridges seen in other genera whose fossilized remains include evidence of the integument. *Platecarpus* was common in the North American interior sea-way, remains occurring in the Niobrara chalk as well as in later deposits ranging from Alabama in the south, through Wyoming, South Dakota and Manitoba, to as far north as the Anderson River in Canada's Northwest Territories.

Probably a slower swimmer than members of the mosasaurine group, *Platecarpus* may have been an open-ocean form, possessed of an especially powerful bite and making up in aquatic manoeuvrability what it lacked in speed to prey on the more evasive types of fish. Analysis of fossil *Platecarpus* stomach contents have disclosed only fish bones and a vertebra of the massive neoteleost ('spiny teleost') fish, *Cimolichthys*, indicating that victims as long as 1.2m (4ft) were sometimes consumed. One interesting specimen of *Platecarpus* incorporated a series of co-ossified tail bones exhibiting an unmistakable bite mark: in one of the tooth holes the tip of a shark's tooth was found. This suggests a battle beneath the waters of the Cretaceous sea from which the mosasaur escaped with its life, although the wound to its tail subsequently became infected and led to the onset of spondylitis, with extensive abscess formation.

Prognathodon seems to have been a descendant of *Platecarpus* and occurred in the later stages (Campanian–Maastrichtian) of the Cretaceous period; it possessed a deep, blunt muzzle and very short powerful jaws armed with massive teeth. The skull of this advanced genus parallels that of the later members of the Mosasaurinae in the lack of the varanoid kinetic structure present among early mosasaurs. *Prognathodon* must have been capable of administering an immensely powerful bite and ammonites may have been its principal prey. Present in the Campanian rocks laid down along the North American interior sea-way, *Prognathodon* was also present in the Late Cretaceous of Europe and New Zealand.

Other derivatives of the *Platecarpus–Prognathodon* line were *Dollosaurus*, from the Campanian of the Donetz basin in the Ukraine, which had a rather short snout and only about a dozen pairs of teeth in each jaw, and *Plesiotylosaurus*, which lived in the Late Cretaceous seas that covered what is now California and possessed a relatively long, slender snout, its skull being of the advanced mosasaurian type that lacked evidence of kinesis.

Plioplatecarpus itself, about 8m (25ft) long, occurred on both sides of the proto-Atlantic, persisting in Belgium and northwestern Africa until the very end of the Cretaceous, and seems to have developed from *Platecarpus* as a belemnite-eater. Certainly one specimen of this mosasaur has been found with belemnite endoskeletons lodged between the lower jaw and the neck vertebrae; furthermore the weakly implanted teeth, restricted to the front of the jaws, parallel the dentition of the 'black fish' *(Globicephala)* which, in modern seas, lives on squids and cuttlefish. As in many later mosasaurs, *Plioplatecarpus* had evolved much more efficient forepaddles, with a massively proportioned humerus and an enlarged scapula to support its powerful musculature (Fig. 10.5).

Ecteneosaurus, which lived in the Niobrara Sea, and had a very slimly contoured snout, seems to have been an early offshoot from the *Platecarpus* central stem of the Plioplatecarpinae while *Selmasaurus* appears to be a member of this subfamily but had largely lost its cranial kinesis.

▶ **Fig. 10.5** ***Plioplatecarpus.***

▶ **Fig. 10.6** ***Tylosaurus*.**

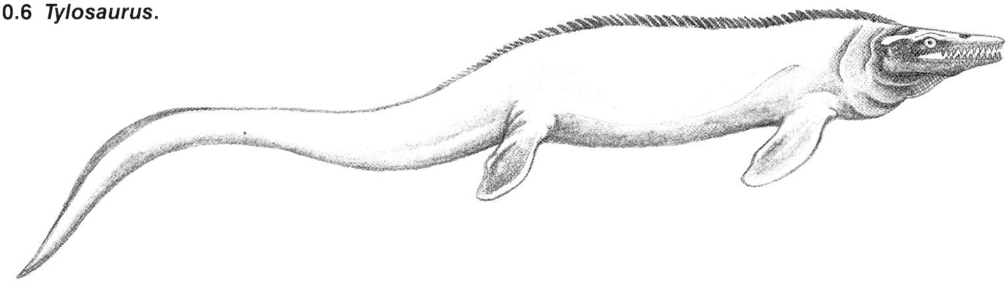

Igdamanosaurus, from Niger, in northwestern Africa, is poorly known but had a blunt-toothed, crushing dentition.

The Tylosaurinae comprised elongate, slenderly proportioned mosasaurs that may well have been diving forms, living in deeper offshore waters. *Tylosaurus* itself attained a length of about 9m (28ft), and was present in the North American inland sea from Niobrara times through the Campanian stage of the Cretaceous period, but then seems to have become extinct in the western hemisphere, although it persisted in the New Zealand area until the end of the period. Remains of either this or a closely related form have been discovered even further south, on Seymour Island, in Antarctica.

Tylosaurus had a fully kinetic skull with elongate, strongly constructed jaws and stout teeth. The rather small flippers and only slightly deepened tail suggest that it was not a very rapid swimmer (Fig. 10.6) but lend support to the suggestion that the subfamily were divers: *Tylosaurus* is one of the mosasaurs in which the occurrence of vertebral necrosis is most pronounced. The bones of *Tylosaurus* are notably cancellous and, in life, may have been impregnated with fat to aid buoyancy, as in whales.

Hainosaurus was probably a giant descendant of *Tylosaurus,* attaining a length of 15m (50ft), whose remains have been found in Belgium and in Manitoba, Canada. Whereas *Tylosaurus* had fewer than 40 vertebrae in the spinal column anterior to the chevron-bone-bearing caudal vertebrae, *Hainosauras* had over 60 but, behind this point, the two genera possessed a similar caudal count of just over 30 vertebrae. Fossil turtle bones have been found in the body cavity of *Hainosaurus,* which gives us some indication of this monster's prey.

Another tylosaurine, *Goronyosaurus,* has recently come to light in the very Late Cretaceous (Maastrichtian) of Nigeria and Niger but the remains of this creature are somewhat fragmentary. It seems to have been a sea dragon of formidable size, however, with an estimated length of about 7m (23ft), but the eyes were proportionately rather small and the premaxillary bones at the end of the nose exhibit an unusual number of large openings for nerve terminations. Perhaps *Goronyosaurus* hunted in the murky waters of sheltered bays and lagoons, using a highly sensitized snout rather than vision to locate its prey.

At the end of the Cretaceous, the mosasaurs vanished with astonishing suddenness, along with the dinosaurs, pterosaurs and plesiosaurs (the ichthyosaurs had already been extinct for some time). Their career was short, a mere 16 million years compared with the 135 million years that the dinosaurs were terrestrial lords of creation, but, despite an imperfect adaptation to life in the seas, they were nonetheless astonishingly successful. Their remains occur from the Arctic to the Antarctic, and from the Pacific to the Atlantic. Admittedly the disposition of the continents was different in Cretaceous times, with Antarctica less far south and the continents of the eastern and western hemispheres much closer together. In addition, the climate was universally milder, with palm trees in western Canada and redwoods and sycamores growing in northern Canada only 640km (400 miles) from the Cretaceous north pole – which was then located in the Chukchee Sea, north of the Bering Strait. Even so, in the shallow seas of the Late Cretaceous world, the mosasaurs would have been almost unchallenged as major predators, with only some of the long-necked elasmosaurian plesiosaurs rivalling them in size and power.

No one will probably ever know why the mosasaurs, or the dinosaurs and the other great reptiles, perished so abruptly. The advent of modern bony fishes (teleosts) late in the Mesozoic has been put forward to account for the extinction of other marine reptiles, which had been accustomed to preying on the older, more primitive fish stocks. But mosasaurs evolved late in the Age of Reptiles and, seemingly, had no difficulty in adapting to teleosts as a source of prey. On the other hand, the ammonites also perished at the end of the Cretaceous and there is no doubt that at least some mosasaurs lived extensively on these shellfish.

▼ **Fig. 10.7 Mosasaur ancestor: *Aigialosaurus*, about 1.5m (5ft) in length, from the Cretaceous of Europe, 95 million years ago.**

The cause seems likely to have been primarily climatic and geographical changes, notably the draining of the shallow Cretaceous seas as falling sea levels caused the oceans to withdraw from the continents and the land began to rise with the initiation of a new phase of mountain building. Perhaps these upheavals were accompanied by extensive vulcanism, or coincided with the impact of a massive extra-terrestrial body but, for whatever reason, the world of the Mesozoic passed into history, taking with it the mosasaurs.

The origins of these magnificent sea dragons are almost equally as mysterious as their end. One clue may be a poorly known group of extinct lizards assembled in a special family of their own, the Aigialosauridae (Figs. 10.7 and 10.8). Their rare fossil remains occur in the Cretaceous rocks of Europe but are usually badly crushed and dif-

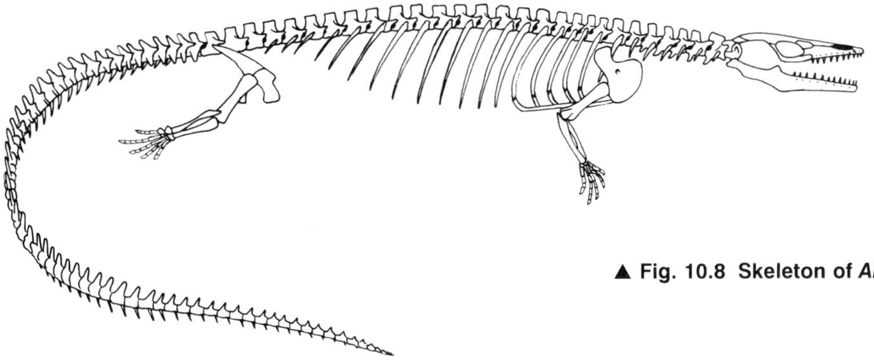

▲ **Fig. 10.8 Skeleton of *Aigialosaurus*.**

ficult for palaeontologists to prepare. Up to about 2m (6½ft) in length, the aigialosaurs had a slender, mosasaur-like skull with an elongate facial region and a typical hinge joint half way along the lower jaw, but a skeleton that was otherwise typical of terrestrial varanoid lizards, including a characteristic oblique articulation between the vertebral centra. However, the limbs seem to have been in the process of conversion to paddles, with shortened bones and broad extremities, so it is quite probable that this obscure group of apparently semi-aquatic forms represents a transitional stage between the varanid lizards and the mosasaurs that occurred about 100 million years ago. Some researchers have disputed the alleged aquatic limb specializations of aigialosaurs. M.W. Caldwell, R.L. Carroll and H. Kaiser, working at McGill University, Montreal, have concluded that these enigmatic forms were probably much more terrestrial than aquatic, despite the occurrence of their fossil remains in rocks laid down beneath the sea. They suggest further that aigialosaurs and mosasaurs should be placed in a superfamily of their own, distinct from the varanoids.

Another poorly known group of small and, in all likelihood, aquatic, Early Cretaceous lizards that are believed to be members of the varanoid assemblage are the Dolichosauridae. Like the aigialosaurs, they have been found only in Europe but seem to be rather more specialized than those putative mosasaur ancestors and perhaps represent an early unsuccessful off-shoot from aigialosaur stock. The dolichosaurs were only 1m (3¼ft) or so in length and had short-faced skulls, long bodies and relatively small limbs, the forelegs being shorter than the hind legs. Whatever their nature and origin, the dolichosaurs quickly disappeared, leaving the mosasaurs to become the largest, most powerful and most voracious varanoids of all time.

CHAPTER 11

Dragons Past, Dragons Future

The varanoids are an ancient race. Monitor lizards shared the Mesozoic world with the dinosaurs, over 65 million years ago, and their origins probably trace to an anguoid stem. The anguoids were once a significant group in evolutionary terms but are now a rather unimportant assemblage, typified by the alligator lizards *(Gerrhonotus, Elgaria)*. Some, however, are ponderous armoured forms, like the galliwasp *(Diploglossus)* and a number of extinct species that seem to have been relatively common some 50 million years ago, and there are various snake-like species with reduced limbs, such as the glass snake *(Ophisaurus)* and slow worm *(Anguis fragilis)*.

The first monitor-like lizards were the Necrosauridae, which appear in the Late Cretaceous, and, although clearly varanoids – the hypapophyses of the neck vertebrae, for example, exhibit separate epiphyses in characteristic monitor fashion – they also display features which are notably more primitive than anything found in living members of the group. The external nostrils are still located at the end of the snout; the intra-mandibular hinge in the middle of the lower jaw is poorly developed; the frontal bone has a weak descending process; there is a trapezoidal suture between the basisphenoid and the basioccipital (the result of an extended posterolateral process on the basisphenoid); the junction between the supraoccipital and the parietal elements is loose; and there is a prominent conch (or tympanic crest) on the quadrate.

In the closing stages of the Age of Dinosaurs, necrosaurids seem to have been relatively abundant both in North America and in Asia – areas that were connected, in the Late Cretaceous, across what is now the Bering Strait and which supported a varied and flourishing population of dinosaurs. Upper and lower jaw fragments in the Lance formation (very Late Cretaceous) of Wyoming have been described as *Colpodontosaurus,* while *Parasaniwa,* from the same area and strata, has a slenderly proportioned lower jaw containing about 13 pairs of trenchant, weakly compressed teeth possessing enlarged, slightly striated bases. Asian necrosaurids of the Late Cretaceous comprise *Ekshmer and Parviderma* – small and poorly known forms of even earlier (Campanian and late Turonian) age than their North American relations, dating back as far as 90 million years ago, together possibly with the uncertainly identified *Chilingosaurus* from northeastern China.

By the beginning of the Cenozoic era, the only necrosaurid still clinging on in Asia seems to have been *Ekshmer* but, in North America, there was little *Provaranosaurus,* with about 20 pairs of slender, high-crowned teeth in the long lower jaw. The Late Palaeocene in Europe, some 57 million years ago, saw the first appearance of *Necrosaurus* itself, with a skull up to 7cm (3in) long, 13–18 pairs of trenchant, laterally compressed teeth and robustly proportioned limbs.

The fortunes of necrosaurids seem to have been waning in North America at the beginning of the Eocene, 55 million years ago, although *Provaranosaurus* appears still to have been present, while only a rather questionable report of *Ekshmer* suggests a continuing occurrence of necrosaurids in Asia. Europe finally became a congenial last refuge for this old and conservative family, with *Necrosaurus* occurring widely there and eventually extending its geological range into the succeeding Oligocene. Throughout the known history of the group, however, the Necrosauridae have been in the nature of relict forms, left over from a hypothetical earlier stage in varanoid evolution. True monitor lizards had already appeared beside the necrosaurids tens of millions of years before the dinosaurs became extinct.

Generally characterized by external nostrils located well back from the end of the snout, development of a hinged joint in the middle of the lower jaw, fused nasal bones, paired frontals and narrow parietal elements with a longitudinal crest, the first monitors occur in Late Cretaceous strata, some 80 million years old, in North America and eastern Asia, sharing this conjoined region with innumerable dinosaurs.

Of special interest is *Estesia,* discovered in the Gobi Desert in 1990 by an American expedition and named in honour of the late Richard Estes, a noted authority on fossil lizards. With a skull about 20cm (8in) long and jaws containing knife-edged teeth, *Estesia* seems to be an early varanid but may constitute a fossil link between the monitor lizards and the helodermatids because a series of canals at the base of its teeth seem likely to have been venom channels.

Telmasaurus was present in both North America and the Gobi Desert region and still retains many primitive features held over from necrosaurid ancestors, e.g. a trapezoidal suture between the basisphenoid and basioccipital, a loose supraoccipital/parietal contact, and a large quadrate conch. It is also unique among varanids in possessing fused frontal bones, although traces of a suture are present on the ventral surface of these two elements.

Saniwides is an exclusively Asiatic form, with a skull about 4.5cm (1¾in) long, that also retains the trapezoidal basisphenoid/basioccipital suture and loose supraoccipital/parietal contact but has a reduced quadrate conch and paired frontal bones. Occurring as a fossil in rocks that are some 70 million years old, *Saniwides* had rather thick, blunt teeth (about 20 pairs in the upper jaw and 15 pairs in the mandible).

Almost equalling some of the largest living varanids in size, *Palaeosaniwa* was present in North America during the closing stages of the Cretaceous period but seems not to have survived the end of the Mesozoic era, 65 million years ago, despite one contested claim that it was present in the succeeding Palaeocene period. The vertebrae of *Palaeosaniwa* measure up to 4cm (1½in) in length and the head was apparently protected by dermal cranial shields arranged in a regular pattern – an apparently primitive feature, redolent of the group's believed anguoid origins.

It seems probable that the varanids originated in eastern Asia, one group (the *Saniwides–Palaeosaniwa* lineage) crossing into North America via the Bering region, which was then dry land (varanid vertebrae have been reported from as far north as Ellesmere Island in arctic Canada), while a westward migration of monitor stock colonized south-central Asia and Africa.

What these earliest monitors looked like in life, and how they lived, is a matter for speculation. Existing varanids display no bizarre or highly specialized characteristics but remain readily adaptable to a wide range of habitats and food. Some progressive features are apparent, however, notably a relatively high body temperature and concomitantly high activity levels, specialized chemosensory attributes (through the medium of Jacobson's organ) and the rapid, skilful capture of hidden or elusive prey.

The fossil evidence, scant though it is, suggests that the monitor lizards of 60 million years or more ago probably resembled their modern descendants in these features. They were about 0.5–1.5m (20–60in) in length and would have hunted over quite wide individual ranges, occasionally taking to the branches of trees or, if necessary, entering the water of streams and lakes. Chemoreception would have been employed to seek out prey and they must have fed on a large variety of small prey animals, with carrion doubtless being eaten when available; clawed feet and powerful jaws were employed to tear meat from carcasses. The specialized diets of some living forms, however, are probably adaptations evolved subsequently, for example, fruit-eating in the butaan, mollusc-eating in the Nile monitor, predation on large mammals in the Komodo dragon.

Early on in the Tertiary, when the embryonic Atlantic Ocean had only recently, geologically speaking, effected the separation of North America from Europe, these two land areas still shared a very similar fauna. The 60-million-year old Middle Palaeocene of Wyoming has yielded two varanid vertebrae that seem to be the first evidence of *Saniwa,* a genus closely related to the living *Varanus* that subsequently occurs quite plentifully in the Early Eocene of Europe and North America; in Nebraska, this genus survived into the Early Oligocene (some 35 million years ago) before finally dying out – the last-known New World monitor. *Saniwa* does exhibit a degree of specialization in possessing unusually long neck vertebrae for a varanid, but also retains numerous primitive characteristics, for example the presence of palatal teeth, only moderate withdrawal of the nostrils from the end of the snout, a long posterior prolongation of the maxillary bone so that the last two or three cheek teeth are situated beneath the eye, and low vertebral neural spines (especially along the tail). In addition, the postorbital and postfrontal bones remain separate in *Saniwa* – a condition encountered in small or juvenile specimens of *Varanus* – and the cervical ribs begin on the fifth neck vertebra (a feature that is occasionally observed in living monitors, which usually only have ribs on the last three or four cervicals). The distribution of *Saniwa* seems to have been determined by the tropical or subtropical climatic belt that, in early Cenozoic days, lay directly across what is now the North Atlantic region; an alleged occurrence of this genus in the Early Miocene of Argentina (20 million years ago) seems to be of very questionable veracity.

Possibly intermediate between *Saniwa* and *Varanus* is a Middle Eocene genus from Spain, *Iberovaranus,* that is known only from fossil body and tail vertebrae. The modern genus was unquestionably present by the Early Miocene in Kenya *(Varanus rusingensis,* a blunt-toothed presumed mollusc-eater, up to 2m (6½ft) in length, from Rusinga Island). By the Middle and Late Miocene, there were also species in Europe *(Varanus hofmanni, Varanus lungui, Varanus semjonovi, Varanus tyrasiensis,)* and Asia *(Varanus pronini),* although much of the material on which these species have been based is extremely fragmentary, consisting in some cases of just a single, isolated bone. By the Middle Miocene, *Varanus* had also reached Australia, where it evolved in spectacular fashion during the ensuing Pliocene and Pleistocene; this island continent remained cut off from the rest of the world until a fall in sea levels during the ice age glaciations created land bridges between New Guinea, the Solomon Islands and Australia.

Despite progressive global cooling, southern European temperatures were still warm enough to support a monitor population during the Pliocene, which began 7 million years ago and ended just over 5 million years later. Species included *Varanus marathonensis,* which may be referable to the subgenus *Psammosaurus* and hence related to the extant *Varanus griseus,* and *Varanus deserticolus* from Hungary, that is probably really attributable to *Varanus marathonensis.* Asian representatives of *Varanus* during the Pliocene included *Varanus sivalensis,* from the Siwalik hills of the Indian subcontinent, and *Varanus darevski* from Tadzhikistan, which was slightly smaller than the living *Varanus griseus,* and possibly ancestral to it, but with a proportionately higher skull, short sharp snout and teeth of relatively greater size. By the end of the Pliocene, climatic fluctuations were beginning to restrict varanids to more or less their present geographical distribution, although they still apparently clung on in Europe on the continent's southern fringes *(Varanus marathonensis* in Italy as recently as perhaps about 200 000 years ago). Australia continued to be a prolific centre of varanid evolution during the Pleistocene, with *Varanus giganteus* making its appearance at this time (a fossil vertebra from New South Wales seems to be attributable to this species). The living *Varanus bengalensis* was apparently established in India by Pleistocene times, Java harboured *Varanus bolkayi* and, on Flores, there was *Varanus hooijeri* – apparently a blunt-toothed mollusc-eater about the size of the Nile monitor that is not, however, regarded as a close relative of the Komodo dragon found on Flores today.

Generally speaking, varanoids are still flourishing at the present time. There are about 40 species, including helodermatids and the obscure little *Lanthanotus*, and none of them are seriously endangered, if indeed any of them are endangered at all. Their remarkable adaptability has enabled monitor lizards to cope exceptionally well with the encroachment of human activities onto their environment. In many areas, urbanization and agricultural development have inevitably reduced their freedom to roam at will through forest, bush and desert. Even so, some species have managed to take advantage of tropical farming techniques: for example, the yellow monitor *(Varanus flavescens)* of the Indian subcontinent seems to have colonized fish farm parks and irrigated areas (e.g. rice paddies), thus offsetting the effects of habitat loss caused by river control and the annexation of land for cultivation.

The hunting of monitors for meat is little more than a local activity to supply an immediate domestic requirement. The flesh has no status as an international delicacy in the way that, for instance, shark fins do, and there is no significant trade in it. Nonetheless, occasional efforts are made to popularize monitor lizard steaks, notably in Australia, where 'roast goanna' can be prepared by throwing a freshly killed animal onto a hot fire to crisp the skin for about 10 minutes, then removing the intestines as soon as the carcass starts to bloat and returning it to the fire for a further 40 minutes (cooking each side for 20 minutes). When well done, the meat is served with yams and small bush bananas that have been baked in the ashes.

Monitor skins do have a market, although they are a less significant item of international trade than crocodile hides. Monitor-derived leather is used for wallets, shoes, belts, handbags, watch straps and similar small luxury or giftwear items. The species primarily involved are: *Varanus salvator, Varanus niloticus, Varanus exanthematicus, Varanus flavescens* and *Varanus bengalensis*, with some demand also for the hides of *Varanus rudicollis, Varanus indicus* and *Varanus griseus*. All are relatively large species, yielding a reasonably sized hide when fully grown or at any rate approaching maturity. Annual trade in water monitor *(Varanus salvator)* skins may reach more than 1 million whole skins a year, mostly originating in Indonesia (Sumatra, Kalimantan, Java), Thailand, Malaysia and the Philippines; their ultimate destinations, via Singapore, are Japan, the UK, North America and Europe. The majority of these skins are from animals just short of full maturity and yield a hide about 25–30cm (10–12in) wide that is usually cut down the mid-ventral line in a way that will optimize the dorsal colour pattern. The most valuable types show well-defined transverse rows of rings and typically come from Sumatra, Kalimantan and western Java, being known in the trade as 'ring-marked' or 'Java lizard' hides. The almost black skins from some coastal regions of peninsular Malaysia and Thailand, Sulawesi (known as 'macassar' hides) and eastern Java and Nusa Tenggara (designated 'anpenang' hides) are of less value and often turn out to be marred by small holes caused by ectoparasite infestation.

Hides of *Varanus bengalensis* are worth considerably less than those of *Varanus salvator,* fetching only about $3 in 1987, and trade in them tends to fluctuate widely: nearly 0.5 million skins in 1984, for example, but only 24 000 skins in 1986. Most skins from this species end up in Japan.

Some concern has been expressed about the number of yellow monitor *(Varanus flavescens)* skins that are traded each year – up to 0.5 million – because this species does seem to have suffered substantial population curtailment in the western and central regions of its range, which extends across the northern part of peninsular India. The hide sells relatively cheaply because it is of small size and, due to the large, oval dorsal scales, rather coarse grained (traders refer to it as 'oval grain lizard'). There is probably a need to investigate the present and past status of *Varanus flavescens* throughout its range, and to consider the maintenance of exploitation controls on this species, although some evidence suggests that, at least in Bangladesh, it may be more numerous than has hitherto been supposed.

Native hunters catch monitor lizards by excavating their burrows, chasing them with dogs, or employing baited traps. Digging out and trapping may be quite an efficient method of capture, particularly if practised by tribal groups skilled in animal collection, and could conceivably almost exterminate a local population of monitors. Pursuit with dogs is labour intensive and probably a good deal less productive.

Generally speaking, monitor populations seem at present able to withstand the level of harvesting being imposed on them. *Varanus bengalensis,* for example, occupies such an extraordinary range of habitats that populations are likely to be very resilient – extensive hunting in one locality will probably result in augmentation of numbers by immigration from a neighbouring area, where breeding has proliferated beyond the capacity of the environment to support all the newly emergent juveniles. *Varanus bengalensis* is found from open semi-desert to dry woodlands and evergreen tropical forest, and is probably absent within its range only from the two extremes of sand desert and dense rainforest. Such an adaptable reptile, that has even succeeded in colonizing agricultural habitats where some plant cover remains, is unlikely to become endangered in the immediate future.

There is a small trade in live monitors for the domestic pet trade, amounting to perhaps 10 000 or so individuals a year; *Varanus exanthematicus, Varanus salvator* and *Varanus niloticus* are the main species concerned. Monitor lizards are not satisfactory pets for people living in northern cities. Many lizards bought for this purpose probably do not survive long, because either they are not properly looked after, or their new owners soon tire of them and find a way to dispose of their unwanted acquisitions – the bathroom route is allegedly widely favoured. Small, brightly coloured juvenile monitors no doubt appeal to tourists seeking exotic mementoes of overseas trips but, since the three species of varanid most abundantly represented in the pet trade all grow to a considerable size, any purchases that do survive to adulthood are likely to provide their owners with a serious problem: a water monitor that has matured into a 1.8m (6ft) adult is going to be something of an embarrassment in an apartment!

Attempts to employ monitor lizards as biological controls of vertebrate pests have proved a failure. The introduction of these lizards to Pacific islands in order to keep down rats only resulted in the rats becoming nocturnal to avoid the exclusively diurnal monitors; the monitors then turned their attention to domestic poultry and the indigenous ground-nesting birds.

Nonetheless, there is every reason to believe that monitor lizards, together with their helodermatid relatives, and even the obscure *Lanthanotus,* can contrive to survive fairly resiliently in competition with burgeoning human populations. Even the monstrous Komodo dragon, which, for such a large reptile, is restricted to a very limited area in the Indonesian islands, probably numbers about 5000 individuals, although, by the mid-1990s, it seems to have vanished from the small island of Padar. However, plans to re-establish it there were being made.

Some 80 million years since the most ancient known varanoids shared the late Mesozoic world with giant dinosaurs, these immensely successful, highly adaptive reptiles still seem to have a long future before them.

▶ The Bengal monitor *(Varanus bengalensis)* is one of the species of monitor lizard whose skin is sought by hide dealers for small luxury and giftware items, such as wallets, belts, shoes or watch straps.

Published Scientific Names of Living Varanids

Numerous species of *Varanus* have been published in the scientific literature over the years but, in the light of later research, many have been found to constitute junior synonyms of previously promulgated taxa and hence invalid under the zoological rules of nomenclatorial priority, or alternatively represent only subspecies. (The listings given below are not exhaustive.)

Varanus (Odatria) acanthurus Boulenger 1885
  Odatria ocellata Gray 1845 (non *Varanus ocellatus* Heyden 1830)
  Varanus acanthurus brachyurus Sternfeld 1919
  Varanus acanthurus primordius Mertens 1942
  Varanus acanthurus insulanicus Mertens 1958
Varanus (Odatria) baritji King & Horner 1987
Varanus (Indovaranus) bengalensis (Daudin 1802) [*Tupinambis*]

The oldest published name for this species is *Lacerta monitor* Linnaeus 1758, which was based on figures that appeared in Seba's *Illustrations of Natural History*. Unfortunately this name, together with *Lacerta dracaena* Linnaeus 1766 and *Stellio salvaquardia* Laurenti 1768, was applied to a composite specimen of *Varanus salvator*, and plenary powers were sought from the International Commission of Zoological Nomenclature to suppress *Varanus monitor* (Linnaeus 1758) in favour of *Varanus bengalensis*. Synonyms of *Varanus bengalensis* include:

  Lacerta dracaena Linnaeus 1766
  Stellio salvaquardia Laurenti 1768
  Lacerta argus Daudin 1802 in part
  Tupinambis cepedianus Daudin 1802
  Tupinambis elegans Daudin 1802 in part
  Varanus guttatus Merrem 1820
  Varanus punctatus Merrem 1820
  Varanus taraguira Merrem 1820 in part
  Monitor gemmatus Guérin-Meneville 1829/38
  Tupinambis cepedeanus Wagler 1830
  Monitor heraldicus Gray 1831
  Monitor nebulosus Gray 1831
  Monitor inornatus Schlegel 1839
  Varanus bibroni Blyth 1842
  Varanus lunatus Gray 1845
Varanus (Odatria) brevicauda Boulenger 1898
Varanus (Odatria) caudolineatus Boulenger 1885
  Varanus laudolineatus Lucas 1901 (in error)
Varanus (Tectovaranus) dumerili (Schlegel 1839) [*Monitor*]
  Varanus macrolepis Blandford 1881
  Varanus heteropholis Boulenger 1892
  Varanus heterolepis Barbour 1912
Varanus (Odatria) eremius Lucas & Frost 1895
Varanus (Empagusia) exanthematicus (Bosc 1792) [*Lacerta*]
  Tupinambis albigularis Daudin 1802
  Monitor exanthematicus capensis Schlegel 1804
  Varanus ocellatus Heyden 1830
  Monitor albogularis Gray 1831
  Varanus gilli Smith 1831
  Monitor microstictus Rueppell 1845
  Regenia albogularis Mueller 1878
  Varanus microstictus Boettger 1895
  Varanus occellatus Tornier 1897
  Varanus occipitalis Tornier 1897
  Varanus xanthematicus Loveridge 1929
  Varanus angolensis Schmidt 1933
  Varanus exanthematicus ionidesi Laurent 1964
Varanus (Empagusia) flavescens (Hardwicke & Gray 1827) [*Monitor*]
  Varanus russeli Heyden 1830
  Varanus picquoti Duméril & Bibron 1836
  Monitor exanthematicus indicus Schlegel 1844
  Varanus diardi Hallowell 1856
Varanus (Varanus) giganteus (Gray 1845) [*Hydrosaurus*]
Varanus (Odatria) gilleni Lucas & Frost 1895
Varanus (Odatria) glauerti Mertens 1957
Varanus (Odatria) glebopalma Mitchell 1955
Varanus (Varanus) gouldi (Gray 1838) [*Hydrosaurus*]
  Varanus ocellarius Theobald 1878
  Varanus gouldiae Berney 1936
  Varanus gouldi rosenbergi Mertens 1957
  Varanus gouldi flavirufus Mertens 1958
Varanus (Psammosaurus) griseus (Daudin 1803) [*Tupinambis*]
  Tupinambis ornatus Daudin 1803
  Varanus scincus Merrem 1820
  Tupinambis arenarius Geoffroy 1827
  Varanus caspius Eichwald 1831
  Varanus terrestris Schinz 1834
  Varanus ornatus Gray 1845
  Varanus caspicus Gray 1845
  Varanus striatus Owen 1845
  Varanus arenaceus Gervais 1848

Varanus ornatus Carlleyle 1869
Varanus griseus Boulenger 1885
Psammosaurus arabicus Hemprich & Ehrensberg 1899
Varanus griseus koniecznyi Mertens 1954
Varanus (Varanus) indicus (Daudin 1802) [*Tupinambis*]
Varanus guttatus Merrem 1820
Monitor douarrha Lesson 1830
Monitor kalabeck Lesson 1830
Monitor chlorostigma Gray 1831
Monitor doreanus Meyer 1874
Varanus indicus rouxi Mertens 1926
Varanus tsukamotoi Kishida 1929
Varanus leucostigma Hediger 1934
Varanus indicus spinulosus Mertens 1941
Varanus (Varanus) karlschmidti Mertens 1951
Varanus indicus jobiensis Ahl 1932
Varanus (Varanus) irrawardicus Yang Datong & Li Simin, 1987
Varanus (Odatria) kingorum Storr 1980
Varanus (Varanus) komodoensis Ouwens 1912
Varanus (Varanus) mertensi Glauert 1951
Varanus bulliwallah Worrell 1956
Varanus (Varanus) mitchelli Mertens 1958
Varanus (Polydaedalus) niloticus (Linnaeus 1766) [*Lacerta*]
Lacerta monitor Linnaeus 1758 in part
Stellio saurus Laurenti 1768
Lacerta capensis Sparrmann 1783
Lacerta tupinambis Lacépède 1788 in part
Tupinambis elegans Daudin 1802 in part
Tupinambis stellatus Daudin 1802
Tupinambis ornatus Daudin 1802
Monitor pulcher Leach 1819
Varanus (Philippinosaurus) olivaceus Hallowell 1856
Varanus ornatus Gray 1845
Varanus grayi Boulenger 1885
Varanus (Varanus) panoptes Storr 1980
Varanus panoptes rubidus Storr 1980
Varanus panoptes horni Böhme 1988
Varanus (Odatria) pilbarensis Storr 1980
Varanus (Odatria) prasinus (Schlegel 1839) [*Monitor*]
Monitor viridis Gray 1831
Monitor kordensis Meyer 1874
Monitor beccari Doria 1874
Varanus prasinus bogerti Mertens 1950
Varanus (Dendrovaranus) rudicollis (Gray 1845) [*Uaranus*]
Varanus scutigerulus Barbour 1932
Varanus swarti Mangili 1962
Varanus (Papusaurus) salvadori (Peters & Doria 1878) [*Monitor*]
Varanus (Varanus) salvator (Laurenti 1768) [*Stellio*]
Lacerta monitor Linnaeus 1758 in part
Lacertus tupinambis Lacépède 1788 in part
Tupinambis elegans Daudin 1802 in part
Monitor nigricans Cuvier 1809
Tupinambis bivittatus Kuhl 1820
Monitor saurus Lichtenstein 1825
Monitor marmoratum Cuvier 1829
Monitor exilis Gray 1831
Hydrosaurus marmoratus Wiegmann 1834
Varanus vittatus Lesson 1836
Varanus cumingi Martin 1838
Varanus binotatus Blyth 1842
Monitor bivittatus philippensis Schlegel 1844
Monitor bivittatus var. *celebensis* Schlegel 1844
Monitor bivittatus var. *javanica* Schlegel 1844
Varanus crocodilinus Owen 1845
Hydrosaurus nuchalis Guenther 1872
Monitor togianus Peters 1872
Varanus manilensis Martens 1876
Varanus salvator andamanensis Deraniyagala 1944
Varanus salvator macromaculatus Deraniyagala 1944
Varanus salvator philippinensis Deraniyagala 1944
Varanus salvator kabaragoya Deraniyagala 1947
Varanus salvator nicobarensis Deraniyagala 1947
Varanus (Odatria) semiremex Peters 1869
Varanus boulengeri Kinghorn 1923
Varanus (Varanus) spenceri Lucas & Frost 1903
Varanus ingrami Boulenger 1906
Varanus (Odatria) storri Mertens 1966
Varanus primordius Mertens 1942
Varanus storri ocreatus Storr 1980
Varanus (Odatria) telenesetes Sprackland 1991
Varanus (Odatria) teriae Sprackland 1991
Varanus (Odatria) timorensis (Gray 1831) [*Monitor*]
Monitor timorensis Mertens 1876
Varanus timorensis scalaris Mertens 1941
Varanus timorensis similis Mertens 1958
Varanus (Odatria) tristis (Schlegel 1839) [*Monitor*]
Odatria punctata Gray 1838
Varanus punctatus var. *orientalis* Fry 1913
Varanus tristis centralis Mertens 1957
Varanus (Varanus) varius (Shaw 1790) [*Lacerta*]
Tupinambis variegatus Daudin 1802
Varanus belli Duméril & Bibron 1836
Varanus mustelinus De Borre 1870
Varanus various Berney 1936
Varanus (Varanus) vietnamensis Yang Datong & Liu Wanzhao 1994
Varanus (Empagusia) yemenensis Böhme, Jager & Schätti 1989

Selected Bibliography

Auffenberg, W. (1979) 'A monitor lizard in the Philippines.' *Oryx*, **15**: 39–46.

Auffenberg, W. (1980) 'The herpetofauna of Komodo with notes on adjacent areas.' *Bull. Fla St. Mus.*, **25**: 39–156.

Auffenberg, W. (1981) *The behavioral ecology of the Komodo monitor*. 406pp. University of Florida Press.

Auffenberg, W. (1983) 'The food and feeding of juvenile Bengal monitors (*Varanus bengalensis*).' *J. Bombay Nat. Hist. Soc.*, **80**: 119–24.

Auffenberg, W. (1984) 'Notes on feeding behaviour of *Varanus bengalensis* (Sauria, Varanidae).' *J. Bombay Nat. Hist. Soc.*, **80**: 286–302

Auffenberg, W. (1988) *Gray's monitor lizard*. 419pp. University of Florida Press.

Auffenberg, W., Rahman, H., Fehmida, I., & Perveen, Z. (1989) 'A study of *Varanus flavescens* (Hardwicke & Gray) (Sauria: Varanidae).' *J. Bombay Nat. Hist. Soc.*, **86**: 286–307

Baird, I.L. (1960) 'A survey of the periotic labyrinth in some representative recent reptiles.' *Univ. Kansas Sci. Bull.*, **41**: 891–981.

Banerjee, V., & Banerjee, N. (1969) 'Seasonal variations of erythrocyte number and haemoglobin content in a common Indian lizard, *Varanus monitor* (Linnaeus).' *Zool. Anz.*, **182**: 203–7.

Bartholomew, G.A., & Tucker, V.A. (1964) 'Size, body temperature, thermal conductance, oxygen consumption, and heart rate in Australian varanid lizards.' *Physiol. Zool.*, **37**: 341–54.

Bellairs, A. d'A. (1949) 'Observations on the snout of *Varanus*, and a comparison with that of other lizards and snakes.' *J. Anat. Lond.*, **83**: 116–46.

Berger, P.J., & Heisler, N. (1977) 'Estimation of shunting, systemic and pulmonary output of the heart, and regional blood flow distribution in unanaesthetized lizards (*Varanus exanthematicus*) by injection of radioactively labelled microspheres.' *J. Exp. Biol.*, **71**: 111–21.

Bogert, C.M., & Martín del Campo, R. (1956) 'The Gila monster and its allies.' *Bull. Amer. Mus. Nat. Hist.*, **109**: 1–258.

Böhme, W., & Horn, H-G., eds (1991) 'Advances in monitor research.' *Mertensiella*, **2**: 268pp.

Böhme, W., Joger, U., & Schätti, B. (1989) 'A new monitor lizard (Reptilia: Varanidae) from Yemen, with notes on ecology, phylogeny and zoogeography.' *Fauna of Saudi Arabia*, **10**: 433–48.

Branch, W.R. (1982) 'Hemipenal morphology in platynotan lizards.' *J. Herpet.*, **16** (1): 16–38.

Brattstrom, B.H. (1968) 'Heat retention by large Australian monitor lizards.' *Amer. Zool.*, **8** (Abstract 144): p.766.

Brattstrom, B.H. (1973) 'Rate of heat loss by large Australian monitor lizards.' *Bull. S. Calif. Acad. Sci.*, **72**: 52–4.

Bukowski, F., & Bond, P. (1989) 'A predator attacks *Sphenodiscus*.' *The Mosasaur*, **4**: 69–74.

Caldwell, M.C., Carrol, R.L., & Kaiser, H. (1995) 'The pectoral girdle and forelimb of *Carsosaurus marchesetti* (Aigialosauridae), with a preliminary phylogenetic analysis of mosasaurids and varanoids.' *J. Vert. Paleont.*, **15**: 516–31.

Callison, G. (1967) 'Intracranial mobility in Kansas mosasaurs.' *Paleont. Contrib. Univ. Kansas*, Paper 26: 15pp.

Cogger, H.G. (1959) 'Australian goannas.' *Aust. Mus. Mag.*, **1**: 71–5.

Condon, K. (1987) 'A kinematic analysis of mesokinesis in the Nile monitor (*Varanus niloticus*).' *Exp. Biol.*, **47**: 73–87.

Cooper, W.E. (1989) '"Strike-induced" chemosensory searching occurs in lizards.' *J. Chem. Ecol.*, **15**: 1311–20.

Cowles, R.B. (1930) 'The life history of *Varanus niloticus* (Linnaeus) as observed in Natal, South Africa.' *J. Entom. Zool.*, **22**: 1–32.

Deraniyagala, P.E.P. (1957) 'Reproduction in the monitor lizard *Varanus bengalensis* (Daudin).' *Spolia Zeylanica*, **28**: 161–6.

Deraniyagala, P.E.P. (1958) 'Pseudocombat of the monitor lizard *Varanus bengalensis* (Daudin).' *Spolia Zeylanica*, **29**: 159.

Dobie, J.L., Womochel, D.R., & Bell, G.L. (1986) 'A unique sacroiliac contact in mosasaurs (Sauria, Varanoidea, Mosasauridae).' *J. Vert. Paleont.*, **6**: 197–9.

Dryden, G.L. (1956) 'The food and feeding of *Varanus indicus* on Guam.' *Micronesia*, **2**: 72–6.

Dryden, G.L., Green, B., Wickramanayake, D., & Dryden, G.G. (1992) 'Energy and water turnover in two tropical varanid lizards, *Varanus bengalensis* and *V. salvator*.' *Copeia*, **1992**: 102–7.

Fleay, D. (1950) 'Goannas, giant lizards of the Australian bush.' *Animal Kingdom*, **53**: 92–6.

Harrisson, H. (1961) 'The earless monitor lizard.' *Discovery*, **22**: 290–93.

Harrisson, H. (1966) 'A record size *Lanthanotus* alive.' *Sarawak Museum J.*, **1966**: 323–33.

Hecht, M.K. (1972) 'The osteology, growth and functional anatomy of the largest lizard, the fossil *Megalania*.' *Yb. Amer. Phil. Soc.*, **1972**: 372–5.

Hecht, M.K. (1975) 'The morphology and relationships of the largest known terrestrial lizard, *Megalania prisca* Owen, from the Pleistocene of Australia.' *Proc. R. Soc. Victoria*, **87**: 239–50.

Heisler, N., Neumann, P., & Maloiy, G.M.O. (1983) 'The mechanism of intracardiac shunting in the lizard *Varanus exanthematicus*.' *J. Exp. Biol.*, **105**: 15–31.

Ishimatsu, A., Hicks, J.W., & Heisler, N. (1988) 'Analysis of intracardiac shunting in the lizard, *Varanus niloticus*: a new model based on blood oxygen levels and microsphere distribution.' *Respiration Physiol.*, **71**: 83–100.

Jacob, D., & Ramaswami, L.S. (1976) 'The female reproduction cycle of the Indian monitor lizard, *Varanus monitor*.' *Copeia*, **1976**: 256–60.

Johnson, C.R. (1976) 'Some behavioural observations on wild and captive sand monitors, *Varanus gouldii* (Sauria: Varanidae).' *Zool. J. Linn. Soc.*, **59**: 377–80.

Kauffman, E.G., & Kesling, R.V. (1960) 'An Upper Cretaceous ammonite bitten by a mosasaur.' *Contr. Mus. Paleont. Univ. Michigan*, **15**: 193–248.

Kauffman, E.G. (1990) 'Mosasaur predation on ammonites during the Cretaceous – an evolutionary history.' In Boucot, A.J., ed. *Evolutionary paleobiology of behaviour and co-evolution*. Elsevier pp.148–9.

King, N., & Horner, P. (1987) 'A new species of monitor (Platynota, Reptilia) from northern Australia and a note on the status of *Varanus acanthurus insulanicus* Mertens.' *Beagle*, **4**: 73–9.

King, E., & King, D. (1975) 'Chromosomal evolution in the lizard genus *Varanus*.' *Aust. J. Biol. Sci.*, **28**: 89–108.

Lingham-Soliar, T. (1991) 'Locomotion in mosasaurs.' *Mod. Geol.*, **16**: 229–48.

Loop, M.S. (1976) 'Auto-shaping, a simple technique for teaching a lizard to perform a visual discrimination task.' *Copeia*, **1976**: 574–6.

Losas, J.B., & Greene, H.W. (1988) 'Ecological and evolutionary implications of diet in monitor lizards.' *Biol. J. Linn. Soc.*, **35**: 379–407.

Mertens, R. (1942) 'Die Familie der Warane (Varanidae). 1. Allgemeines; 2. Der Schädel; 3. Taxonomie.' *Abh. Senck. Naturforsch. Ges.*, **462**: 1–116; **465**: 1–118; **466**: 1–160.

Mertens, R. (1957) 'Two new goannas from Australia.' *W. Aust. Nat.*, **5**: 183–7.

Millard, R.W., & Johansen, K. (1974) 'Ventricular outflow dynamics in the lizard, *Varanus niloticus*: responses to hypoxia, hypercarbia and diving.' *J. Exp. Biol.*, **60**: 871–80.

Oelofsen, B.W., & van den Heefer, J.A. (1979) 'Role of the tongue during olfaction in varanids and snakes.' *S. Afr. J. Sci.*, 75: 365–6.

Parry, N.E. (1932) 'Some notes on the water monitors in the Garo Hills, Assam.' *J. Bombay Nat. Hist. Soc.*, **35**: 903–5.

Pianka, E.R. (1968) 'Notes on the biology of *Varanus eremius*.' *W. Aust. Nat.*, **11**: 39–44.

Pianka, E.R. (1969) 'Notes on the biology of *Varanus caudolineatus* and *Varanus gilleni*.' *W. Aust. Nat.*, **11**:76–82.

Pianka, E.R. (1971) 'Notes on the biology of *Varanus tristis*.' *W. Aust. Nat.*, **11**: 180–83.

Prakash, R., & Sahai, R. (1960) 'On the presence of atrioventricular bundle in the heart of *Varanus monitor* (Linné).' *Proc. Ind. Sci. Cong.*, **47**: 484–5.

Rich, T.H., & Hall, B. (1979) 'Rebuilding a giant.' *Aust. Nat. Hist.*, **19**: 310–13.

Rieppel, O. (1979) 'A functional interpretation of the varanid dentition (Reptilia, Lacertilia, Varanidae).' *Gegenbaurs Morph. Jb.*, **136**: 797–817.

Russell, D.A. (1964) 'Intracranial mobility in mosasaurs.' *Postilla*, 86: 19pp.

Russell, D.A. (1967) 'Systematics and morphology of American mosasaurs (Reptilia, Sauria).' *Bull. Peabody Mus.*, **23**: 240pp.

Smith, H.C. (1931) 'The monitor lizards of Burma.' *J. Bombay Nat. Hist. Soc.*, **34**: 467–73.

Smith, M.A. (1932) 'Some notes on the monitors.' *J. Bombay Nat. Hist. Soc.*, **35**: 615–19.

Sprackland, R.G. (1970) 'Further notes on *Lanthanotus*.' *Sarawak Museum J.*, **18**: 412–13.

Sprackland, R.G. (1972) 'A summary of observations of the earless monitor, *Lanthanotus borneensis*.' *Sarawak Museum J.*, **20**: 323–7.

Sprackland, R.G. (1976) 'Notes on Dumeril's monitor lizard, *Varanus dumerili* (Schlegel).' *Sarawak Museum J.*, **24**: 287–91.

Sprackland, R.G. (1991) 'Taxonomic review of the *Varanus prasinus* group with descriptions of two new species.' *Mem. Qd Mus.*, **30**: 561–76.

Stirling, E.C. (1912) 'Notes on the habits of the large Central Australian monitor (*Varanus giganteus*) with a note on the "fat bodies" of this species.' *Trans. R. Soc. S. Aust.*, **36**: 25–33.

Storr, G.M. (1980) 'The monitor lizards (genus *Varanus* Merrem 1820) of Western Australia.' *Rec. W. Aust. Mus.*, **8**: 237–93.

Tercafs, R.R. (1963) 'Transmission of ultra-violet, visible and infra-red radiation through the keratinous layer of reptile skin (Serpentes and Sauria).' *Ecology*, **44**: 214–18.

Walsh, T., Rosscoe, R., & Birchard, G.F. (1993) 'Dragon tales.' *The Vivarium*, **4** (6): 23–6.

Wells, R.W., & Wellington, C.R. (1983) 'A synopsis of the class Reptilia in Australia.' *Aust. J. Herpet.*, **1** (3–4): 73–129.

Wilson, S.K., & Knowles, D.G. (1988) *Australia's Reptiles.* pp.316–21, 353–61. Collins, Australia.

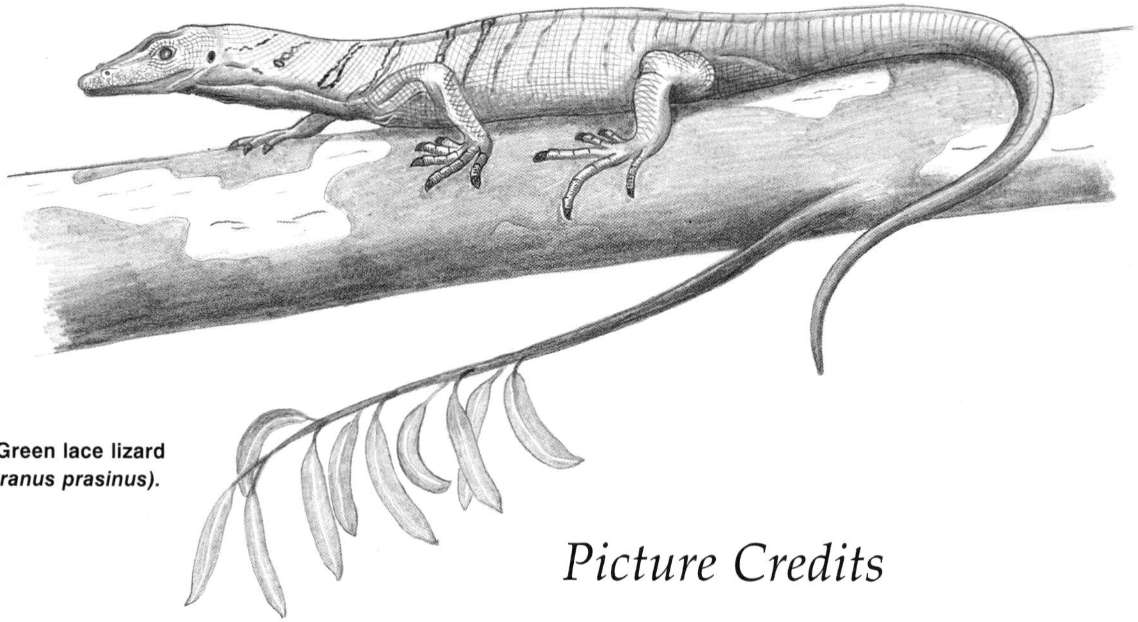

▲ Green lace lizard *(Varanus prasinus).*

Picture Credits

Ardea: p. 118 (Hans and Judy Beste)
Bruce Coleman: p. 38 (Jen and Des Bartlett), pp. 6, 43, (Erwin and Peggy Bauer), p. 86 (Fred Bruemmer), p. 95 inset (John Cancalosi), pp. 22, 30, 39, top and bottom (Mark Carwardine), pp. 2-3 (Alain Compost), p. 107 (Stephen J. Doyle), p. 70 (Peter Evans), p. 127 bottom (Jeff Foott Productions), pp. 82, 90 (C.B. and D.W. Frith), p. 111 (Frithfoto), p. 66 (Gordon Langsbury), p. 10 top (M. R. Phicton), p. 74 (Dr Eckart Pott), pp. 79, 83, 94-5 (Fritz Prenzel), pp. 11, 50 (Hans Reinhard), p. 10 bottom, (Austin J. Stevens), pp. 62 top, 63 inset, 127 top (Rod Williams), p. 151 (Gunter Ziesler)
FLPA Ltd: p. 62 bottom (Eric and David Hosking)
Mark O'Shea: pp. 46, 98 99
Still Pictures: pp. 14-15, 62-3 (Xavier Eichaker)

Line drawings by Rodney Steel.

Index

Page numbers in *italic* refer to illustrations